Science and Religion in America
1800-1860

Herbert Hovenkamp

SCIENCE and RELIGION in AMERICA
1800-1860

University of Pennsylvania Press / 1978

Designed by Adrianne Onderdonk Dudden

Library of Congress Cataloging in Publication Data

Hovenkamp, Herbert.
    Science and religion in America, 1800–1860.

    Bibliography: p.
    Includes index.
    1.   Religion and science—History of Controversy
—United States.   I.   Title.
BL245.H66   215   78-53332
ISBN 0-8122-7748-1

Contents

Acknowledgments

I am most indebted to William H. Goetzmann, a master historian whose knowledge of the nineteenth century is exceeded by no one. No one has a greater capacity than he to make innovative but nevertheless workable suggestions and criticisms. Robert M. Crunden, to whom I am equally grateful, obliterated an earlier version of this manuscript with harsh comments, every one of which it richly deserved. My wife Beverly put up with my esoteric interests and foul disposition without complaint. I relied on her constantly.

Alexander Vucinich always welcomed me when I tried to profit from his encyclopedic insights into European science. With his departure from Austin, the University of Texas lost one of its greatest scholars. Howard Miller read this manuscript in its earlier stages and provided valuable comments and suggestions.

I am also grateful to Jeff Meikle, with whom I discussed my ideas almost daily, and who was always willing to take time out from his own work. I likewise thank Shirley Showalter, David Tanner, and Mark Smith, all of whom were quick to distinguish when I had something to say and when I was talking nonsense. Finally, I thank Darla Tarletz, who, while not a historian, is a master at sorting out confused and contradictory ideas and at setting misguided scholars back on the right track.

Introduction

During the first half of the nineteenth century, American Protestants became increasingly fascinated by the sciences. They developed a sophisticated natural theology built on the premise that nature contains clear, compelling evidence of God's existence and perfection. The Protestant believed that in order to do natural theology he had to be an "empiricist"; like Francis Bacon in the seventeenth century, he had to observe carefully the facts of nature, always avoiding useless speculation or "hypotheses." Secondly, the natural theologian had to be a scientist; he had to understand the natural phenomena he observed. Natural theology was a discipline in which Christian philosophy and empirical science merged.

To America's post-Enlightenment Protestants, science appeared to provide a special set of opportunities. Most of them believed that the science of the Enlightenment had not been particularly conducive to orthodox Christian belief. At the same time, however, most orthodox Protestants felt that Enlightenment science had been far too speculative, based much more on abstract systems than on carefully collected data. The new "Baconian" science of the nineteenth century promised to be much more supportive of their own Christian beliefs.

For American Protestants, the result of this optimism was the enthusiastic incorporation of the natural sciences into their college curricula. In the beginning of the nineteenth century, American colleges began hiring full-time scientists. They did not engage them, however, to conduct research or to develop new technologies, but to teach young students that nature, like history and scripture, revealed the perfections and sovereignty of God.

In this way nineteenth-century American Protestantism conducted a broad experiment in the unification of knowledge and belief. Above all, Protestants tried to create a religion free from all doubt. The orthodox Protestant did not want to confess anything he could not prove, so he devised a "scientific" theology that could prove everything.

By 1860, however, the experiment had clearly failed. The facts that looked like the great hope of Christianity in 1800 proved to be its nemesis a half century later. American Protestants had attempted to make religion into a science. It became, however, a pseudoscience, whose "facts" would not hold up in the face of the more convincing facts of geology or biology. Through those years orthodox Americans taught a difficult lesson, although many refused to learn it themselves: facts and values are not easily mixed. When religion becomes scientific, it ceases to be religious. Their religion without doubt became a religion so dubious that only the most closed-minded, blindly committed could take it seriously.

The first half of this work discusses people who were chiefly theologians and philosophers; the second half is concerned primarily with scientists. However, this book has been organized as a history of science and not as a history of religion. The people in it were selected and arranged because of the way they responded to important scientific issues, not because of their membership in any particular religious denomination or institution. Nevertheless, the nineteenth-century Americans treated here did hold some important religious commitments in common. Almost all were Protestant. A nation with no influential

Catholic or Jewish universities and almost exclusively Protestant religious publications developed an overwhelmingly Protestant understanding of the relationship between science and religion. Most of the Americans described here were also united by their "orthodoxy." That is, each of them believed he was the beneficiary of a long and powerful religious tradition. That tradition included a commitment to two broad Christian principles: first, that God created nature and that the evidence of his creative activity is obvious; secondly, that God provided additional, completely reliable information about himself in the Holy Bible. Although the orthodox Presbyterian and the orthodox Unitarian might disagree about many of the details, they shared those two fundamental beliefs. Invariably, the rebels who departed from orthodoxy doubted or compromised at least one of them.

That dual religious commitment had always been a central aspect of Christian belief. For evangelicals, however, it became one of the casualties of the nineteenth century. Most orthodox Protestants had no trouble reconciling Christianity and geology in 1800; but most found it almost impossible to reconcile biology and Christianity in 1860. After the Civil War, science and American Protestantism became increasingly divided. Many scientists became anti-Christian, convinced that orthodox Christianity was inherently opposed to science. On the other hand, orthodox Protestants became increasingly distrustful of the sciences, always fearing that ultimately they might have to compromise even more of their Christian faith.

At the risk of gross oversimplification, I also add a word on the period itself. To say it was "Romantic," while true, is to say far too many things at the same time. In a way this book is an extended definition of what it meant to be "Romantic." Perhaps it is sufficient here simply to say that after 1800 many American intellectuals began to realize that space, time, and the varieties of experience were all much greater than most of them had imagined before. More than any previous age, the Romantic era was fascinated by the remote, the changing, and the challenging.

But such fascinations entailed considerable risk, and they created a particularly uncomfortable tension in Protestant orthodoxy. First of all, Protestants believed wholeheartedly that no matter how big the world was, God was bigger. At the same time, however, they believed that the world conveyed a message to Christian man. To that extent, the world had to "make sense." There had to be identifiable lines between the true and the false, between the known, the unknown and the unknowable. The Romantic world was not only bigger than the historical Christian world, it was also infinitely more difficult to understand. As the universe began to appear more mysterious, and as God himself became a greater mystery, many Protestants began to feel they could accept these new complexities only with great difficulty. Many began to feel that they could not accept them at all.

Science and Religion in America
1800-1860

1

Orthodoxy and Empiricism

John Witherspoon and his wife Elizabeth arrived at the College of New Jersey at Princeton with mixed feelings. He was a man with a dynamic and tireless constitution, who, in spite of efforts to the contrary, frequently appeared academic and far removed from the worldly politics of eighteenth-century religion and education. She, an equally dynamic woman who had somewhat rudely stepped out of her role as wife of a prominent Scottish minister and let it be known that she did not intend to leave her civilized home to create a new one in the American wilderness. But a charming young American medical student at Edinburgh named Benjamin Rush convinced her that America was not the savage wasteland she had imagined. They now received as warm a welcome as could be hoped for by any new college president's family. Dozens of distinguished gentlemen met them at the docks when they disembarked from the *Peggy* on 7 August 1768. Then there followed a few days of intended rest, always disturbed by dozens of queries concerning the embattled and divided Presbyterian Church back in Scotland, and at the same time an overload of information about the equally embattled Presbyterian Church in America.

Witherspoon had been called to Princeton in order to close a breach that threatened immediate schism in American Presbyterianism. In the twenty-five years since the Great Awakening, Presbyterians and Congregationalists, Baptists and even Anglicans had faced growing contention within their ranks. The issues were broad, dividing two very different political philosophies, two views of education, and two sharply antagonistic ideas about the nature of religious experience. The College of New Jersey had been caught squarely in the middle of the Presbyterian conflict. Founded by Jonathan Dickinson, one of the few leaders who retained the respect of both sides of the revival controversy, the institution managed for a while to preserve the unity of the Presbyterian Church. Late in his life, however, Dickinson opted for the New Side, prorevivalist party. From that time on the college presidency remained firmly in revivalist control. Only when the fifth president, Samuel Finley, died in 1766 did that tradition come to an end.

The church itself was a shambles. The New Side stood for revivalism and the Holy Spirit, but it also stood fiercely for orthodoxy and was inclined toward a narrow antiworldliness, so much so that many antirevivalists were considering joining the more cosmopolitan Anglican Church. The threat that Anglicanism might grow stronger in New Jersey exacerbated Presbyterian fears that Tories were plotting to take over evangelical churches, educational institutions, and perhaps even the government itself. Fearing this, Governor William Franklin made it clear that "the sooner Presbyterians buried their differences and united their forces the better would be their position to cope with that branch of the Christian Church which they called 'the enemy.' "[1] The Princeton trustees received this as a mandate to return the school to the middle of the road.

The members of the Old Side were eager for compromise. They quickly presented the trustees with a petition proposing the appointment of a president, two professors in the sciences, and one professor of divinity. The antirevivalists suggested that the president and one of the professors be selected from the

Old Side, while the two remaining professors be taken from the New Side. This, they said, would balance the faculty.[2]

But they underestimated the strength of the New Side. The proposal was rejected and the trustees were caught in a stalemate. They finally decided to choose an orthodox clergyman from Scotland who had not been involved in the struggle and would not be inclined to side with either party. He could then select his own faculty. The plan was eventually acceptable to everyone, and then began the long period of communication between the New World and the Old that led to the immigration of the Reverend John Witherspoon to New Jersey.

The new president was a little more headstrong than most of the trustees had anticipated. No sooner had he taken office than he started making changes. Witherspoon found that the division in the church had taken its toll on the College. Instruction was weak, the library was small, and much of it was inappropriate to the needs of the students. More seriously, the school was badly in debt. Witherspoon fought on all fronts at once. Immediately after becoming settled he went on an extensive fundraising tour into Virginia. He added his own remarkable collection of three hundred books to the college library and arranged for further gifts from Scottish benefactors back home. He also began buying scientific equipment: the famous Rittenhouse orrery, a "terrestrial globe," and dozens of maps. He reinforced entrance requirements, which had grown lax through the years, and redefined the curriculum.

All of these things contributed to the respectability of the College and made its standards more like those of Harvard and Yale. But none of them had the effect of his most lasting contribution: the introduction of Scottish Common-Sense Realism. Scottish Realism became much more than another philosophical theory taught in a particular set of lectures on the little campus. It became an evangelical world-view that permeated every classroom and which eventually influenced hundreds of ministers, countless schoolmasters, and dozens of practicing scientists and physicians. In Witherspoon's lectures lay a Scottish Realist theory of education, a Scottish Realist approach to philosophy, and, most importantly, a highly distinctive Scottish Realist method of scientific investigation.

Scottish Common-Sense Realism was a unique product of the Scottish Enlightenment of the eighteenth century. It was the answer of the orthodox to John Locke, David Hume, and Bishop George Berkeley. Locke had argued that at birth a man's mind is an absolute blank—a *tabula rasa*. Every bit of information he stores in his head reflects something communicated to him through his senses. The senses provide the mind with "ideas," representations of the world that appear as images inside one's head. A man's knowledge about the physical world is nothing more than the sum of the ideas implanted in his mind by his senses, together with his memory of former, similar ideas. Furthermore, his knowledge of the spiritual world—of God, life after death, or the meaning of life—could come only as a result of inferences from these empirical ideas, or else from ideas generated by a special revelation from God—the Bible. Gone was Calvin's *Semen Religionis*, the seed of religion or consciousness of God born into every man. If a man had any knowledge about God, he had it by his own experience.

Scottish Realism managed to come to terms with John Locke—at least to a point—but not with David Hume. Hume was an unorthodox product of the early Scottish Enlightenment. Born in Edinburgh in 1711 and nearly always a resident there, Hume devoted his life to a study of Locke and the empirical philosophy. He accepted Locke's suggestion that man is born with an empty mind and that everything he ever knows must come through his senses. At the same time, however, Hume realized that Locke did not follow consistently the way of thinking that he himself had described. While professing to know only what could be derived from his senses, Locke nevertheless believed a great many things that he accepted purely on faith and without sensory evidence. For example, he believed without proof that his senses were giving him reliable information about the external world. If his senses were the only link between the ideas in his mind and the outside world, then what was to assure him that his eyes and ears were not telling him lies? Furthermore, Locke accepted on faith that there is an essentially honest God who gives men reliable information about himself. Why could he not just as easily believe in Descartes' wicked demon, giving men false information about a God who really did not exist?

The conclusion was obvious. If man knows nothing but what his senses tell him, and if his senses can tell him nothing about the most fundamental questions he could ask about the universe, then he could not know the answers to these questions. Hume's position resulted in one of the most absolute scepticisms in Western philosophy. If all that Hume said were actually true, man would no longer have convincing grounds for knowing anything at all.

One possible answer to Hume's position came from George Berkeley, an early eighteenth-century Anglican Bishop. Berkeley agreed with Locke and Hume that all of a person's knowledge consists of ideas of external objects. Perhaps this is so, he reasoned, because nothing but the ideas themselves exist. If the whole world were composed of nothing but ideas—no inert physical objects "out there" in space—and if man's knowledge consists of those same ideas, then in a very real sense one could say that man knows the external world directly. Nothing can exist, said Berkeley, except in the minds of perceiving beings. But, he went on to say, God perceives everything and at all times; the world is in fact the sum of God's ideas. Man, as it were, shares in God's ideas and therefore has accurate knowledge about the world.

Most people found Berkeley's solution unacceptable. Common sense told them that the world really contains hard rocks, soft babies, living organisms—not simply countless incorporeal "ideas" shared by a collection of perceiving minds. Berkeley's reasoning seemed to contradict the obvious.

Scottish evangelicals demanded something different. And an answer came from Aberdeen, only a few miles from Hume's hometown. Thomas Reid was a rather late bloomer in philosophy. Although he was a year older than David Hume, he did not begin writing until thirty years after Hume's first publication. Reid's *Inquiry into the Human Mind on the Principles of Common Sense* was so well received that it earned him a chair of moral philosophy at the University of Glasgow.

Reid began his *Inquiry* with an attack on the general Lockean theory of ideas. Locke, he said, had confused two quite distinct meanings of the word "idea." "To have an idea" refers to a subjective *act* in which the mind focuses its attention upon some external object. However, Locke made the idea itself the object of knowledge. In Locke's paradigm it would not be correct to say that men have ideas about *things*; they only "have ideas" about ideas. Building on this error, argued Reid, it was quite easy for Hume to say that one cannot know any part of the external world. "Mr. Hume's system does not even leave him a *self* to claim the property of his impressions and ideas."[3]

Implicit in Reid's thought was a notion that the mind is a functioning instrument that performs processes, not simply a stockpile of nonmaterial objects called "ideas." Locke and Hume had argued that man can know only what comes to him through his senses. He cannot perceive objects but only ideas. Therefore, he can know only ideas and not objects themselves. Reid agreed that man can know only what he learns through his senses, but he rather cleverly added that it is *ideas*, not objects, that cannot be verified—not if "idea" means a bit of information inside one's brain. Man knows objects; but he knows them by means of ideas.

Reid's greatest service to philosophy involved the union of knowledge and belief. Locke had intended to show what people can *know* about the world; he was not particularly concerned with what someone might happen to *believe* about it. Hume went a step further by showing that people can "know" nothing about the external world, not if "knowing" means being logically certain about something. Reid's notion was quite similar to Hume's in one respect: both believed that on the basis of empirical data alone no one can ever construct an unassailable argument for the reality of the external world. At some point one would have to accept some kind of statement that is unverifiable, perhaps like "I believe that my senses are giving me reliable information"; or perhaps, "I believe that the picture of the world presented by my mind is something like the world that actually exists." In Reid's words, "when I perceive a tree before me, my faculty of seeing gives me not only a notion of simple apprehension of the tree, but a belief of its existence . . .; and this *judgment* or *belief* is not got by comparing ideas, it is included in the very nature of the perception."[4] The unverifiable belief that what I am looking at really exists is forced upon me by the act of perception, not by logical argument. This feeling is so powerful that it is as convincing as logical demonstration.

Because everyone has it, Reid called this feeling "Common Sense."

Although Reid rejected much of Lockean sensationalism, he did not return to the older rationalisms of the Continent, such as that of Descartes. He was an empiricist who still believed that all of man's knowledge of the external world comes to him through his senses. For Reid, as for Kant several years later, the mind's rational powers were not useful for creating new "knowledge." They served instead to establish necessary nonempirical connections between bits of empirical data. Reid called these necessary connections "self-evident principles." They included mathematical and logical axioms, and also certain principles that Reid "derived" from empirical data, such as "whatever begins to exist must have a cause that produced it." Reid believed that although such a statement is not verifiable, everyone whose senses are functioning properly must believe it. These beliefs are also a part of "Common Sense."

Reid's "self-evident principles" included a number of necessary presuppositions of empirical science. These statements were by their nature unprovable, but science could not proceed without them. Included among them were, "those things did really happen which I distinctly remember." No one can verify his memory in any absolute sense, but everyone must use it and trust it. Another such statement was "that in the phenomena of nature what is to be will probably be like to what has been in similar circumstances." This unprovable statement—the predictibility of nature—is a necessary presupposition of all inductive reasoning.[5]

Witherspoon learned Common Sense Realism by reading the works of Reid and his two most popular followers, James Beattie and Dugald Stewart. When he came to New Jersey, Witherspoon used these new ideas to begin a rapid transformation of the College at Princeton. He frequently shrugged off the controversies generated by the Great Awakening. Instead, he began his own intellectual debate with the tutors—the young graduates who coached the students through their daily lessons. Jonathan Edwards, Jr., Joseph Periam, and John Blair had been following in the steps of the late Jonathan Edwards, the great theologian of New England Calvinism. But Edwards had died an idealist. He, like Berkeley, had denied the existence of a material world. By the 1760s, idealism had spread through the College and had led to discussions of such metaphysical niceties as the nature of Being-in-General, of absolute space, and of the difference between contingent and necessary existence. Witherspoon would have none of it. He first "reasoned against the system"; then, as he often did, he mocked it. Finally he forcefully insisted that the three idealist tutors resign. After that, Scottish Realism became the official philosophy of the College of New Jersey.[6]

Through Witherspoon's development of Princeton as one of the most impressive fortresses of Protestant orthodoxy, the Scottish Realist method of understanding the world became practically identified with the evangelical point of view. In the late eighteenth century, "empirical science," which at that time referred chiefly to the sort of experimenting advocated by Francis Bacon in the seventeenth century, was not considered a threat to Christianity. The threats were deism and atheism, and those beliefs did not derive from experimentation but from rationalization, from men who allowed the logical powers of their minds to carry their thoughts to scepticism about God and his works. The Scottish Realists had only to look at Voltaire and Hume to see two very different men who drew their conclusions not from conducting experiments with nature but rather from sitting in front of their fires and thinking about the problems of knowledge, causation, free will, and divine providence. These men were not physicists but metaphysicians; their conclusions were not "evidences" but "mere hypotheses." Witherspoon and the evangelicals of his time saw that such speculation always tended toward infidelity.

The Common Sense intellectual of the late eighteenth century believed in three sources of knowledge. First, he could not deny the existence of reason: the logical powers of men to make relationships between ideas; to discern causation, moral purpose, and ethical responsibility; and to present arguments for the existence of God. Reason distinguished men from animals. By 1780, however, evangelicals were generally agreed that the Enlightenment had placed more emphasis on reason than it deserved. The second source of knowledge was nature. Men could collect the data of the natural world, arrange them, and mold them into conclusions about man himself and his environment.

The third source of knowledge was scriptural revelation from God, knowledge available to anyone who could read or hear a sermon.

The Scottish Realist believed that nature and Scripture were the two ways in which God spoke most directly to man. Calvinists referred to them respectively as "natural revelation" and "special revelation." The Scriptures contained a set of facts in exactly the same way that nature contained facts, and learning from the Bible was an empirical process. One had to receive the data, analyze and organize them, and draw valid conclusions. Conclusions venturing too far beyond the explicit data were unacceptable "hypotheses," like scientific statements that did not have enough facts to support them. In order for the chemist or botanist to do his work he must have certain training and equipment. The theologian or moral philosopher must have a comparable set of tools: a knowledge of Greek and Hebrew, an education in the principles of biblical interpretation, lexicons and commentaries on the work of his predecessors, and rules for systematizing his findings into some logical pattern. The tools and data sources for scientist and theologian were different, but the methods of investigation were essentially the same. The development of this method of religious and philosophical investigation generated a new form of Protestant orthodoxy.

One historian of American philosophy has defined "orthodoxy" as the systematizing, recording, and disseminating of a particular body of knowledge, rather than speculative creation of new ideas.[7] The orthodox in any area are those who build upon a well-established system for describing facts, perhaps making refinements or improvements, always creating new distinctions, writing new interpretations, and making cautious additions. American Scottish Realists were proud of their orthodoxy. They composed dozens of classroom texts in philosophy. They insisted that all philosophical conclusions be correctly derived from given data. They shunned speculation. As Reid told them, "Conjectures and theories are the creatures of men, and will always be found very unlike the creatures of God. If we would know the works of God, we must consult themselves [sic] with attention and humility, without daring to add anything of ours to what they declare."[8] To allow each tutor to read widely in the Greek philosophers, Calvin, Descartes, or Locke, and then develop and teach his own system, was to invite trouble. With this in mind, America's Common Sense evangelicals began to produce teaching books in moral philosophy, divinity, and finally the natural sciences. The job of the instructor was to explain and answer questions about the assigned reading. To be sure, a tutor could slant the discussion in such a way as to satisfy his own beliefs, but the body of the work done in the classroom was always based on the facts given in the text, on work that had the prior approval of the college.

By this means knowledge became sterile. When thinking ceased to be original but was merely passed on from one student to the next, it stagnated. What one learned in the moral philosophy class was taught not because it was exciting or relevant or even helpful; it was taught because it was orthodox, because it had first been taught by someone whom the church or college recognized as an authority.

John Witherspoon's American successor was Samuel Stanhope Smith. Born in Pequia, Pennsylvania, in 1750, and having "a mind of no common order," Smith had everything it took to become the genius of orthodoxy. He began to study languages at the age of "six or seven," and he distinguished himself in his father's small academy "for his improvement in every branch to which he directed his attention." Arriving at Princeton at age sixteen, he was quickly caught up in Berkleian idealism and came "in great danger of making shipwreck of his religious principles." Fortunately, Witherspoon arrived just in time to take over the college and save Smith from his captors. Young Samuel then turned from New Divinity idealism to the works of Reid and Stewart, "the influence of which was quickly perceptible, in bringing back this gifted young man into the regions of common sense. . . . When his mind had once become steadfast in the right, it became so for life." After graduation Smith entered upon a short ministerial career and marriage to Witherspoon's oldest daughter. Seven years later he was president of Virginia's new Hampden-Sydney College. However, failing health kept him from doing an adequate job. In 1779 Witherspoon, always in correspondence with his young protégé, asked him to return to Princeton and take the chair of moral philosophy. That call was the beginning of a distinguished career for Smith. Witherspoon was soon "afflicted with total blindness, and many bodily infirmities, which in a great measure, incapacitated him for the duties of his office as President." Throughout the 1780s Smith performed nearly all of Witherspoon's tasks and began to assume much of the intellectual leadership of American Presbyterianism. With Witherspoon's death in 1794, Smith formally became president of the College.[9]

Smith Americanized the Scottish tradition that was carried across the ocean by Witherspoon. In Scotland the primary interest of philosophers had been Hume's empirical scepticism. But Hume never affected America as much as he had affected England and Scotland. American colleges were generally too pragmatic and too concerned with the developing sciences to worry much about the problems of religious knowledge.

In the 1780s the College of New Jersey was doing relatively well. It was larger and its curriculum more varied than at any previous time. But it still lagged far behind Harvard, Yale, and most European universities in the sciences.[10] Smith helped to correct this situation by his entrance into one of the most important scientific debates of his day: the controversy over the origin and physical nature of man.

Smith began investigating the problem in order to defend the Christian faith. His great scientific work, *An Essay on the Causes of the Variety of Complexion and Figure in the Human Species*, was a response to an earlier Scottish Realist, Lord Kames.[11] Kames had compiled his researches in physical anthropology into his 1774 *Sketches of the History of Man*, a popular book that came out in several editions throughout the remainder of the century.[12] Kames argued that the always perfect God had precisely fitted each race of mankind for its earthly home. Differences in body structure and color correlated perfectly with differences in environment. However, said Kames, that relationship was not the result of adaptation. Kames denied that species are able to adapt permanently to diverse environments. But how, then, could each race of man be so perfectly suited for its geographical climate? To Kames's readers the solution seemed obvious: Kames would suggest that there had been as many creations as there were races of men, that all men had not descended from a single "Adam and Eve." But to suggest that would have been heresy, and Kames was unwilling to go quite that far. Instead, he concocted a bizarre miracle that divided the Adamic race into different subgroups, "fitted for different climates." However, in the eyes of many evangelicals the damage had already been done. Although he did not assert multiple creations, Kames did hypothesize the existence of an extrabiblical miracle to account for the existence of the different races of men.

Smith's response to Kames immediately drew the attention of the scientific community to himself. By studying migration patterns and the experiences of people who had moved from one part of the world to another, Smith concluded that men were able to adapt permanently to new environments and pass these adaptations on to their offspring. In this way one original creation, with no intervening miracles, could account for all of the varieties of color and form among humans. By arguing this way, Smith hoped to do two things. First of all, he wanted to defend the veracity of scripture against the attacks of a writer who had at least implied that the Bible contains inconsistencies with the scientific record. Secondly, however, Smith tried to show that scientific investigation rightly conducted will never lead to conclusions that contradict the written Word of God. Smith gave most of his attention to the latter task.

Smith's certainty about science gave him "pleasure to observe . . . that the most extensive and accurate researches into the actual state, and the powers of nature, have ever served . . . to confirm the facts vouched to us by the authority of holy writ." Kames's suggestion that science and the Bible were inconsistent was a result of nothing more than his failure to understand true empirical science. "His dissertation commences with a speculative argument drawn from his own ideas of propriety, and the wisdom of providence."[13] Kames, quite simply, had used a speculative "hypothesis" rather than depending exclusively on the evidence. For Smith, "hypothesis" and "evidence" were mutually exclusive. "Evidence" was the stuff of which scientific conclusions were made. "Facts" always led to true knowledge of nature, God, and the self.

The *Essay's* statements on the origin of man, its defense of divine revelation and of the legitimacy of scientific investigation, made Smith a temporary hero among Presbyterians. But trouble was soon to follow. Smith was too innovative for his more orthodox colleagues. In the 1790s he pushed the trustees to approve the reduction of training in the classical languages to one year. This, he told Benjamin Rush, would give students more time to learn the infinitely more practical modern European languages and, more importantly, to study natural philosophy.[14] He appointed Princeton's first scientist to the faculty, the young chemist John Maclean. Smith spent a great deal of Presbyterian money on scientific apparatus. Finally, to the dismay of many of the college's constituents, he persuaded the trustees in 1799 that students should be allowed to come to the College to study exclusively "such subjects of science as they or their parents may select." The trustees listened to Smith's arguments and decided rather reluctantly that perhaps the idea was not so bad, provided that such students receive "certificates of proficiency" and not the standard academic degree.

The new program signaled trouble for the Presbyterian ministry, and therefore for Samuel Stanhope Smith. Intellectual influences from Europe, especially France, were growing increasingly secular. Jeffersonian democracy in America was not particularly religious. Rather than fighting the ways of the world, Smith was granting young Presbyterian boys the opportunity to obtain an essentially secular education in an institution that had been founded in order to preserve evangelical orthodoxy. In the early years of the nineteenth century, dozens of eager young students were sent to Princeton by parents hoping someday to have sons preaching or perhaps teaching in a new western academy. One by one these boys found the scientific, secular curriculum much more fascinating than classical languages and theology. In 1806 Henry Kollock, the College's only professor of theology, resigned for lack of students. By 1808 the Presbyterian Church faced a severe ministerial shortage, and Princeton—although it had plenty of students—was not producing nearly enough young candidates to fill the need.[15]

Smith's personal problems in dealing with his students only exacerbated his problems with the Church. A rather pompous man, proud of his oratory and attractive appearance, Smith alienated many students and found it difficult to command respect. Several crises in discipline resulted. The fire that destroyed Nassau Hall in 1802 was widely suspected to be student arson. In 1807 a student riot did severe damage to the buildings and grounds, and several students had to be dismissed. From 1806 to 1807 enrollment dipped from 200 to 112, and the corresponding loss of tuition income put the college in a critical financial position.[16]

The rumbling of conservative voices in the Church and the College grew louder by 1810. Ashbel Green, Samuel Miller, and Archibald Alexander, all conservative Old School Presbyterians, began campaigning for a divinity school, a seminary distinct from the college and designed exclusively for the training of ministerial candidates. In August 1812, the trustees approved plans for the new seminary. The chemist John Maclean resigned in protest against an act he thought subversive of sound educational principles. Smith followed him one day later.

Then the reaction set in. From the moment the seminary was created, the College received only secondary consideration from the trustees. Smith's job as president went to Ashbel Green, a reactionary whose interest was more in rigid orthodoxy than in liberal education. The result was predictible. While Harvard and Yale confronted and acquired dozens of new ideas from Europe, Princeton remained content to rely on Reid, Witherspoon, and the body of orthodox Calvinism. With the passing of Smith, the new method introduced into America by Witherspoon became frozen and lifeless.

Smith has posed a difficulty for historians because he does not seem to fit into the subsequent Princeton tradition of intellectual orthodoxy and doubt about science. Some historians have chosen to omit Smith from the "Princeton tradition."[17] Others, however, argue that there are really two traditions, perhaps even two currents in American evangelical thinking of the early nineteenth century.[18]

The more progressive tradition represented by Smith is, oddly enough, most similar to the oldest tradition in American religion. Seventeenth-century Puritans believed that God's word and work could not possibly conflict. Science and theology were merely two different ways of coming to know and appreciate God. Smith, in effect, did nothing more than dress up this tradition in more sophisticated, nineteenth-century garb. His science tried to be more empirical and less speculative; his theories were more complex; and his understanding of the Bible was more inductive. But the basic idea was the same: the study of science could do nothing but good for the student of God's word. Furthermore, the Baconian method of investigation was the only reliable way through which man could come to know both God's word and his works. Fallen man did not have the purity of mind nor the analytic power to arrive at God from within; knowledge of God had to come through something external—facts of nature and facts of scripture.

The other view was much less worldly. It also held in theory that God's testimony in the Bible did not contradict His testimony in nature. But science is not nature, just as theology is not the Bible. Both are merely man's interpretations of God's revelations of Himself. Both, as activities performed by fallen man, are likely to be filled with errors.

Archibald Alexander objected to Smith's scientific curriculum, not because he believed that science was bad, but because he feared that man's misunderstanding of nature could lead to heterodoxy or infidelity. Beyond that was a problem of influence. In spite of the fact that the spiritual growth of the flock was always more important than knowledge of God's work in the world, science persistently proved more interesting to young men than divinity. Conservatives viewed the development of the scientific curriculum with growing distrust. As Alexander explained, "the great extension of the physical sciences, and the taste and fashion of the age, have given such a shape and direction to the academical course that I confess it appears to me to be little adapted to introduce youth to the study of the Sacred Scriptures."[19]

However, John Witherspoon, Samuel Stanhope Smith, and Scottish Realism did leave one very important legacy with both liberals and conservatives: the insistence that all knowledge, both natural and scriptural, must be based on facts and not "hypotheses." Both sides reacted with equal vigilance against the Enlightenment's complex epistemologies, abstract and speculative metaphysics, and heavy reliance on reason. Error was sure to be the result of such speculation. As Smith told his students, "the extreme refinements of reason, which arise from the natural ambition of human pride, to extend its authority beyond its proper sphere, always tend to dogmatical error in bold and ardent minds, or to the cold indifference of scepticism, in minds of the opposite character."[20]

As a result of these two contravening traditions, a tendency developed in evangelical thinking of the early nineteenth century to pay lip service to science and natural evidence, but always at a distance. To talk about scientific method, about sticking to the facts, and about the great strengths of Bacon and the Scottish Realists was one thing. To turn from theology to scientific research was quite another.

In short, there was significant doubt in evangelical belief that nature always reveals the perfect Word of God. Most evangelicals tried to believe that only "bad" science could lead men away from God. But as scientists began to suggest more threatening geological and biological theories, evangelical doubts would grow stronger. Perhaps even good science, if pursued in the wrong spirit, was of questionable religious value. To be sure, the attack on science *per se* was an extreme position, advocated by only a few. But Archibald Alexander's resentment as he watched students turn from their Greek manuals to the laboratories of philosophical apparatus survived that champion of Protestant orthodoxy by many years.

2

Knowing and Believing

The Scottish Enlightenment did not come exclusively to Princeton. President Witherspoon was among the first to carry the ideas of the conservative Scottish evangelicals to America, but there were other prophets, and they went to a large number of American colleges. David Tappan, Hollis Professor of Divinity at Harvard and a Moderate Calvinist like many of his Presbyterian colleagues, introduced the books of the Scottish Realists into his classrooms in the 1790s. By 1810 Scottish philosophy was well entrenched at Harvard, and it became an integral part of the growing Unitarian movement. Harvard moral philosophers Levi Frisbie, Levi Hedge, James Walker, and Francis Bowen read and taught the Scottish philosophers to their students into the middle of the century.[1]

When Tappan died in 1803 and was replaced by a liberal, conservative Calvinists left to form Andover Theological Seminary as an evangelical alternative to Unitarianism. Those who left Harvard to join Andover carried Scottish philosophy with them and taught it throughout the period of Andover's dominance of New England Congregationalism. For years the philosophical leader of Andover was Scottish Realist Leonard Woods, Jr., a conservative Calvinist. He was later replaced by Edwards Amasa Park, who was much more liberal than Woods but equally influenced by Scottish Realism. The Unitarian Controversy and its impact on New England thought is real enough, but one thing certain is that Scottish Realism was not at issue: both sides accepted it implicitly and its ideas dominated the thought of three or four generations of Harvard and Andover professors and clergymen.[2]

Yale's Timothy Dwight read the Scottish philosophers avidly and taught them to his students in the 1790s. In fact, it was a combination of Edwardsian Calvinism and Scottish Arminianism that led to the successive modifications of orthodoxy that characterized the New Haven Theology. This system for making Calvin more palatable to people rapidly losing their interest in complex theologies was filled with Common-Sense Realism. Nathaniel Taylor, its foremost advocate in the 1820s, read widely in the Scottish philosophers.[3]

What began at Princeton, Harvard, Andover, and Yale spread widely. For sixty years the men who taught the most popular courses in moral and analytic philosophy, who questioned and licensed ministerial candidates, who produced the scientific thinkers and wrote the college textbooks, were disciples of the Scottish Enlightenment. Francis Alison introduced it to the College of Philadelphia; Samuel Stanhope Smith carried it to Hampden-Sydney College, Virginia; Mark Hopkins taught it at Williams College, Massachusetts.

The reason for Scottish Realism's popularity is not hard to explain. Evangelical Protestants found it very difficult to enter the nineteenth century. It was a time of great uncertainty, countless theological heterodoxies, and dozens of internal divisions in American churches. Princetonians spent much of their lives worrying about what the Enlightenment could do to their young men. Yale's Timothy Dwight practically equated infidelity with the French Revolution. Harvard Unitarians vigorously attacked deists and others who doubted revelation and miracles. The Age of Reason was banging hard on the doors of America's Protestant churches, and their clergymen and intellectual leaders were determined not to let it in.

To make matters worse for churches and colleges, the most influential threats were not isolated in Europe; many of them originated at home. Reasonable thinking had given America great statesmen and fine leadership in the Revolution—but it had also created religious radicals: Jefferson, Paine, and Ethan Allen.

Allen's *Reason the Only Oracle of Man* (1784), was an exercise in sceptical metaphysics. Allen speculated that Reason was the only means by which man could come to know God. Reason indicates, said Allen, that the world had no beginning in time, that "from the necessary attributes, perfections, eternity and infinity of God, we may demonstrate that creation must also have been eternal and infinite." Moses' account of the creation was obviously a fabrication; how could an inspired narrative suggest that God created the sun, moon, and stars after he created light? Allen eventually included the entire Bible in his attack. Revelation from God, he reasoned, must be rational in order to be understood; therefore "a revelation must consist of an assemblage of rational ideas intelligibly communicated." But this fact precludes any supernatural origin; a "rational" revelation "could be nothing more or less than a transcript of the law of nature, predicated on reason, and would be no more supernatural, than the reason of man may be supposed to be."[4] Allen thought it was irrational to believe in miracles. He insisted that the Bible could not be infallible because it had been fallibly translated and copied. In short, *Reason the Only Oracle of Man* was a systematic attempt to undermine practically every belief that American Protestantism, both evangelical and liberal, supported.

Thomas Paine was even more scandalous; he was everything American evangelicals loathed. Unstable, frequently intoxicated, twice accused of immoral conduct in his job, he was far too colorful to suit the orthodox as either philosopher or patriot. "A mongrel between pig and puppy," equally patriotic John Adams would call him. "Begotten by a wild boar on a bitch wolf."[5] By 1794 Paine was an old man and his patriotism was behind him. His religious views were not. He wrote *The Age of Reason* as a manifesto of his mature beliefs. His work showed a greater consciousness of science than Allen's book. Paine saw astronomy, with its exact mathematics, perfect circles, and orderly, predictible phenomena, as the best possible evidence of a supreme being. To that point he was a good theist and even the evangelicals could agree with him. But Paine found it unreasonable that the same God who created a perfectly functioning solar system would commit a blunder that necessitated sending his own "son" to die for the sins of the world. He found it quite irrational to think that a god who speaks to man so precisely through nature would also want to speak through the Bible, a book full of historical inaccuracies and internal contradictions, which attributes immoral acts to the Old Testament God, and which is full of scientific errors. All of this made Paine think that "it would be more consistent that we called it the word of a demon than the word of God."[6]

Perhaps because of Paine's popularity during the American Revolution, perhaps because his book was more sophisticated and timely than Allen's, Paine drew the brunt of the evangelical reaction. No one was more incensed than Presbyterian Elias Boudinot, director of the United States Mint in Philadelphia. Boudinot had been shocked to discover that, due to overprinting, thousands of copies of *The Age of Reason* had been sold at auction in Philadelphia for a cent and a half apiece, "whereby children, servants, and the lowest people, had been tempted to purchase [it] from the novelty of buying a book at so low a price."[7] Boudinot's angry response was *The Age of Revelation: or "the Age of Reason" Shown to be an Age of Infidelity.* Boudinot charged Paine with being unscientific and inconsistent. By any reasonable criteria for historical verification Paine would be forced to agree that the witnesses of biblical miracles were sufficiently reliable and numerous to establish a case. Furthermore, Paine was inconsistent when he said that Jesus was "an excellent moralist" but not divine. Jesus himself claimed to be divine; and if he was not, then he was a liar.

Paine's attacks on the inspired Bible were fairly representative of the deism of the Enlightenment. Deism had attempted to make a clean break with the authoritarian, dogmatic thinking of post-Reformation orthodoxy. Reason was the mechanism by which a person could keep himself free from heavy reliance on such authorities as Aristotle, the Church Fathers, or John Calvin. However, the use of reason alone severely limited the number of statements one could make about God. This led Enlightenment theologians like Thomas Paine or Joseph Priestley to suggest a sort of "theological reductionism"—a Christianity that contained only those doctrines that a reasonable, "enlightened" person could accept. Evangelicals were also in favor of being reasonable, up to a point. But such reductionism was carrying things a little too far, for the doctrines most important to historical Christianity—the Trinity, the Atonement, and the infallibility of the Bible—would have to be excised through this process. Protestant evangelicals and moderates who considered themselves intellectually sophisticated did not want to sound antirational, and they often argued that reason and authority were not mutually exclusive but rather were two different means by which one can know God. They believed that one particular authority, the Holy Bible, and reason supplemented each other perfectly. Revelation says that "the heavens declare the glory of God" and thereby suggests that man can discern the workings of God in nature. But at the same time, the Bible says much more about God than can be acquired by the mere studying of the nodes about a stem or the movement of the planets.[8]

Orthodox Protestants needed to find a sophisticated, reasonable thinker who could justify and explain this use of reason and revelation together—a man who would symbolize the Protestant commitment to a complete and rational world-view, built on both nature and Scripture. By the beginning of the nineteenth century, orthodox Protestants had agreed that Francis Bacon was such a symbol.

Bacon symbolized facts and knowledge, not speculation. More important, he symbolized the use of a single method of gathering information about both God and the world. The "Baconian method" suggested a process that was shrewd and analytic, that did not accept things unless they were founded upon hard evidence. It symbolized the uselessness of metaphysics (although the men who praised the method most involved themselves in endless metaphysical controversies). It symbolized the belief that knowledge about God and knowledge about the world are of the same kind, that in the process of investigating one a person always makes discoveries about the other. In short, by citing Bacon the orthodox could convince themselves that they were doing theology "scientifically," and that the conclusions to which they came were just as irrefutable as the conclusions of the natural scientist or mathematician.

After 1810 the influence of Baconianism grew geometrically in America. By 1823 Edward Everett, editor of the *North American Review*, could say that "at the present day, as is well known, the *Baconian* philosophy has become synonymous with the *true* philosophy."[9] Not many orthodox Americans disagreed. Characteristically, however, Everett's article said nothing about how one uses the Baconian method. The fact was that those who most lauded Baconianism had a severely limited understanding of the methods of scientific investigation. Most could simply chant with Presbyterian Albert Barnes that Baconianism "consists in a careful and patient examination of *facts*, or the phenomena of the universe, and deriving from the observation of those facts the principles of a just philosophy."[10] Nearly everyone who talked about Baconianism put words like "fact" and "hypothesis" in bold print or italics, as if each was the first preacher of a bold new gospel. But by 1840 the gospel of Baconianism was neither bold nor new, and more analytic minds were beginning to realize that simply to say that Baconianism consists in "a careful and patient examination of *facts*" was not to say very much at all. Only then did American defenses of empirical method become substantially more sophisticated.

This early lack of clarity led to a wide variety of ideas about how the word "Baconianism" must be applied in science. One historian believes that the term came to have three meanings.[11] First, it meant "empiricism," or the idea that scientific statements must rest solidly on observed facts. Secondly, it meant "antitheoretical": that science must avoid "hypotheses" and not go beyond immediate observation. Finally, "Baconianism" frequently meant the identification of all science with taxonomy. American scientists usually used the second or third meaning when they discussed method. However, nonscientists, especially theologians and moral philosophers, thought primarily in terms of the first two meanings. For the clergyman or professor writing on natural theology, "Baconianism" meant in some very unclear way that learning about God and the universe necessitated a method that relied on "facts" and not "hypotheses." John Brazer, Harvard-educated pastor of the Unitarian North Church in Salem, Massachusetts, argued in an 1835 Dudleian lecture that "a priori" or deductive reasoning is "wholly independent of all facts, and cannot be applied to the authentication of any fact."[12] There was only one true method for ascertaining *facts*, such as the existence of God, and that was "the *inductive* mode of Reasoning." Still talking orthodox Baconianism, Brazer further asserted "that a being, whom we call God, or Deity, exists, is a proposition to be proved, in the same way as the proposition that a certain law of relative forces reigns among the orbs of the planetary system; —namely, by that great organ or instrument of inquiry called the *inductive process* of reasoning; whose principles were first fully developed by Lord Bacon." So much for the description of the rigorous method to be applied. After telling his listeners that he would carefully dissect nature on his laboratory table, and find inside irrefutable evidence of God's existence, Brazer launched into the same kind of speculative reasoning that theologians had been indulging in for more than a millenium: "Now, if it can be shown, that in the works of nature, or in the material universe around us, order, beauty, harmony, and concurrence of means to ends prevail, which are precisely similar to those which . . . are uniformly connected with mind or intelligence, . . . then the inference is irresistible that these . . . must be referred to mind or intelligence as their producing cause." Brazer's "rigorous," fact-seeking method became the most speculative of metaphysical essays—a rehash of the teleological argument, the principles of causation, and the nature of creative intelligence.[13]

It was not entirely the Americans' fault that they talked one kind of investigative method and practiced another. This scientific duality was very much a part of British philosophy, where Baconianism was supposedly practiced in its purest form. Americans looked to England for scientific and philosophical guidance. When Samuel Tyler, perhaps the greatest American defender of the Baconian method in the 1840s, wanted to defend his philosophy from the Continental charge that it led to materialism and atheism, his answer was to cite England's great books on natural theology as proof that good empirical method always led to the discovery of God's greatness. Tyler admired the work of Bishop Butler and William Paley, but he reserved his loudest praise for the *Bridgewater Treatises* as the finest of all works designed to prove that the course of nature and the providence of God are always in harmony. Regarding the *Treatises*, Tyler noted that "the more Baconian philosophy has been cultivated, the more has natural theology advanced." Furthermore, said Tyler, the essential correctness of the Baconian philosophy is borne out by the fact that because of it "all the great discoveries of modern science have been British and not Continental."[14]

The *Bridgewater Treatises* began as a great project to unify theology with the sciences. Before his death in 1829 the eighth Earl of Bridgewater, Francis Henry Egerton, had charged the executors of his estate with selecting eight authors to write scientific studies demonstrating the "Power, Wisdom, and Goodness of God" as manifested in creation.[15] Among the most powerful of the *Treatises* was William Whewell's *Astronomy and General Physics Considered with Reference to Natural Theology.* Whewell tried "to show how the views of the creation, preservation, and the government of the universe which natural science opens to us, harmonize with our belief in a Creator, Governor, and Preserver of the World."[16] Whewell found evidence of God in every mechanism of the universe.

The *Bridgewater Treatises* covered a variety of subjects, although no one handled them quite as well as Whewell. The list of eight titles included books on physics, the natural sciences, and human anatomy. At its end was a study of a truly sublime subject: Thomas Chalmers' *On the Power, Wisdom, and Goodness of God as Manifested in the Adaptation of External Nature to the Moral and Intellectual Constitution of Man.* Chalmers attempted to apply the inductive method to the tracing of the "marks of a divine intelligence in the mechanism of human society, and in the frame-work of the social and economical systems to which men are conducted."[17]

Americans loved the *Treatises.* Mark Hopkins, a bright young physician and professor of moral philosophy who would one day be the president of Williams College, reviewed Whewell's book in 1833 and found in it a scientific answer to "the deplorable atheism of such men as LaPlace." Whewell used clear evidence of God working through the cosmic mechanism, rather than unfounded speculation about a self-sufficient universal machine.[18] Warren Burton, the liberal minister of the East Cambridge Unitarian Church, agreed. He regarded Whewell's effort as a clear demonstration that "all the changes of nature proceed from the instantaneous impulses of [God's] almighty will."[19]

Two things are quite clear about American religion and science in the 1820s and 1830s. First, Americans were very excited about something they called the "empirical" or "Baconian" method of acquiring factual knowledge, and many believed that this method was the only one a Christian could use. Secondly, for all the excitement, no one had a clear idea of how to go about using the method. "Baconianism" was not really a tool; it was a symbol—something to use in the opening paragraphs of essays in order to show that one was on guard against rationalism, deism, speculative science, or anything else that might approach infidelity. To use the name of Bacon in an introductory statement was to guarantee an audience. After that one could go on to the business at hand, which was essentially to do Christian metaphysics in the same way it had been done for nearly two thousand years.

Baconianism gave security to threatened evangelicals. It allowed men who only grazed the surface of science to believe that their theological picture included a complete and perfect scientific world-view. It permitted the minister as philosopher of science to believe that he knew more about "science" than the practicing physician or botanist, simply because the former had a complete perspective on the way God works in the universe. To the orthodox, Baconian science, properly used, could never lead men away from God. Any time a scientist *did* appear to be departing from orthodoxy, something was sure to be wrong with his methods, motives, or data. The evangelicals saw Baconianism as a missing link, a method that would apply to theological as well as physical investigation. It confirmed the evangelical's belief that there was an external unity imposed upon the world, that all its pieces somehow fit into place with one another. It also confirmed his belief that theology is a science—a truly empirical science. This belief could lead the introverted, intellectual minister from the smallest Congregational Church in New England to believe that he held the key to the universe and the answers to the most ultimate questions his parishioners could ask.

Orthodox Protestants of the 1820s and after generally saw Baconianism as a full-scale attack on metaphysics. In 1824 Samuel Gilman, a Unitarian Clergyman from Charleston, South

Carolina, craftily defined "metaphysics" as "that which ascribes imaginary and plausible causes to existing appearances, and speculates upon the nature of what is hidden and unknown."[20] Metaphysics was bad because it did not make observation the basis of its conclusions. A Baconian like John Brazer could "show" from the "works of nature" that physical objects have "mind or intelligence as their producing cause" and still not be engaged in metaphysics. After all, he began his investigation by looking at nature—and that is not the method of metaphysics but of science. It is *science* ("philosophy"), said Gilman, that *"ascertains* the causes of phenomena, and learns from *experience* the properties of things." For example, "when Newton discovered and applied the law of gravitation, he was, strictly speaking, the philosopher." That activity involved observation. However, "when he ascribed that gravitation to the influence of a subtle, etherial fluid, pervading all bodies . . . he was only the metaphysician." So by a curious twisting of the definition a scientific hypothesis (untested) becomes a "metaphysical" statement, while the statement, "the harmony of nature proves the greatness of God" is not metaphysical at all but quite scientific. Such statements of natural theology, said Gilman, always employ "the severest inductive philosophy."

This definition of "metaphysics" allowed Baconians to make an important distinction between their own scientific method and the method of the Enlightenment, a distinction between "knowing by observing" and "knowing by proving." According to one orthodox writer's belief, "the maxim, that nothing is to be believed which cannot be proved, that is, logically proved . . . has occasioned a deplorable waste of intellect, even in our own times."[21] In the writer's eyes, the belief that "mathematical demonstrations" are the only sure way to knowledge had led to the distrust of the senses characteristic of Descartes, Hume, and Berkeley. Bacon, quite naturally, was responsible for "the overturn of this idea."

In 1833 Andover theologian Leonard Woods, Jr., carried this epistemological discussion one step further. Woods also believed that men seek knowledge by two different methods. In addition, however, he argued that this knowledge comes from three distinct sources. He described these sources in the "order of their relative dignity." The first is the "*divine revelation* contained in the Old and New Testaments." The second is *"the human mind itself."* The third, *"the external world,* of which we are informed by our senses." Getting at this knowledge, said Woods, involves several intellectual processes. "Reflection" is the process of using the mind to "sort the unorganized data." "Science" is reflection developed in one particular area of investigation. Finally, "philosophy" is reflection that "takes a comprehensive survey of the world of truth, in all its departments, and unites them together in one general point of view."[22]

Woods believed that a Christian must study all three sources of knowledge equally, for "whatever is furnished by each of these sources is supplemental of some deficiency in the others; so that [none] can be thought perfect except as a part of a system which comprises them all." The history of philosophy is a history of error, explained Woods, because every school has emphasized one source of knowledge at the expense of the other two. Those "who have concentrated their reflection upon the *mind*—the inherent laws, original ideas, and spontaneous forms of thought" become sceptics, rationalists, or *"idealists."* This error, said Woods, is most characteristic of the Germans. Others, who have "chiefly prevailed in France," have considered "the *outward world* as the only sphere of real existence, and sensation as the only inlet of true knowledge." This error always leads to *"sensationalism"* and *"materialism."* Both idealism and sensationalism, he explained, eventually reject revelation and yield agnosticism or atheism.[23]

The third error strikes much closer home, although Woods did not regard it as quite as serious as the first two. Some persons, because of "a superstitious regard for Revelation, have confined their attention to its doctrines, considering the intellectual and physical sciences as useless and profane." This emphasis, said Woods, leads to a "sour bigotry." In this way Woods chided his contemporaries who had not kept up with the times and who were growing increasingly wary of the secularizing influences of the sciences.

Not all Baconians agreed completely with Woods' tripartition of the sources of knowledge. John Brazer argued in his 1835 Dudleian lecture that reason is not a "source" of knowledge, but only a means by which the mind organizes facts. His was a more Kantian idea that facts have to do with the content of knowledge, while reason has to do with the form into which knowledge is placed. Statements of "reason," such as logical and mathematical propositions, do not convey any information about the external world. They are merely mechanisms for establishing relationships between mental categories or for explaining the definitions of words. In Brazer's framework a good Baconian acquires knowledge in two steps. First, he performs an investigative operation in order to collect data. He then performs a reasoning operation in order to organize and classify these data.

Before 1850 America had two outspoken proponents of this limitation on the use of reason: Samuel Tyler and Alexander Bryan Johnson. Johnson is one of America's neglected intellectuals, a man always out of step with his times. When he wrote philosophy in the 1820s, few people understood him or cared to. Later, when his method became more popular, his works were already out of print and forgotten. He was born in Gosport, England, in 1786. His family moved to New York in 1801. When his father retired in 1810, Alexander inherited his business and began a long and successful career in finance and economics.[24]

But Johnson's hobby was the analysis of language. In 1828 he published the first results of his thinking as *The Philosophy of Human Knowledge, or a Treatise on Language*. Not entirely satisfied, he expanded his work into *A Treatise on Language*, published in 1836.[25]

Like other Baconians, Johnson despised metaphysics. Unlike his contemporaries, however, Johnson's argument against metaphysics was essentially linguistic. Creation, Johnson reasoned, is boundless. It consists of an infinite number of objects that have no relation to one another. Man's understanding, however, is not infinite. In order for him to comprehend the world he employs reasoning to classify his experiences. In general, Johnson noted, men have found that their five senses make a good classification mechanism; so they have divided their experiences into "sights," "sounds," "tastes," and so on. When someone uses the word "star," for example, he is always talking about a "sight." However, if someone should talk about "gold," it is possible that he is describing a feel, a sight, or perhaps even a taste. Gold can be experienced in all these ways. Metaphysical problems arise, explained Johnson, when people confuse different kinds of sense perceptions. Bishop Berkeley, for example, observed that the word "round" describes both a "sight" and a "feel." He did not know, however, that "the duality of nature controls the oneness of the name." Berkeley believed that "true roundness" must be either a "sight" or a "feel," but not both. He decided "in favour of the feel, and hence he proclaimed roundness to be invisible." Berkeley's problem was that he was studying words instead of things; he was confused by the fact that one word, "roundness," describes two distinct sense perceptions: the "feel" of roundness and the "sight" of roundness. The "problem" Berkeley discussed was merely a pseudoproblem created by the nature of language.

Johnson believed that David Hume had committed the same kind of error. At one point in *An Enquiry Concerning Human Understanding,* Hume's universal observer is backing away from a table. The table, quite naturally, becomes smaller in his field of vision. "The table which we see seems to diminish as we recede from it," explained Hume; "but the *real table* suffers no diminution." How, exclaimed Johnson, could Hume make a distinction between "the table which we see" and the "real table"— as if we were not seeing the "real table" at all? Obviously, Hume did not realize that in the first instance he was talking about the "sight table," but in the second he was describing the "feel table." Hume's entire sceptical method, argued Johnson, was based on a false distinction between "the world which we see" and the "real world," as if those two worlds were different things.

The process of reasoning, as Johnson saw it, is a process of manipulating words. Those who rely on reason too heavily believe that they are saying something about the world. Actually, however, they are talking about nothing but language. For example, rationalists are very fond of speaking about absolutes, such as "absolute truth." However, said Johnson, the phrase "absolute truth" has no meaning. Johnson studied three propositions: "I am speaking"; "I am standing"; "several persons are present." Each of "these assertions is a truth," Johnson explained, if the conditions described are satisfied. However, the word "true" in each of these cases refers to an entirely unique observation. To say that "I am speaking" and "several persons are present" are both "truths" is not to say that there is some powerful similarity between these two sentences. However, the fact that many statements can be described by the word "true" has fooled people into believing that "truth" is a unity. "If we seek among these truths for truth itself, believing it to be a unit, we are seeking in nature for what is merely a contrivance of language." Nevertheless, many philosophers have written disquisitions on this "contrivance of language," and their books are littered with speculation about "the nature of truth" or "beauty and truth." Such philosophers, said Johnson, have allowed the process of reasoning to run wild.[26]

While Johnson had few disciples, Samuel Tyler was acclaimed by his Baconian contemporaries as "the greatest philosopher America had yet produced," a man who would go down in history beside "Aristotle, Bacon, Locke, and Thomas Reid."[27] Tyler argued that the Baconian method is not a "new mode of reasoning," but merely a "new method of investigation." A new method was necessary because philosophers could no longer accept simplistic explanations for diverse phenomena, such as Aristotle's attempt to make fire "the principle of all things."[28] That kind of theorizing always leads to rationalism, because it makes men think that everything can be reduced to a few general principles and that the manipulation of these principles within the mind is the method by which learning takes place. Rationalism convinces the intellectual that because he knows the general principles and the illiterate peasant does not, he therefore employs a different way of thinking than the ordinary one. On the contrary, Tyler insisted, Baconian thinking is the most common kind of all: "the spirit of this philosophy is that in order to become philosophers truly so called, men must cast off that intellectual pride, which vainly strives to find out the secrets of nature by mere reasoning."[29]

Tyler attacked the idea that reason is a "source" of knowledge by citing the problem of Descartes, who reasoned that his own mind was such a source, but was then obliged to verify it. The result was that he had to "prove his own existence, God's existence, before he [could] reason about the world around him."[30] Descartes had failed to see that the source of knowledge must lie outside himself. Tyler regarded as "the most profound and comprehensive remark ever uttered by man" the first aphorism of Bacon's *Novum Organon*: "man, as the servant and interpreter of nature, is limited in act and understanding by his observation of the order of nature; and neither his knowledge nor his power extends further."[31]

The pursuit of a purely Baconian method frequently led to difficult theoretical problems. In their zeal to eliminate everything unverifiable from science some Baconians forgot that the predictive and generalizing aspects of science depend on unverifiable concepts. To divest science of these concepts would make scientific explanation impossible. For those who came closest to identifying science with taxonomy the problem was most serious. To extreme Baconians, terms like "theory" and "law" were part of metaphysics, not of true science. As a result, predictive statements like "the sun will rise tomorrow" gave Alexander Bryan Johnson endless trouble. It is certainly not a verifiable fact that the sun will rise tomorrow, not until tomorrow arrives and the sun is actually rising. Likewise, the statement "all men must die" cannot be a "fact" by Baconian standards until all men are actually dead. Johnson tried to avoid this problem by suggesting that predictive statements refer "to an internal feeling of expectation, which is excited in us naturally by our uniform experience."[32] In other words, the scientist who says "the sun will rise tomorrow" actually means "I have a feeling that the sun will rise tomorrow." But that meant that Johnson's imaginary scientist was not talking about nature at all, but about himself. Johnson must have realized that his solution to the problem of scientific prediction would not work, for he never developed it in great detail. For him, the problem of scientific law remained unsolved.

For other Baconians as well, the problem of scientific prediction involved the ability to talk about scientific "law" without talking "metaphysics." Clement Long, a young Andover graduate just entering the Presbyterian ministry, suggested a solution that was common among Baconians. In 1833 Long reviewed John Abercrombie's *Inquiries Concerning the Intellectual Powers*, a book that attempted to solve the problem of scientific prediction. However, Long rejected as too metaphysical Abercrombie's theory that the laws of nature are statements of "general facts" or of "uniform effects." After all, one can never see a "general fact," he can only see a fact. A "law," explained Long, is "that which *governs*," and only one being does that. The sun does not rise tomorrow because of some "general fact." It rises because God makes it rise.[33]

It was a curious state of affairs. Long was suggesting a theological explanation of nature's uniformity in order to eliminate the need for any "metaphysical" explanation. By the Baconian criterion for determining true knowledge, a criterion that accepted the "facts" of the Bible as well as those of nature, such an explanation was perfectly legitimate. After all, God's divine government is a verifiable fact—one has merely to look in the Bible. It would be contrary to the "data" to suggest that something other than God makes the sun rise; and it would certainly be hypothetical speculation to suggest that there is some *tertium quid*, a scientific "law," responsible for nature's regularity.

This sort of scientific Antinomianism had been an undercurrent in American thought for some time. Antinomianism of the variety propagated by Anne Hutchinson in seventeenth-century Massachusetts had included a fierce rejection of Natural Law. For this reason the Hutchinsonians threw out the Covenant Theology. The Covenant was a legal mechanism designed to come between God and his people. It implied, as Anne Hutchinson saw it, that God ran a bureaucracy—that he established covenants, laws, agencies, and the like to do his work for him. The result was that man's responsibility was not to God directly but to the Covenant. Antinomianism, as the name implies, represented a complete rejection of the "law" paradigm as an explanation for the way God carries on his affairs. It suggested a God who runs everything directly, by his own hand.

One hundred years later Jonathan Edwards acquired the same idea from John Locke. Like the Antinomians, Edwards divested his theology of the Covenant and began insisting that God's sovereignty over the world is direct, unmediated by any kind of law. Edwards' *The Doctrine of Original Sin Defended* included a long essay on causation in which he vehemently argued that natural phenomena are produced by the "*immediate* agency, will, and power of God."[34] The only reason anything happens, said Edwards, is that God wants it to happen: "the whole *course of nature*, with all that belongs to it, all its laws and methods, and constancy and regularity, continuance and proceeding, is an *arbitrary constitution,*" a constitution "which depends on nothing but the divine will."

Edwards gained his insights because he understood Enlightenment philosophers such as Locke and Isaac Newton better than most of his contemporaries. He realized one thing that Newton had wrestled with for years but which most eighteenth-century Newtonians failed to acknowledge: the laws of nature do not explain why objects behave in a certain manner; they only describe the way in which they behave. By giving his theological explanation to natural phenomena, Edwards was suggesting with Newton that science itself should avoid teleological explanations. That task must be reserved for a higher discipline.[35]

One Unitarian reviewer of Whewell's *Astronomy and General Physics* stepped out of phase with his rationalistic colleagues and offered Edwards's explanation for the way the world is run. Warren Burton suggested that the "Deity operates directly upon and through the material universe without the intervention of what philosophers call Laws, —that all the changes of nature proceed from the instantaneous impulses of his Almighty Will." If the universe were governed "by the agency of laws," argued Burton, then God would be an "idle being" and nature would be "but a machine."[36] Built into Burton's criticism of Natural Law was a mortal fear of the objective, impersonal deism that had plagued Christianity for nearly a century. Any option was better than the well-oiled, law-ridden, self-contained universe of the Enlightenment, even if this new paradigm made men infinitely more dependent on the caprice of a mysterious, perhaps even unreasonable, god.

The inductive method implied uncertainty. Even an orthodox Baconian such as Samuel Tyler had to admit that scientific truth is never logically certain. The determination of facts by the Baconian method "is effected by testimony, and not by rules of logic," he wrote in his only contribution to The *American Journal of Science*.[37] Scientists must understand that testimony is always probable, nothing more. Suppose, said Tyler, that an observer discovers that a certain water fowl has webbed feet. He finds another bird and discovers that its feet are also webbed. He inspects another and another. Finally, at some unspecified time when "it is warranted by the probabilities founded in the analogies of nature, and in the constitution of the human mind," the evidence "compels [him] to draw the inference." Tyler's description was no system of inductive logic, nor was it a method for scientific procedure. It was an admission, however, that scientists are not mathematicians, that scientific conclusions can be subject to revision, and that there is always room for doubt and error.

Mid-nineteenth-century America contained no Kierkegaards. But even some of the orthodox could realize that *both* science and religion rested ultimately on human faith. Although they loathed doubt, they would have to admit that not every belief of any Christian religion was "reasonable"—not to the extent that man without a special source of knowledge could arrive at it through a strictly analytic procedure. Some things must simply be believed. Orthodox Unitarian Andrews Norton attacked the German Transcendentalist assertion that the evidence of historical Christianity "consists only of probabilities" by arguing that for any finite being there is "no absolute certainty, beyond the limit of momentary consciousness, a certainty that vanishes the instant it exists, and is lost in the region of metaphysical doubt." Norton was willing to carry the weight of constant doubt even beyond the realm of metaphysics. "In all things of practical import," he wrote his fellow Unitarians and Transcendentalist dissidents, "in the exercise of all our affections, in the whole formation of our characters, we are acting, and must act, on probabilities alone."[38] When another Unitarian, Andrew Peabody, reviewed Norton's *Discourse* a year later he added a final and more difficult sentence: "the evidences, on which the faith of almost the entire Christian world has reposed for eighteen centuries, amount to as high a probability as we usually seek to base our conduct upon in the most important affairs of life."[39] A "high" probability perhaps, but a probability nevertheless. Even Common-Sense Realism and the Baconian method could survive only by sustaining the proper mixture of faith and doubt.

3

Declaring the Glory of God

Orthodox Protestants believed that the Baconian method was useful for both science and theology. For them, doing theology was a scientific activity. It employed the inductive method and drew its data from the world of nature. As orthodox Baconians conceived it, natural theology was also like the sciences in one other respect: its conclusions could be demonstrated empirically. The men who engaged in natural theology believed it could prove, beyond any reasonable doubt, God's existence and sovereignty.

Like the Baconian philosopher, the natural theologian believed that he had to create a system without metaphysics. Today, people often think of "metaphysics" and "natural theology" as roughly interchangeable terms, or else they believe that natural theology is a part of metaphysics. But to a mind like Francis Bowen's, the distance from metaphysics to natural theology was just as great as the distance from metaphysics to science.

Bowen, born and raised in Massachusetts, educated at Harvard, represented the conservative wing of Unitarianism in the 1840s. In 1843 he became editor of the *North American Review* and made his critical reputation on his essays about German idealists and French eclectic philosophers. In 1848 Bowen was invited to deliver the annual set of lectures on the "Application of Metaphysical and Ethical Science to the Evidences of Religion" at Boston's Lowell Institute, America's most famous lyceum.

Bowen's concern with the problem of metaphysics became clear at his first lecture, "The Distinction between Physical and Metaphysical Science." He defined the physical sciences as the study of "things physical, or those which exist distinct from our thoughts." Metaphysics, he said, is the study of those things "which do not exist apart from our thoughts." To Bowen "all the truths of pure mathematics, pure logic, and pure reason are metaphysical truths." Thus anything to which the deductive method is applied is metaphysical; anything to which the Baconian, or inductive, method can be applied, is scientific.[1]

Bowen treated his second audience to an "application" of these definitions. He borrowed a distinction from David Hume and classified "all the objects of human reason" into *"relations of ideas"* and *"matters of fact."* Metaphysics, observed Bowen, is concerned with the relations of ideas, while the physical sciences deal with matters of fact. Theology, as every orthodox Christian knows, is not the study of mere relations between ideas. The existence of God, the historicity and divinity of Christ, the workings of the Holy Spirit—all these things are obviously matters of fact. Theology, quite clearly, is a science just as much as botany and astronomy.

Bowen was participating in a reaction against "metaphysics" characteristic of antebellum American Protestantism. Like his contemporaries, however, Bowen defined "metaphysics" in such a way as to include only those things he wanted to excise from natural theology. The meaning Bowen assigned to "metaphysics" was quite different from the meaning it had been given by Immanuel Kant.

In the *Critique of Pure Reason* Kant had divided metaphysics into three parts: psychology, theology, and cosmology.[2] *Rational psychology*, said Kant, is the sort of thing Descartes pursued in his *Meditations*. It uses reason to establish a principle such as

"I think" or "I exist" and then proceeds to absolute questions about the nature of the self. *Rational theology*, on the other hand, is concerned with the existence of an absolute and perfect being. It studies the existence of a god, his attributes, and his relationship with the universe. This is the branch of metaphysics with which natural theologians have historically been most involved.

The third branch of metaphysics, *rational cosmology*, deals with ultimate questions concerning the nature of the universe. These issues include free will and determinism, cause and effect, and the nature of substance. Men like Bowen and John Brazer who wanted to rid themselves of metaphysics were thinking chiefly of cosmology. To them the contemplation of cause and effect or absolute substance was the worst form of metaphysical speculation. But reasoning about God's relationship with the world or about the evidences of design was not metaphysics at all but a proper application of scientific method.

The biggest factor in determining the Baconian's definition of "metaphysics" was verification. One could never verify the existence or nonexistence of absolute substances; however, he could easily find evidences of design in nature. The natural theologian's job was to arrange these verifiable "evidences" into a cogent argument, such as the cosmological argument for the existence of God.

The cosmological argument began with the observation that natural phenomena exist in cause-effect relationships with each other. Each event has been caused by some previous event, which was in turn caused by some event before that. At what point, asked the philosophers, do we arrive at an event that was not caused by anything else? Such an "uncaused cause" must exist, or else we must believe that the cause-effect chain stretches back into infinity. To the cosmological argument's advocates, belief in an uncaused cause was far more rational than belief in an infinitely old earth, particularly if that uncaused cause was God himself.

By Bowen's time, however, the cosmological argument had been in disrepute for over a century. It had been attacked, some philosophers said annihilated, by David Hume. His refutation had been simple: facts are verifiable, but causes are not. The cosmological argument rests on the postulation of something no one has ever seen. Only a very weak "empirical" argument would be based primarily on "data" that cannot be observed.

Bowen conceded that causes cannot be seen. But that fact, he said, merely demonstrated that causes are not "physical." When we talk of a "physical cause," explained Bowen, we are using an "exertion of mind" that "is applied only by metaphor to the material universe." The very fact that causation is *not* physical implies that it is made of "power, will, and action." Those who would destroy the cosmological argument point out that one cannot verify the existence of a "cause." But that is precisely the point. If a "cause" were a physical object, a visible connection between two events, to be seen, handled, or measured, then it would be quite clear that causation is not divine. However, the fact that we know that causation *must* be present but at the same time cannot perceive it, proves that it is something other than physical, something to be explained only by the will and power of God. Bowen argued that to talk about the "course of nature" is never to talk about nature itself. The events of nature have no "course" of their own. Rather, "all events, all changes, in the external world, are attributable directly to [God's] will and power."[3] At best Hume's battle with causation had been a Pyrrhic victory. He had shown that causation is not verifiable, but in so doing he had not demonstrated the invalidity of the cosmological argument. On the contrary, he had called attention precisely to the reason that it *does* prove God's existence.

One could see this "new look" at the cosmological argument as a little interesting casuistry on Bowen's part; or perhaps one could simply grant that Bowen did not have Hume's mental power. At any rate, those who are bothered by the cosmological argument today generally think that Hume was right and Bowen wrong. However, Bowen and his contemporaries saw it differently. It would never have entered their heads that the sequence of events in nature was simply irrelevant to knowledge of God. On the contrary, nature is where one must begin his study of God. Congregationalist minister Joseph Haven, Jr., the Andover-trained pastor of the Harvard Church in Brookline, saw natural theology built on the cosmological argument as the "foundation" and "firm basis of all other theological science." Religious faith, explained Haven, is based "upon the *conviction* in the mind that there is a God." Theology based on the cosmological argument, however, is more than mere faith. Such theology "rests upon the *certainty*, the clear and decisive *evidence* that there is such a being."[4]

"Evidence" was the biggest word in the natural theologian's vocabulary. That word became so strongly associated with the theological discipline that an orthodox philosopher could title his speech simply "a lecture on the evidences," and everyone would know that he was not speaking about evidences of the permanence of species, or evidences that comets are hot and gaseous. "Evidences" always implied facts relevant to the existence of God, or as verification of the fundamental ideas of Christianity.

As important as the word was to the natural theologian, however, it is nearly impossible to compile a list of precisely what kinds of things could be "evidences." In his *Evidences of the Authenticity, Inspiration and Canonical Authority of the Holy Scriptures*, Princeton theologian Archibald Alexander devoted himself mainly to a broad attack on deism and a refutation of Hume's argument against miracles. But Alexander never bothered himself with a long list of facts taken from nature. Likewise, Congregationalist Mark Hopkins's 1844 Lowell Lectures *On the Evidences of Christianity* contained a great deal of criticism of Hume, but by no stretch of the imagination was there a collection of "data" in support of Christianity.[5]

One thing the written display of the "evidences" almost invariably included, however, was argument by analogy. The "analogical method" had been one of the most important tools of medieval theologians, as well as of English and American Puritans. In the strictest sense the method involved arranging the known similarities between two objects, demonstrating that one of the objects had some additional property, and then concluding that the second object must have that additional property as well. However, in practice the "analogical method" frequently became a much looser procedure of pointing out similarities between natural processes (such as a mother caring for her young) and divine activities (the lovingkindness of God). In this way orthodox theologians found many "evidences" of God's activity in the world. For example, Lutheran pastor James Richards of Auburn Seminary argued in his *Lectures on Mental Philosophy and Theology* that the law of nature, "like produces like," is clearly an analogy designed to explain and defend the doctrine of original sin. After the Fall it was only natural that Adam would produce "in kind"—more sinful people like himself.[6]

Amherst professor of geology and natural theology Edward Hitchcock carried the method a bit further. During the late forties he treated Amherst students to a series of *Religious Lectures on Peculiar Phenomena in the Four Seasons*, the purpose of which was to show how changes in nature are analogically related to God's attributes and activities. Spring, Hitchcock explained, symbolized the Resurrection because it illustrates the rebirth of life. The fact that the same plants come up year after year but each time are composed of a completely new set of atoms demonstrates how man stands in relationship to his "glorified body" at the time of the final Resurrection.[7]

In his study of the metamorphosis of insects, Hitchcock found more evidence of the Resurrection. The chrysalis, for example, passes the winter "enveloped in his silken shroud" but in the spring "bursts from its prison, endowed with new life and beauty." Hitchcock regarded this as one of the most convincing of all "evidences," observing that "the analogy between these metamorphoses" and the reanimation of man is "so striking" that "many able writers on natural theology have considered [it] as direct proof of [man's] future resurrection."

In order to get the full impact of Hitchcock's reasoning we must understand that he was not writing a little devotional piece full of clever symbols. To Hitchcock the "evidence" he had gathered from nature established the truth of the Resurrection doctrine. "The manner in which I have endeavored to defend the scripture doctrine of the resurrection of the body, by an appeal to certain principles of chemistry and physiology," he told his readers, "seems to me quite conclusive." Like any scientific theory, however, it must be independently confirmed. "Yet as I have met with it in no writer," admitted Hitchcock, "I ought not to be over confident in its validity."[8]

Several years later Hitchcock published another set of lectures designed to dig out even more analogical evidences of God in nature. *Religious Truth Illustrated from Science* contained "scientific" lectures on the "Wonders of Science compared with the Wonders of Romance" ("often delivered"), "The Catalytic

Power of the Gospel," and "Mineralogical Illustrations of [Human] Character." Here Hitchcock tried to convince his readers that science always supports biblical testimony and often explains spiritual operations only partly described in the Bible, such as the (catalytic) power of the Holy Spirit to win men's hearts to Christ.[9]

To be sure, some despaired of such excessive uses of analogy. Leonard Woods, Jr., lectured his students at Andover on the "Dangers to be Avoided in Analogical Reasoning," telling them that "whenever analogical reasoning proceeds on the supposition of a *strict* analogy between the attributes and operations of God, and the attributes and actions of man . . . and those of the material or animal world; then errors of one kind or another are sure to be the consequences."[10] In spite of this and other detractions, however, the analogical method remained one of the most frequently used pieces of ammunition in the natural theologian's arsenal.[11]

Natural theology gathered a heavy momentum during the forties, the years in which the "Baconian method" determined practically everything the orthodox theologian thought was important. Natural theologians were able to draw large, enthusiastic crowds of laymen to weekly lectures. The famous Lowell Institute in Boston invited one distinguished natural theologian after another to speak about the "evidences" in front of audiences composed of ministers, students, and laymen.

One of the more elaborate attempts to bring natural theology to the layman was the Virginia Lecture Series. In 1850 the University of Virginia invited fifteen distinguished scholars, each an expert in some area of natural theology, to present lectures on the "evidences of Christianity." The lectures were delivered and published a year later as a final answer to Christianity's sophisticated critics—a one-volume complement to England's *Bridgewater Treatises*.[12]

The broad range of inquiries that the word "evidences" could involve becomes quite clear to anyone who pages through the *Virginia Lectures*. They contain the usual arguments in support of miracles and the veracity and inspiration of the Bible, and the usual answers to deistic objections against revealed religion. In addition, however, Thomas Vernor Moore, Princeton educated pastor of Richmond's First Presbyterian Church, lectured on the "Unity of the Human Race," trying to establish that the biblical position expressed in Genesis was not in conflict with "true" science, but only with those misguided scientists who had "hypothesized" separate creations for the individual races of mankind. Presbyterian Lewis Warner Green gave lectures designed to show that scriptural revelation and geological science were not in conflict.

The *Virginia Lectures* also reveal that natural theology was becoming increasingly defensive. Throughout the thirties and forties theologians had been concerned predominantly with method. Now before they could really use this newly-developed method they were having to face all kinds of scientific "objections." Rather than gathering the evidences that every orthodox Protestant was sure lay waiting in nature, theologians were having to prove that scientific data did not deny the existence of God, the reliability of the Bible, or the truth of Christianity. Bad science, not infidel metaphysics, was the most rapidly growing threat to the Protestant faith. Furthermore, the biggest issue was not scientific methodology but scientific fact. After 1850 natural theology in America began to look less like the metaphysical treatises of the Middle Ages or of Puritan orthodoxy and more like the works of the scientists themselves. A discourse on natural theology could take the form of a book on the unity of the human race or on the evolutionary hypothesis. These works inevitably began with a confident restatement of the old position that science and Christianity can never be in conflict; but there were always explanations to be made. Perhaps the Bible had thus far been misunderstood; perhaps scientists had been misguided or had incomplete information; perhaps a little of both.

The 1850s are a watershed for American natural theology. Up to the middle of the century the work became gradually more sophisticated, more responsive to the natural sciences. It was generally acclaimed by Christians of all persuasions as an effective way of demonstrating the existence and attributes of God. After *On the Origin of Species*, however, the emphases in theology changed dramatically. Liberal churches lost interest in natural theology as a distinct discipline. For them theology became increasingly historical and cultural. Seminaries became more interested in the psychology and sociology of religious belief and less interested in dogmatics. Theologians themselves became more concerned with historical perspective than with absolute truth. The influence of Auguste Comte and Positive philosophy in America was sufficient to make many Congregationalists and even liberal Presbyterians and Methodists acknowledge that dogmatic theology had failed to answer some of man's most basic questions about himself and the world. Increasingly they felt that such problems should be left to the sciences, especially the newly-developing social sciences.

But perhaps the hardest blow to natural theology came from the man who had worked so hard to destroy the old metaphysics. Immanuel Kant had become increasingly influential in America during the 1830s and 1840s, but he overran American philosophy in the 1850s and after. Anyone who wanted a sophisticated philosophy of religion had to come to terms with the Kantian system. Kant had essentially agreed with Locke that all knowledge of the external world must come through the senses, but he added that these data are unclassified and random. The function of the mind is to sort them into some meaningful order. This sorting activity makes the outside world "reasonable" to man, but it also modifies the picture he obtains of the world beyond himself. The result is that one can never know things the way they really are (things-in-themselves); he can only know things the way his mind reconstructs their images.

Kant called the tools which the mind uses in this sorting process "categories." These include causality, necessity, space, and time. One can never "see" a cause. Causation is merely an attribute the mind assigns to phenomena in order to give them a reasonable explanation. The idea of causation explains the relationship between two empirical data that the mind observes occurring together repeatedly, such as the position of the moon and the height of the tide. Hume was correct when he insisted that we cannot perceive causes, said Kant; but he was wrong when he asserted that causation cannot be a part of human knowledge. Causation in fact is a part of knowledge, but it refers to the *form* in which the mind holds that knowledge, not to its *content*. Metaphysical problems occur when we try to treat questions having to do with the form of knowledge as if they were questions of content. As long as the philosopher understands that causation is a mechanism for explaining the relationship between two events, he is arranging data properly and can arrive at new knowledge about the world. However, as soon as he talks about "absolute causation," or "final cause," or any other kind of "causation" that does not relate to empirically observable events, then he is speaking nonsense. To try to apply the category of causation to the question "Did the universe have some cause outside of itself, or did it bring itself about?" is meaningless; that question involves unobservable events. Likewise, to talk about "absolute space" (Is the universe infinite, or does it end somewhere?) or "absolute time" (Did God predestine man before or after the creation of the world?) is absurd when one understands that "space" is the category that describes the distance between two observable objects, and "time" is the category the mind uses to explain the interval between two observable events.

The Kantian attack on general metaphysics, coupled with the positivistic assertion that what cannot be perceived cannot be known, led to clearer ideas about the limits of the scientific method. To talk about Gods, absolutes, and First Causes was simply not scientific. The object of science was to deal exclusively with what could be seen, and natural theology had no place in this new, sophisticated framework.

The most immediate result of Kant's critical philosophy was more precise limitations on the range of conclusions to which natural theology could come. Natural theologians began to concede that their discipline could not produce a great deal of information about God. That was the task of biblical and systematic theology. The function of the natural theologian became more apologetic than informative. His job was to produce a foundation: to show that "God exists" is a rational statement, or to demonstrate that he is good, powerful, and benevolent.[13] With "these things ascertained, and clearly established, natural theology has nothing further to do," wrote Joseph Haven, Jr., in 1849. "Whatever else we wish to know of God, we are to look for it not in his *works*, but in his *word*."[14] While the range of obligatory scientific issues discussed by the natural theologian was becoming constantly broader, the range of theological conclusions he could make became ever narrower.

Already by the 1840s, evangelicals had to face the threat that their optimistic faith in the inductive sciences might backfire. Samuel Stanhope Smith had been convinced that the scientific method, properly applied to natural phenomena, could never lead man away from God. But Smith never had to deal with uniformitarian geology, higher criticism, or the evolutionary hypothesis. Like the evangelicals, most of the advocates of these threatening scientific theories were theists. They were simply more willing to accommodate science than evangelicals were. The rise of the new sciences told orthodox Protestants one thing: if natural theology was going to prevail, it would need a more scientific orientation.

The orthodox natural theologian of the 1850s was, more than anything else, a critic or a popularizer of the sciences. For example, Harvard moral philosopher James Walker's *God Revealed in the Process of Creation* was primarily an attack on evolutionist Robert Chambers.[15] Secondly, however, it was a "proof," taking into account all the latest scientific evidence, that the universe reveals itself as the work of a single, intelligent designer. Walker found his best support in the chemical tables. The rigidly fixed proportions and the beautiful harmony in the structures of chemical compounds convinced him that they could not have been conceived and created by mere chance.

A more sophisticated attempt at scientifically astute natural theology came from Edward Hitchcock. The fact that Hitchcock's appointment at Amherst was as professor of "natural theology and geology" itself illustrates the belief of the day that a good natural theologian is also a competent scientist. Hitchcock's greatest work was his 1852 *The Religion of Geology and its Connected Sciences*, written both to teach geology and to "defend and illustrate" the truth of the Christian religion.[16]

Hitchcock conceded that the Bible is not a scientific textbook and agreed that its descriptions are not to be taken as literal, scientific explanations of how things happened—a concession granted by many Protestants in the 1850s. However, warned Hitchcock, that does not mean that the Bible contains statements that are scientifically false. Like many of his colleagues, Hitchcock drew a rather blurry sketch of what it meant to say that the Bible is "not scientific" but at the same time is not "contrary to scientific fact." He certainly did *not* mean to imply that Moses had a mythological world-view and had therefore written a myth-based description of the world's beginning. Only Trans-

cendentalists or infidels would have suggested that. What Hitchcock meant is that science and the Bible talk about the same
subjects "only incidentally." Genesis 1 is a nonscientist's description of a scientific phenomenon. Although it is truthful, as far
as it goes, it is neither complete nor scientifically precise.

That explanation may have settled some minds, but certainly
not everyone's. The Bible said that the world was created from
first formation to modern man in a period of six days; geology
was beginning to suggest times on the order of several million
years.[17] One could not bring the two explanations together
simply by suggesting that the Bible's explanation is "not scientific." Either the world was created in six days and the Bible is
right, or else it was not created in six days and the Bible is
wrong. In many evangelical minds the answer was that simple,
and any talk about a "prescientific" or "nonscientific" Bible
was merely beating around the bush in order to avoid the real
issues.

But the consequences for natural theology were clear. Hitchcock had broadened the discipline to include any possible connection between science and religion. By this definition the only
people who did not believe in natural theology were those who
thought that science and religion have absolutely nothing to do
with one another. So Benjamin Silliman, James D. Dana—even
Louis Agassiz and Asa Gray—were natural theologians, not
because they wrote on causation but because they argued that
the facts of science have something to say about the truth or
falsity of the Christian religion.

Of course, these men *were* natural theologians. Silliman's
elaborate harmony of geology and Genesis was as much theology as science. Agassiz's idea that a species is an "idea in the
mind of God" was built on as many theological as scientific
presuppositions. By the middle of the century, the domain of
natural theology had become so broad that finally students had
to talk about *everything* as natural theology or else concede that
the discipline had lost its identity. Many American universities
and seminaries were quite willing to make that concession.

If a growing acquiescence in science caused liberal and moderate Protestants to abandon natural theology, a growing fear
and resentment forced more conservative evangelicals to drop
it from their curricula. For conservative Presbyterians and Bap-

tists, *On the Origin of Species* was the final excuse to change the honeymoon with science into a pitched battle for the minds of Protestants. It simply became too risky to tell a young scholar to study biology or geology in order to find absolute assurance of God's providence; chances were good that he would not find that at all but would come away with his doubts confirmed. Rejected by liberal and evangelical alike and caught in the middle of the great religious battles of the Gilded Age, natural theology began to loose its foothold nearly everywhere except in the Catholic seminaries.

Natural theology lost its identity because it became too diffuse. It lost its force simply because fewer people bothered to ask the questions it was designed to answer. By the middle of the century the emphasis in religious education was shifting from apologetics and justification toward religious psychology and sanctification—"Christian Nuture," as Horace Bushnell put it. Bushnell symbolized the passing of one religious consciousness and the conception of another: the vastness of the distance between knowing and believing, between thinking and acting, between Calvin's "sovereignty of God" and Schleiermacher's "feeling of dependence." The dead end of dogmatics in America became for Bushnell the starting point for a new idea of the nature and purpose of religious belief.

Bushnell never directed a general attack on natural theology. In fact, he frequently spoke in support of many of its methods. However, he fostered a theological outlook that permitted natural theology to die a slow death through qualification and neglect. Perhaps Bushnell's single greatest contribution to theological method is that he purged theology of the "spectator view" of gaining knowledge. For Bushnell the theologian was no longer the neutral observer who took in the facts, assembled them, and produced theological dialogue; he was rather a creative force, someone who constantly invented, interpreted, and imagined. Bushnell made subjectivism palatable to the children of orthodox churchmen who had been absolutely opposed to Transcendentalism and subjective liberal theology. He himself came from a moderately orthodox home, although his grandparents and parents never quite found themselves comfortable

in any church. When Bushnell was born, they were Congregationalists simply because that church was nearest home. He
was raised to reject the hard Calvinism of New England theology, but when he attended the Yale Divinity School in the
early thirties he found Nathaniel Taylor's "modernized" Calvinism almost equally unacceptable. Taylor's efforts to modify
the terrible, wrathful God of the Edwardsean tradition had led
to successive rationalizations and modifications of old dogmas:
a new definition of "original sin" that put more emphasis on
individual behavior and responsibility; a new emphasis on man's
"cooperation" with God in the salvation process; and a new,
elaborate rationale of God's love.[18] In all this, however, Bushnell
saw nothing more than a little cosmetic on a theology already
outdated and irrelevant.

He turned momentarily from the Calvinistic tradition to one
of the heretics who was beginning to destroy American Unitarianism—Coleridge. The moment was enough. He was not
able to put the *Aids to Reflection* aside. Its ideas stood completely outside his Calvinist frame of reference: the possibility
that religious belief is not entirely rational; that scientific induction of facts is not the best way to religious knowledge; perhaps most important, that much of religion is an *experience*
indescribable by human language.

They were ideas far too radical for most Yale and Princeton
scholars. Coleridge despised the "evidences." He regarded William Paley as the "archenemy" of Christianity. He found Kant's
attack on the metaphysics of natural theology completely convincing. Scientific reasoning could never yield answers to ultimate questions about God, moral purpose, or the nature of
man. That possibility frightened American theologians, but not
Coleridge.[19] He found the entire effort to arrive at theological
statements scientifically to be "irreligious." Faith implies "fi-
delity" and the constant possibility of doubt. When one uses
"evidences" to prove the Christian religion in the same way
that he proves a theorem of geometry or a rule of science, then
he is trying to create a Christianity that is not religious at all.
Christianity, said Coleridge, cannot be "a theory or a speculation," but a "life and a living process."[20] The true test of the
validity of Christianity is not to be found by scientific analysis
but by human experience. He criticized the cosmological argu-

ment for God's existence for "clandestinely [involving] the conclusion in the premisses," for being a "species of logical
legerdemain not unlike that of the jugglers at a fair, who putting
into their mouths what seems to be a walnut, draw out a score
yards of ribbon—as in the postulate of a first cause."[21] Coleridge
developed a complex theory of intuition and imagination to
account for the human feeling of dependence on God, a feeling
he believed to be the most important aspect of Christianity.
Natural theology, he said, confused nature with the supernatural; it confused science with religion and forced clergymen
to lose sight of what they should really be doing: helping men
to find faith in an unknowable God.

The arguments had challenged more American Protestants
than Bushnell. In 1828 Vermont's James Marsh, an Andover-
educated evangelical "to whom both Unitarianism and Transcendentalism were reprehensible,"[22] brought out the first American edition of the *Aids* and added a long introduction in which
he admitted that the theology of his own tradition was "en-
snared in the metaphysical web of its own weaving . . . and
yet suppose[s] itself blessed with a perfect immunity from the
dreaded evils of metaphysics."[23] Amazingly for a Calvinist,
Marsh had little criticism of Coleridge except that he was frequently difficult to understand. Little did Marsh know as he was
writing, however, that most of his readers would not be the
Andover moral philosophers whom he addressed but rather
the dissidents within Boston and Harvard Unitarianism. A few
years later he was horrified when Transcendentalists made a
Bible of his edition of the *Aids* and used it to attack orthodoxy
on a half dozen fronts.

Marsh's essay on Coleridge exhibits one of the ironies of
American religion in the 1830s: Presbyterian and Congregational evangelicals were much more receptive of European idealism than were Unitarians. In large part Unitarian hatred of
Kant and Coleridge was a reaction against American Transcendentalists—a group much more threatening to Unitarianism
than to Presbyterianism. The articles on Coleridge in the *Christian Examiner* rail at his thought and call him hypocritical,
scandalous, garbled, and infidel.[24] James Marsh was not nearly
as critical, and Yale's orthodox Noah Porter, writing as late as
1847, faulted Coleridge only moderately for his deviations from

evangelicalism and for his "foreign look."[25] Porter concluded that Coleridge's influence on American religion was quite worthwhile because it "opened new fields of inquiry, and put us in possession of other modes of viewing religious truth."

His friendship with Porter undoubtedly made it easier for Bushnell to rely on Coleridge so heavily. Pointing out difficulties in the theological position of one's own institution can be a dangerous task, especially if that institution guards its orthodoxy as well as Yale. Eventually, however, Bushnell carried Coleridge's antirationalism too far. By 1851 even Porter was forced to agree that Bushnell deserved to be tried for heresy.[26]

To Bushnell, the problem of natural theology pointed out most ably by Coleridge was a problem of language. Christianity could not be the product of scientific reasoning because its tenets could not be expressed in scientific terms. Like Coleridge, Bushnell believed that religious language is more expressive of human need than of some actual state of affairs. Bushnell justified his belief in "A Preliminary Dissertation on the Nature of Language, as Related to Thought and Spirit," part one of *God in Christ* (1849).[27]

As an empirical philosophy, Scottish Realism had always asserted that one could "know" only those things that could be perceived. Furthermore, one could speak only about those things that could be known. Words must be "signs of things" or else they are meaningless. Metaphysical problems arise, said Bushnell, when men begin using words—"cause," "law," "absolute" —that do not refer to some specific object or phenomenon. Furthermore, the theological vocabulary of orthodoxy is full of such words: "God," "Heaven," or "Resurrection." If these words do not refer to things that can be seen, then how can they actually have meaning? The Scottish philosophers solved the problem with a rather complex doctrine of analogy. As Hitchcock argued, one *can* observe the cocoon changing into a butterfly, the new buds and leaves in the spring, and the mathematical evidences of design in the movement of the planets and the positions of the nodes on a stem. Men learn the facts of nature by observation, and through the process of analogy they also learn something of the Divine.[28]

But Bushnell presented a new problem. Suppose, he said, that "two human persons . . . be thrown together, who, as yet, have never heard the use of words." Soon, in an effort to communicate with each other these two men would begin pointing to objects and making sounds. There is no rational explanation for why one would use "rock" to describe something and the other "saxum." The important thing is that all these early words would be symbols of particular objects in the user's perception.

But suppose that one of these persons "has a thought or emotion in his mind, or wishes to speak of a spiritual being or world." Thoughts, emotions, and spiritual beings are not objects that can be examined the way rocks can. However, said Bushnell, all people have a commonness of experience. Furthermore, there is a "vast analogy in things, which prepares them, as forms, to be signs or figures of thoughts, and thus, bases or types of words." Thus if one man is about to express an abstract thought to the other, he "will strike at some image or figure in the sensible world, that is itself a fit representation of his thought or emotion." He will then turn "the attention of the other party upon this image," and signify that "he is trying to mirror some internal state. . . . The image becomes, in fact, a common sign or conception of the same internal state—they understand each other."[29]

This was not a very scientific explanation. But Bushnell was not interested in scientific explanations; in fact, he was hoping to get away from them. He was merely trying to show that every language contains two parts: "a literal department, in which sounds are provided as names for physical objects and appearances," and secondly, "a department of analogy or figures, where physical objects and appearances are names as images of thought or spirit, and the words get their power . . . through the physical images received into them."

All of our abstract nouns, therefore, have double meanings. All, that is, except for some of the terms of theology. The word "God" has only its abstract meaning, for nothing in nature is a satisfactory analogy for "God." Theologians, however, often make the mistake of assuming that "there is a literal terminology in religion as well as a figurative." Because of this assumption they begin to evaluate theological definitions "not as signs or images, but as absolute measures and equivalents of truth." However, it is impossible to speak about God or metaphysical truths with scientific precision: "all we can say is, that a mystery transcending in any case our comprehension, the Divine Logos, who is in the world, weaves into nature types of images that have an inscrutable relation to mind and thought. On the one hand, is form; on the other, is the formless."[30]

Bushnell was one of the few mid-nineteenth-century scholars who read Alexander Bryan Johnson's *Treatise on Language*.[31] He agreed with most of Johnson's conclusions about abstract words. Words like "sin," "goodness," or "God" must, according to Locke's *tabula rasa* theory, mean to each person some composite of former experiences that are associated with that word. Perhaps he has performed acts described by others as "sin"; perhaps he has seen someone else's acts described that way. However, everyone has unique experiences; therefore, the word "sin" conjures up different ideas to different people. This is doubly true of the theological word "God," because experiences of God are much less unified and much more loosely defined. Two people using the word "God" can never mean precisely the same thing. All "words of thought or spirit are not only inexact in their significance, never measuring the truth or giving its precise equivalent, but they always affirm something which is false, or contrary to the truth intended. They impute *form* to that which really is out of form." When using such words, theologians must keep in mind that "they are but signs, in fact, or images of that which has no shape or sensible quality whatever; a kind of painting, in which the speaker, or the writer, leads on through a gallery of pictures of forms, while we attend him, catching at the thoughts suggested by his forms."[32]

What a blow to the idea that theology is a science and that theological treatises are equivalent to scientific reports! But Bushnell was not finished. He noted that because words cannot be accurate descriptions of spiritual reality there is always the possibility of self-contradiction. The "loftier" the truths that words 'try to express, the further they will fall short of literal description, and the more confusing and contradictory will be the result. Thus "the most contradictory book in the world is the Gospel of John; and that, for the very reason that it contains more and loftier truths than any other." John's Gospel is only a "quirk of logic" away from being absurd, said Bushnell; but such lofty work is always filled with more truth and genius than that of "a mere uninspired, unfructifying logicker." Logic itself is a "defective, and often deceitful instrument," and the Bible, a book most noteworthy and literary because of its "profound alliance with poetry," should not be subjected to it too strenuously.[33]

The *God in Christ* lectures went on to attack the divisiveness of the church's creeds and the fine distinctions in the doctrine of the trinity (a point not taken lightly by New England Congregationalists and Presbyterians still licking the wounds of the Unitarian controversy).

The orthodox came back hard. The author of a response in the *Princeton Review* found Bushnell guilty of "Sabellianism, Docetism, Appolinarianism, Dutychianism, Pelagianism, and semi-Pelagianism." A review in the *Christian Observatory* contained sixty pages without a kind word.[34]

Most ominous was the fact that Bushnell was gaining a large following among the orthodox. Progressive Congregationalist Edwards Amasa Park of Andover began campaigning for a theology of the "feelings" instead of the "intellect."[35] Young ministers of every denomination eagerly ordered copies of Bushnell's lectures and helped make *God in Christ* a best seller. The growing harrassment by older leaders in the church and the threat of a heresy trial only helped to arouse sympathy for Bushnell and his position.

The damage to New England orthodoxy was permanent. Actually, however, Bushnell was only a catalyst. New philosophy, new social problems, and the hope for new solutions to old problems all helped Americans realize that they needed a new theology focused on faith and feeling rather than dogma and knowledge. The "Dissertation on Language" showed that a scientific natural theology was virtually impossible, but the entire slant of Bushnellian thought was that natural theology was simply irrelevant to the needs of Americans in the 1850s. *Christian Nurture,* in both the early edition and the expanded edition of 1860, angered the hard-line orthodox because it rejected the Calvinistic view of the sudden conversion experience and substituted the liberal notion that a young man grows gradually into grace and expands his religious "sensitivity." That was what the people needed to hear. They needed ethics and not theology. They wanted plans of action and not propositions of dogma. They believed that a man's faith and intuition were more important than his training in the catechism, that the real foundation of faith does not come from dogmatics but from a "perceptive power in spiritual life . . . , an immediate experimental knowledge of God."[36] Bushnell gave groping Protestants reasons to believe what they undeniably already felt: that all the work of the natural theologians—extended analogies, complex disquisitions on causation, incessant criticism and interpretation of new scientific theories and discoveries— did not have very much to do with the act of being religious.

Implicit in all this was a two-fold declaration of independence. The theology of the feelings freed religion from the strictures of scientific exactness. It also freed science from a millstone that had hung around its neck altogether too long. Increasingly after the 1850s there would be a feeling in the colleges and seminaries that scientific language spoke about one world, religious language about another. Intellectual freedom, academic freedom— even religious freedom—demanded it.

4

The Science of Religion

Nearly every controversy over science and Christianity in the nineteenth century touched on the nature of the Bible and its interpretation. One simply could not be religious without giving some thought to Scripture, and even deists who wanted to develop a religion free from any kind of "special revelation" found it necessary to devote many pages to the Bible.[1] Orthodox Christians had to agree with Francis Bacon that theology is grounded chiefly "upon the Word and oracle of God, and not upon the light of nature." After all, wrote Bacon, the Bible says that " 'The Heavens declare the glory of God' "; but it does not say that " 'The heavens declare the will of God.' "[2] Natural theology could go only so far in guiding fallen man from conception to Heaven. Where nature falls silent, the Bible begins to speak.

The questions asked about the Bible's position within religion and in relation to science were numberless, but they can be reduced to a few overriding ones. The first concerned the nature of revelation itself. Deists, German critics, and American evangelicals were all concerned with the ways in which God speaks to man. To Tom Paine the idea that God could "reveal" himself through the Bible to anyone who bothered to read it was "a contradiction in terms." God's revelation to man "is necessarily limited to the first communication," and after that the Bible's words are only something that someone says is revelation.[3] To Theodore Parker (America's foremost exponent of German higher criticism) the Bible could be "revelation" only in a very loose sense—a sense that did not imply inspiration by the Holy Spirit or infallibility. The Bible was a "revelation" in the same way that the intuition was revelation: man in communication with his soul is always receiving revelations from God. To evangelical Samuel Tyler the Bible was the Word of God, pure and simple. God spoke through the Bible in a way in which he speaks no longer, and the minister who quotes Genesis or John from the pulpit is speaking the Word of God just as certainly as if God himself came down from Heaven to preach the morning sermon.

One's attitude toward revelation reflected one's position on how the Bible should be read. Should one study the Bible in the same manner as any book of history or ethics, or is there some special method? For some Baconians there was indeed a special method. The words of the Bible "embrace eternity, with all the facts in that boundless field of experience," Samuel Tyler wrote in the *Princeton Review*.[4] One must read the Bible in order to gather its data, not to criticize it. Biblical "criticism" is no more valid than scientific doubt that the grass is green or the earth round. One cannot deny facts, but only manipulate and organize them. But even Tyler admitted that in order to understand fully the facts of the Bible a certain amount of textual interpretation "by the rules of grammar and logic" would be necessary.

Men of every religious persuasion believed that the Bible needed to be interpreted, but the length to which interpretation could be carried was a subject of endless controversy. To Parker "interpretation" could mean separating fact from fiction and myth; to Andover's Moses Stuart it meant finding the true text and meaning of a passage; to Andrews Norton it meant determining whether or not a passage was genuine (included by the original author); to most of the orthodox it meant deriving correctly a theological dogma or a rule for living. But all sides held in highest esteem the thorough scholar—the man who had a complete knowledge of Hebrew, Aramaic, Greek, and of course German. In that respect there were no anti-intellectuals. The war over the nature of the Bible included some of the most sophisticated battles in American Protestantism.

The question of how the Bible should be read revolved around two issues: inspiration and genuineness. The inspiration question addressed itself to the precise nature of God's participation in the composition of the books of the Bible. Because it involved questions about divine activity it lay outside the boundaries of scientific investigation for all but the most crusading evangelicals. Even those who allowed a "scientific" study of inspiration admitted that the question presupposed the issue of genuineness.[5]

Questions of genuineness were addressed to the true authorship, date, and canonicity of the biblical books. Questions such as: "Did Moses really write the Pentateuch?" "Was Matthew originally written in Greek or in Hebrew?" "Did Isaiah have one or two authors?" concerned the greater number of biblical scientists. Andrews Norton's mammoth *Evidences of the Genuineness of the Gospels* dealt almost entirely with authorship. When Theodore Parker attacked the biblical literalism of evangelicals and Unitarians, he did not do as Thomas Paine and speculate about the reasonableness of a perfect God's having to send man a supplementary revelation. Rather, he tried to show that many of the books of the Bible had not been ascribed to their rightful authors, that many passages were "borrowed" from older non-Hebraic and non-Christian sources, and that many books were written much later than the date Christian tradition had assigned them.

The questions of genuineness and authorship were closely related to new ideas about textual criticism, generally ideas that had come from Germany. "Lower" criticism—critical determination of the most accurate reading of a particular passage—dated back to the early Renaissance. Such internal analysis of the words of the Bible was implicitly more a tool of orthodox than of heterodox critics. The orthodox were more interested in precise determination of the Bible's words. In the early part of the century, when archeology and historical philology allowed scholars to arrive at better readings and clearer interpretations of ancient texts, the orthodox were quick to pick up on the work. Moses Stuart at Andover and his student Edward Robinson established that seminary as an American center for lower criticism.

On the other hand, "higher" criticism was much more problematic for the evangelicals, and they looked at it with more caution. Higher critics began their work with the assumption that biblical statements are historically conditioned and therefore products of the world-view of the age in which they were made. Implicit in this was the assumption that the human authors of the Bible did the writing and not God himself; and higher critics frequently denied such orthodox doctrines as inspiration and infallibility. They hoped to gain from historical study of the texts an insight into the world-view of the authors, to reconstruct the development of religious consciousness in the Old and New Testaments, and often to separate those parts of the Bible that are historical from those considered fiction or myth. Obviously, one could carry the pursuit of higher criticism to various lengths. Orthodox Unitarian Andrews Norton found historical criticism most useful in his attempt to prove that the books of the New Testament are historically reliable sources for the events that occurred during and shortly after the life of Christ.[6] However, he was horrified when German David F. Strauss used higher criticism to excise everything supernatural from the Gospels, so much so that he published a new edition of the *Internal Evidences of the Genuineness of the Gospels* containing a long refutation of Strauss's position.[7] Before the Civil War, Theodore Parker was the only important American scholar to accept the severest implications of the higher criticism, and even he found Strauss' *Das Leben Jesu* occasionally too rationalistic and subjective to be good biblical science. Many Harvard Unitarians (J. S. Buckminster, Andrews Norton, Edward Everett, George Bancroft, George R. Noyes) dabbled in higher criticism, but only to the extent that it supported their own positions: that the Bible is historically reliable, that miracles can be verified by generally accepted criteria for historical verification, that most of the books of the Bible have been assigned to their rightful authors.[8] Congregational and Presbyterian evangelicals generally rejected even this limited use of higher criticism. Andover editor and professor of Old Testament Bela Bates Edwards attacked the whole idea of "erecting . . . a standard of judgment . . . to which everything is made to bow without appeal." To Edwards this involved too much "the setting up of one's own feelings, or intellectual and moral judgment, as the final arbiter." Such an approach was simply unscientific.[9]

What the scriptural interpretation of America's evangelicals lacked more than anything else was a sense of history. The orthodox believed that all of the Bible's statements were absolutely true and that absolute truth always stands still, just as much as the facts of nature are always the same. It was contrary to the evangelical persuasion to accept such things as historical conditioning, prescientific world-views, or myth-based religion. They demanded a theology thoroughly grounded in historical fact. If there were no historical resurrection, then there could be no Christianity, and the idea that a Christian faith could be built on a "resurrection-myth" was as absurd as the suggestion that one could write a scientific article about the environment of some imaginary island, or a lab report describing the dissection of a nonexistent flora.

The comparison is not as ludicrous as it may sound. Evangelicals of the same cast of mind as Samuel Tyler thought that the Bible really was a kind of "lab report." Kentucky's Episcopal Bishop Benjamin B. Smith argued that biblical theology was a "strictly inductive science" and that "as the beautiful and living carpet which covers and adorns the earth is the proper field of the botanist, so the Bible is the proper field of the theologian; and the words and facts of the Bible are as much the materials of his science to the one, as plants and trees are to the other."[10] Andover's Leonard Woods, Jr., agreed, and insisted that the method of biblical investigation must be the same as "that which is pursued in the science of physics," regulated "by the maxims of *Bacon* and *Newton.*"[11]

Samuel Tyler himself contributed to the *Princeton Review* a long article on scriptural interpretation in which he tried to formulate the science along strictly Baconian lines. Tyler insisted that a good evangelical scholar always try to understand one passage of the Bible by referring to other passages. "In a word," he wrote, "we must make scripture the infallible rule of interpreting scripture; just as we make nature the infallible rule of interpreting nature."[12] The Bible must be its own final authority. To attempt to verify the facts of the Bible by reference to some independent source was a task roughly analogous to verifying the credibility of one's own senses. It was one step further than logic could go.[13] The reason was simple: "revelation," said Tyler, "teaches a knowledge which nature does not." One does not try to verify one with the other. Good scriptural study is "limited in all its speculations by the definite facts of revelation, and does not pretend to see beyond. And this inductive method of interpretation corresponds with the nature of Christianity."[14]

Some evangelicals had a greater concern for historical development than Woods or Tyler. Andover's Old Testament scholars found themselves in constant theological struggle with Harvard's Unitarians. The result was the development of a rather sophisticated evangelical method of biblical scholarship. Moses Stuart argued that lower criticism was the acceptable means of Bible interpretation because it was more scientific than higher criticism. It did not rely on a large number of assumed presuppositions about what can and cannot be historical; it was governed by rules of grammar that could be universally applied to all writings; it left nothing open to supposition or conjecture.[15]

Stuart, a Yale graduate trained chiefly by Timothy Dwight, began his teaching career at Andover in 1810. With little more than the ordinary ministerial training in the biblical languages and without the benefit of a German education, Stuart taught himself the rudiments of criticism. He purchased every German theological work he could and aroused the suspicions of many of his colleagues who were becoming aware of the unorthodox nature of German biblical science. However, Stuart gave them little cause for alarm; he spent his life defending the Bible from every kind of critic.[16]

Stuart did deviate from the position of Samuel Tyler by suggesting to his students that the Bible should be "interpreted as other books." Only by this means, he argued, can we have a truly scientific biblical criticism, for "the principles of interpretation, as to their substantial and essential elements, are no invention of man, no product of his effort and learned skill; nay, they can scarcely be said with truth to have been discovered by him. They are coeval with our nature." In other words, the scientist must accept certain universally considered criteria for carrying on his work or else he is not a scientist. Stuart would contend that the development of methodology is not a creative process but a logically necessary response to given data. Regarding scripture, "if God has implanted in our rational nature the fundamental principles of the hermeneutical art, then we may reasonably suppose that when he addresses a revelation to us, he intends and expects that we shall interpret it in accordance with the laws of the nature which he has given us."[17]

Implicit in Stuart's thought was the idea that the Bible was written by pretechnical men to other people of their own times. He had sufficient historical consciousness to agree with German critics that the Biblical writers express "the common views of their age and time," at least "on all subjects not pertaining directly to the development of moral or religious truth.[18]

This view prompted Stuart to take issue with Edward Hitchcock over alleged "scientific statements" in the first chapter of Genesis. Hitchcock, always eager to find analogies between science and religion, thought that Genesis was full of geological statements about the earth's composition and formation. He contributed a long article on "The Connection Between Geology and the Mosaic History of the Creation" to Andover's *Biblical Repository*, in which he tried to deal with apparent discrepancies between geology and the Genesis account. Hitchcock set up a geological analogy to the Genesis paradigm of creation, describing six geological epochs to correspond with the creation days. He found in Baron Cuvier support for the idea that "the cosmogony of Moses assigns to the epochs of creation precisely the same order as that which has been deduced from geological considerations."[19] In spite of the fact that Hitchcock regarded Genesis one as a figurative story of the creation of the world, he believed that the biblical account somehow "mirrored" modern geologic history. This view was untenable to Moses Stuart. The creation story did not pertain to "the development of moral or religious truth" and it was ridiculous to assume that the author of Genesis would create a figurative account that corresponded item-by-item with nineteenth-century science. Stuart insisted that "the discoveries of modern science and of recent date" cannot "determine the meaning of Moses' words."[20] Quite obviously, said Stuart, the writers of the Bible were "not commissioned to teach geology." Any geological statements the Bible might contain were purely incidental and "altogether in the popular way of speaking." On that ground Stuart saw no validity in Hitchcock's criticism that biblical scholars did not bother to study geology. The study of modern geology could only get in the way of any attempt to arrive at exactly what Moses meant when he wrote the words of Genesis. If anything, one would have to study the "geology" of Moses' contemporaries. However, Stuart was not arguing for that either; rather he supported a scriptural interpretation based on philological considerations alone, with nothing of modern science allowed to get in the way. The whole point of his "Examination of Genesis I, in Reference to Geology" was simply that one cannot examine the Bible "in reference to geology" or any other science.

For Stuart, the Bible interpreter was a specialist—a philologist; not a chemist, botanist, or geologist. The 1830s was an age of rapidly increasing specialization in the sciences. By the middle of the century, clergymen would no longer be called to fill college chairs in the natural sciences. Stuart's insistence that the textual critic stick to a narrow area was in part a recognition of the need for this kind of specialization. In part, however, it was a reaction to the *Naturphilosophie* of German higher critics that allowed them to use contemporary philosophy and social science to interpret scripture. It was also an answer to less critical men such as Hitchcock and Benjamin Silliman, who would continue for some time to study the Bible "in the light of modern science." Moses Stuart was really defining the limits of biblical science. The result was the compartmentalization of its method, and for good or ill Americans would continue to compartmentalize the sciences throughout the remainder of the century. The suggestion that biblical interpreters and geologists have nothing to say to each other would sound innocuous enough in 1900, but to the evangelical mind assured of the unity and thorough consistency of all knowledge it was quite disturbing.

Hitchcock's indignant reply to Stuart appeared in the next number of the *Repository*. To Stuart's proposition that "no discovery of modern science can be of any service in ascertaining the meaning of the Mosaic writings, because Moses had no reference to such discovery," Hitchcock replied that in "numerous" cases "modern science" had done exactly that. But Hitchcock's example sounded quite irrelevant: "It is scarcely 200 years since the Christian world . . . understood Moses and the other sacred writers to teach that the sun, moon, and stars, really rose and set each day. . . . And what changed the opinion of philologists as to these points? Nothing surely but 'the discoveries of modern science.' "[21] How Galileo's discovery cast new light on biblical interpretation Hitchcock did not bother to say. However, he then asked a rhetorical question that indicated his complete misapprehension of Stuart's point: "Could philology, without astronomy, have ever discovered this principle?" Stuart certainly never meant to imply that the philologist, by studying the words of Genesis alone and not dabbling in astronomy, would eventually come to the conclusion that the earth in fact goes around the sun. Rather he argued that the entire question is simply irrelevant to the meaning of Moses' words.

A more incisive criticism of Stuart's strictures on scientific interpretations of Genesis 1 came from a writer who called himself "K" in an article in the *American Journal of Science*. "K" found Stuart frequently violating his own maxim that "the digging of rocks and the digging of Hebrew roots are not yet precisely the same operation."[22] In arguing that philology ought to ignore geology completely Stuart spent too much time pointing out geology's internal contradictions and difficulties. That in itself was a violation of Stuart's principle.

Implicit in Stuart's theory of scriptural interpretation was an idea of revelation already popular among German evangelicals and which would become a standard part of mainstream American theology in the second half of the century. Although he would never state it explicitly, Stuart's method assumed that only the doctrinal and ethical parts of the Bible were actually infallible revelation from God. The rest was simply the statements of men speaking their own minds to their contemporaries. Men of Hitchcock's frame of mind would always be bothered by the problem of how the creation story could describe an "evening" and a "morning" before the sun had been created, because they believed that God always spoke the truth and that the truth cannot be historically conditioned. Hitchcock *had* to find an answer, no matter how hard he had to strain scripture or science. To Stuart, however, the description of the creation of the sun in Genesis 1:14–16 was not the words of an omniscient God at all, but of a very limited, primitive Moses.

Stuart identified scientific biblical criticism with lower criticism. Unitarians George R. Noyes and Andrews Norton were also quite concerned with good scientific method, but unlike Stuart they believed that certain elements of higher criticism could be used to make scientific conclusions about the Bible. While Stuart, for example, accepted the entire biblical canon as given and defended it vigorously, Noyes used largely philosophical considerations to maintain that the teachings of Jesus were inconsistent with those of the Old Testament.[23] Noyes concluded that the New Testament was clearly inspired and authoritative, but that the Old Testament was of dubious authority and mixed value.[24]

Noyes' opinions were too near the fringes of American theology to receive much airing outside Boston and Cambridge. However, his teacher, Andrews Norton, was both popular and successful in making use of all kinds of biblical criticism. Norton grew up in an atmosphere that gave him a much better preparation for biblical criticism than Stuart's. He was trained for the ministry at Harvard under Henry Ware, the controversial Hollis Professor of Divinity whose appointment had precipitated the departure of evangelicals to Andover Seminary. After taking his A.M. degree in 1809, Norton began to associate closely with Boston's liberal clergy, particularly with Brattle Street's new pastor, Joseph Stevens Buckminster—a man whose youth, aggressiveness, and excellent education were coupled with a set of theological opinions that alienated half his congregation while inspiring the other half to constant intellectual energy.[25] Buckminster, charter member and cofounder of Boston's Anthology Club and a frequent contributor to its *Monthly Anthology*, had written his most powerful words against the dogmatic orthodoxy of his day. He did not so much attack biblical literalism as suggest that the Bible does not support the vast dogmatic systems that had been derived from it. Buckminster also wrote countless articles on the canonicity and authorship of various Bible books and passages, and no doubt inspired his young disciple Norton to the same kinds of interests. In 1806–7 Buckminster went to Europe, ostensibly for his health. But he spent the time collecting books and returned to America with three thousand volumes. In 1811 Harvard recognized his scholarly abilities and appointed him as the first Dexter Lecturer on Biblical Criticism. Unfortunately, however, he died in 1812, before his lecture series could begin. William Ellery Channing was appointed as Buckminster's successor but found the job too demanding and resigned after one year. Andrews Norton succeeded him.

Norton was the most absolute of liberals—fiercely intellectual, often pedantic, and so obstinate in his views that critics and friends alike would dub him the "hard-headed Unitarian pope." In spite of his saw-toothed personality, however, Andrews Norton in 1812 was a very precocious and highly esteemed scholar. In the year of Buckminster's death, Norton had been called upon to defend Unitarian liberalism from the attacks of Calvinistic evangelicals, and he used the opportunity to challenge the orthodox theory of scriptural interpretation. Norton let it be known that he could not accept a literalistic approach that made "no allowance . . . for the inadvertance of the writer, and none for the exaggeration produced by strong feelings." Evangelicals too often viewed the writers of the Bible as mere copyists or secretaries. Furthermore, their biblical literalism often led them to interpret words out of context and pay too little attention "to the circumstances in which [the author] wrote, or to those of the persons, whom he addressed."[26] In his Harvard lectures several years later, Norton would suggest that inspiration (which he never doubted) should not be applied to the words of Scripture, but rather to the writers at the time of their writing. They spoke God's word, but in their own language and in relation to their own problems.[27]

Norton's theological perspective supported two theses: 1) all Christian theology must be supported clearly by the Bible; 2) the Bible does not support the vast dogmatic system of New England Calvinism. Norton combined the liberal trend toward theological "reductionism" with the belief that the Bible supported a small number of "great truths" upon which all of Christianity rests. The task of the biblical scholar is to affirm that the Bible is actually the Word of God. The duty of the theologian is to discover and explain the "great truths" of Christianity. The former was Norton's task, and to it he devoted his full-time attention after he resigned from his Harvard position in 1830. The result was the three volume *Evidences of the Genuineness of the Gospels,* and later the *Internal Evidences of the Genuineness of the Gospels.*[28]

The *Evidences* was designed to show that the Gospels were a completely reliable guide to the life and teachings of Jesus. Norton's book was largely a response to such German works as J. G. Eichhorn's *Einleitung in das Neue Testament.* Eichhorn had suggested that the Gospels were second-century variations of an original, lost story of the life of Jesus and were not to be considered reliable historical data. Norton responded that the Gospels were written by the men whose names they bear and that they "remain essentially as they were originally composed."[29]

The reviewers regarded Norton's work as a landmark in biblical scholarship.[30] Moses Stuart accepted it as a "phenomenon in our literary hemisphere" and found good science all the way through, with Norton constantly replacing German hypotheses with American facts.[31] The one criticism Stuart found of the evidences he seriously overstated: "Norton rejects altogether the idea of *inspiration* in respect to the Gospels." What troubled Stuart was Norton's description of certain things as "erroneously referred by Mark" or instances when John "misplaced" words or "blended" together "fiction and miracle." Stuart was not yet willing to allow that the Gospel writers made these kinds of errors. That, he said, would rob Christianity of its foundation, for "any mere conviction of the genuineness of the Gospels . . . will never move the mass of men to yield to their *authority.*"[32] Even this tiny bit of higher criticism was carrying biblical science too far. The difference between Stuart and Norton was not nearly as great as the difference between Norton and Eichhorn, but the difference was there just the same. Stuart worked entirely from within the text of the Bible. He accepted its books as completely reliable and then sought to see them in historical perspective. Norton was looking for a method that would objectify the Bible in order to facilitate scientific studies of its origin. He could talk about Gospel *fallacies,* while Stuart would discuss only *prescientific world-views.* But even Norton was not ready to admit as many "fallacies" as some higher critics could find. That job went to Theodore Parker, America's disciple of the demythologizing school of DeWette and Strauss.

What Kant and Coleridge had been to natural theology and metaphysics, Hegel and Strauss were to the inspired Bible. Perhaps no one had a more profound sense of the meaning of history than Georg Wilhelm Friedrich Hegel. To him all aspects of man's existence were a product of historical development. Hegel was an idealist who saw the entire universe as a single mind, usually the mind of God. For this reason he believed that thinking and activity are largely the same process: action is the working out of the thoughts of God. Thus history has a *rational* as well as a merely factual explanation: one can talk about *why* things happen at the same time he is narrating the fact that they have happened. To the historian this view of history as a rational process meant that historical events, like the controversy between church and state, for example, had to be "explained," not merely described. Hegel's more radical followers (including Feuerbach and Marx) picked up on the idea that contemporary institutions are the result of a rational developmental process; however, at the same time they were convinced that the "reason" that had gone into the development of these institutions was frequently ill-conceived and badly motivated. For example, religion claimed to be concerned with metaphysics and things not belonging to this world. In its actual historical development, however, religion came to have a great deal to do with politics, education, and economics. Left-wing Hegelians like David Friedrich Strauss reasoned that the only way to rediscover religion's true relationship with other aspects of the world was to work the historical process in reverse—to trace backwards into time the development of religion, always being careful to excise everything fictional, mythical, and unessential. Once a person arrived at Christianity's real historical kernel, he could obtain a picture of religion working in its proper relationship with the rest of society. By getting at the historical fact of the life of Jesus of Nazareth, Strauss hoped to see Christianity as it was first conceived, before it developed in so many unfortunate directions.

Strauss was controversial in the 1830s not so much for the fact that he thought the life of Christ had to be rewritten as for the criteria he established for determining what is history and what is myth. He argued that men of different historical periods viewed reality in different ways. A first-century Gospel writer might easily give a mythical explanation for an idea he could not understand, in the process changing that idea into an "event" (such as the turning of water into wine, or the resurrection from the dead). Strauss worked with the uniformitarian premise that because miracles are foreign to modern experience, they were not experienced by men in the first century either. Anything that could not be given a natural explanation by modern science could not have happened and must be a myth. Strauss believed that every historical event must have been caused by previous events, that the whole of history was one natural chain. A miracle would be an unexplainable break in such a chain and would disrupt the entire Hegelian scheme of history as a rational, developing process.[33]

Strauss' book was the logical conclusion of a long tradition of critical historical thinking in Germany. Hermann Samuel Reimarus, a reclusive German scholar about whom little is known, wrote "The Aims of Jesus and His Disciples" to suggest that most of the gospel miracles were fictitious, created by disappointed disciples after Jesus' death. Reimarus' work was more polemic than history, but his followers, the "rationalistic" historical critics, did try to be more objective. Like their deist counterparts in England and America, the rationalistic critics accepted only those parts of Christianity which seemed reasonable. Unlike British and American deists, however, they focused most of their attention on the historical books of the New Testament. Johann Jakob Hess's three-volume *History of the Last Three Years of the Life of Jesus* (1768–72) did not deny the historicity of miracles but attempted as much as possible to minimize their importance, emphasizing instead Jesus' ethical teachings. Hess believed that Jesus' birth and resurrection were both miraculous and historical. However, he tried to provide natural explanations for smaller, less significant miracles. Franz Volkmar Reinhard's 1781 *Essay upon the Plan Which the Founder of the Christian Religion Adopted for the Benefit of Mankind* explained the gospel miracles as natural events whose actual causes were hidden. Reinhard reasoned that it would be both rational and easy for God to bring about a perfectly natural event that is merely "an obvious exception to what can be brought about by natural causes, so far as we know them."[34]

Gospel historians frequently attempted to give natural explanations for Christ's miracles, but none carried these quite as far as Heinrich Paulus. Paulus suggested in his 1828 *Life of Jesus as the Basis of a Purely Historical Account of Early Christianity* that the writers of the gospels were too primitive to understand a wide variety of natural phenomena. Whenever a gospel writer saw something that he could not comprehend he invented a "miraculous" explanation. The result was that the gospels contained neither miracle nor myth. The miracles were historical, but they were not supernatural.[35]

The theory sounded good enough. However, when Paulus attempted to explain the causes of alleged miracles he ran into trouble. For Christ's miracles of healing, he suggested that perhaps Jesus had discovered a number of medicines known to him alone. Christ's walk on the water, said Paulus, was merely an illusion of the disciples. Jesus appeared to still the storm when he was in the fishing boat with his disciples because at the precise moment he spoke the boat became sheltered from the wind by a coastal mountain. The apparent dead who were raised had actually lapsed into comas. These unsatisfactory rational explanations for the miracles in Paulus's "rational" life of Jesus made his book unacceptable to many critics. Strauss began his own *Life of Jesus* by attacking Paulus's suggestion that the gospel miracles could be given such explanations, for they were even less rational than literal acceptance of the gospel story. Instead, Strauss opted for an explanation already given for parts of the Old Testament by Wilhelm Martin de Wette and Johann Gottfried Eichhorn: that the world-view of Christ's contemporaries was largely mythical; their method of communication was to describe religious ideas as historical facts.

Strauss's reasoning came from Hegel's thesis that everything which happens in the world is part of the thinking process of a single great mind. Each thought and each event is a small part of a cosmic process of mental maturation—the development of a universal "self-consciousness." At the time of early man this universal self-consciousness was in its infancy and perceived things as an infant would perceive them. As it matured, however, its explanations grew more scientific. Andrews Norton and the evangelical Bible scholars had a thoroughly Lockean theory of knowledge. They believed that each man is born knowing nothing, but that in the process of growing up he acquires a mature understanding of the world. For Norton an adult of the first century A.D., had as mature a world-view as a nineteenth-century adult. Strauss, on the other hand, began with the premise that the New Testament writers wrote when the universal self-consciousness was in an adolescent state. They had no mature idea of reality analogous to the scientific view of the nineteenth century. The ancient writers did not see history as part of a great cause-effect chain. They made no distinction between natural and supernatural. They communicated their most lofty ideas by creating myths or epics, so that intangible ideas could be clothed in tangible forms. For example, the writers of the New Testament translated the Old Testament idea of Messianic expectation into the stories of Jesus' miraculous birth and resurrection. They translated the historical Jesus' rejection of the Jewish temple ritual into the account of the rending of the temple veil at the time of his death.[36]

To Strauss, the idea that the content of the New Testament histories was mythical rather than historical had the effect of strengthening rather than weakening the gospel message. Facts have no religious value; faith in an historical fact is faith in nothing at all. Faith, said Strauss, must be built on *meaning*, not on factuality or historicity. Because he was strongly influenced by positivism, Strauss's idea of fact was tied very closely with scientific verification. To say that faith depends on historical fact is to say that the content of faith is something that can be empirically established. But implicit in the nature of religious belief is the demand that its content be unverifiable. For example, as soon as I have verified that Christ rose from the grave, then my faith in the resurrection is no longer religious belief at all but mere scientific knowledge. Strauss wanted to avoid completely that kind of rationalization of the Christian faith. To say that the historical content of the Christian faith is mythic was a neat way of keeping the objects of faith and of scientific investigation in their own separate corners.

That idea may have sat well with American Transcendentalists, but never with the orthodox. American Protestantism was thoroughly committed to factuality. The "facts" of the Bible were meaningful precisely because they described events that had actually occurred. For evangelicals and Unitarians nothing existed between the historical and the nonhistorical—no myths, symbols, epics, or poetic expressions. Either Jesus actually rose from the dead and Christianity is the only true religion, or else he did not rise and Christianity is false.

Perhaps the first evangelical to give Strauss written acknowledgment was conservative Presbyterian Charles Hodge, Princeton theologian. Hodge had apparently not had time to read Strauss but had heard that in *Das Leben Jesu* "infidel theology appears to have reached its consummation." Most of his very short review was devoted to a sketch of the way in which German theology was rapidly departing from historical commitment and approaching Strauss's pantheism, which "acknowledges no God but the God incarnate in the human race."[37]

The superficiality of Hodge's discussion suggests that many evangelicals did not really consider Strauss a serious threat. In a day when conservative Presbyterians and Congregationalists were still debating predestination, infant damnation, and the infidel tendencies of the New Haven Theology, *Das Leben Jesu* was about as intimidating as a Hindu preaching in Sanskrit from atop Plymouth Rock. Strauss and the evangelicals simply did not share enough common ground even to begin a debate. With one outstanding exception, the leading evangelical journals gave Strauss little space.

Ironically, the only full-length review of Strauss by a mainstream evangelical was among the most sophisticated American responses to *Das Leben Jesu*. Horatio Balch Hackett, an Andover-educated professor of New Testament at Newton Seminary, was a painstaking scholar who produced little written work but was always thorough. He provided his readers with a brief history of higher criticism and attacked its method for violating "too many principles of language and common sense to maintain its ground against the stricter views of philology." Hackett told his readers about myths, explaining that they are religious ideas *"clothed in a historical form,"* and that form can be "a pure fiction, having no foundation whatever in any actual occurrences, but arising solely from the tendency of the human mind to give to spiritual truths an outward representation." He argued that by Strauss's criteria for separating myth from reality "all history loses its certainty, and becomes a mere phantom, an illusion." For "no biography was ever written . . . which may not be resolved into a set of myths as easily as the account of the Saviour contained in the Gospels." Hackett's arguments against Strauss were essentially the same as Moses Stuart's arguments in support of lower criticism: the method to be applied in biblical scholarship must be the same as that used in all kinds of historical and textual criticism. Strauss's criticism leaves us with very little "historical" information about the life of Jesus, but if we used the same criteria we would have little knowledge about any aspect of the ancient world: "All confidence in the past [would be] destroyed," concluded Hackett; "all distinction between the ideal and the actual [would be] annihilated, and men [could] be sure of nothing which has taken place at any period remote at all from their own time, whatever be the testimony by which it is supported." So, he concluded, Strauss lacked the scientific objectivity necessary to do biblical criticism.[38]

The Unitarians had more common ground with Strauss than the evangelicals did. For some years they had been sending bright students to Germany to study with notable theologians. They were well acquainted with the development of Continental philosophy, especially with the influence of Kant and Hegel. They generally had a greater sense of history than the trinitarian evangelicals. What there was of a controversy over Strauss in America took place almost entirely among Unitarians, the conservatives attacking him and Theodore Parker rather cautiously coming to his defense.[39]

Unitarian historian George Edward Ellis faulted the entire "German pattern for Scriptural criticism" for treating "words and opinions and theories and institutions after the same manner as the old Dutch fashion of gardening applied to trees, plants and hedge-rows,—shaping roots into letters, converting nature's waving line of beauty into the painful distortions of art, and reducing the rule which God has appointed into methods which man prefers." Furthermore, said Ellis, Strauss had ignored the ordinary rules of evidence, particularly the great principle "established in the courts, in the forum, and in historical science, that in a comparison of independent witnesses and testimonies there will always appear some discrepancies . . . which no skill can reconcile."[40] Ellis's mention of the principles of evidence was probably a reference to a book published in that same year by Harvard law professor Simon Greenleaf and entitled *An Examination of the Testimony of the Four Evangelists, by the Rules of Evidence Administered in Courts of Justice.* Greenleaf had attempted to bring the gospels "to the tests to which other evidence is subjected in human tribunals."[41] He concluded that if we reject the gospel narratives because of discrepancies between them then we would have to reject as well stories of the American Revolution, or of any other event described by mutually contradictory accounts. This would probably make the writing of all history impossible. Greenleaf's judgment was inescapable: if historians and juries could accept the testimony of four independent witnesses, regardless of minor discrepancies, then Strauss and other biblical scholars must accept them as well.[42]

Francis Bowen chose to review Strauss's *Das Leben Jesu* and Greenleaf's *Examination* together, noting that it "is hard to conceive of two works more unlike in their scope, character, and purpose." Bowen found Greenleaf superior to Strauss in almost every respect. He saw Strauss's "absurd application of an absurd theory" as sufficient to "mark it as one of the most signal of all failures in speculation," and he "heartily" advised Strauss to *"leave the ministerial profession."* Bowen's review was still another comparison of the diligent, empirical scholar with the flamboyant, reckless speculator—one work an excellent specimen "of clear and shrewd English common sense," the other "of German erudition, laborious diligence, and fertility in original speculation."[43] For Bowen the approaches of Greenleaf and Strauss were the different approaches of the scientist and the metaphysician, and there was no doubt about who was the abler biblical critic.

Theodore Parker had actually been given the privilege of writing the first full-length review of Strauss to appear in the *Christian Examiner.* Largely an extensive and thorough analysis, his article left little time for Parker's own conclusions about Strauss's method. Clearly, however, Parker was one of the few people in the United States who could honestly appraise Strauss's work. Parker was relieved that in the third German edition of *Das Leben Jesu* Strauss had retracted some of his doubts about the genuineness of the Gospel of John (although Strauss would reinsert those doubts in the fourth edition). But he attacked Strauss's claim that he had begun his study "without any 'presuppositions.' " Parker identified Strauss's presuppositions as the notion "that the idea precedes the man, who is supposed to realize the idea; that many men, having a certain doctrine, gradually and in a natural manner, refer this doctrine to some historical person, and thus make a mythical web of history." In addition, Strauss had presupposed that "a miracle is utterly impossible." Finally, he had assumed "that the Ideal of Holiness and Love, for example, like the Ideal of beauty, eloquence, philosophy, or music, cannot be concentrated in an individual. In a word, there can be no incarnation of God."[44]

But Parker was not nearly as critical of Strauss as he could have been. He had too much respect for Strauss as "a lover of truth" and "a serious and earnest spirit." In spite of his criticisms of the mythic theory, the idea clearly fascinated Parker. A year later Parker would borrow from Strauss a title for a sermon—the most daring ever preached before the small West Roxbury congregation that he served as pastor. "The Transient and Permanent in Christianity" showed a much more critical Parker than the Strauss review had. He attacked the doctrine of biblical infallibility and the biblically derived doctrines of orthodoxy, including the divinity of Christ. "The theological doctrines derived from our fathers," he told his congregation, "seem to have come from Judaism, heathenism, and the caprice of philosophers, far more than they have come from the principle and sentiment of Christianity."[45]

Parker continued to toy with mythical theories in spite of conservative opposition, and by 1842 his transformation was complete. The lectures he delivered that year in Boston's Old Masonic Temple, eventually published as *A Discourse on Matters Pertaining to Religion*, reveal that he had come to accept most of the controversial opinions of Strauss he had criticized in his earlier review.[46] In 1842 he told his audience that the authorship, dates of composition, and source material of the synoptic gospels were in doubt. He suggested that the gospels contained as much myth or fiction as they did historical fact. Furthermore, he had come to agree with Strauss that the historicity of all gospel miracles was doubtful.[47]

Evangelicals and Unitarians alike had something to say about Theodore Parker and the Bible. Conservative New Hampshire

Unitarian Andrew Preston Peabody reviewed "Mr. Parker's Discourse" for the *Christian Examiner* four months after it was delivered. Peabody was aghast that Parker should talk about the books *"between the lids of the Bible,"* especially when all he had to say about them was that they had been brought together *"by caprice or accident."*[48] The unnamed author of an article in the Baptist *Christian Review* was even more outraged than Peabody. The reviewer made long comparisons between the work of Parker and that "of that celebrated apostle of infidelity, Thomas Paine," and found it "curious" that "the bitterest infidel of the past age, writing to overthrow Christianity," and "a professed successor of the holy apostles, standing in the Puritan pulpit" should use the same arguments against the Bible.[49]

A Discourse on Matters Pertaining to Religion aroused orthodox reviewers just as much as the sermon on the "Transient and Permanent" had. John Hopkins Morrison, a Unitarian pastor from Massachusetts, found Parker's repeated assertions that some of Christ's miracles had been borrowed from older pagan accounts, that the gospels contradict one another, and that Jesus was "mistaken" in his interpretation of the Old Testament, too much to bear. Painstakingly, Morrison answered dozens of Parker's allegations about biblical statements, each time pointing out how Parker had misinterpreted or misunderstood. He found through it all that Parker suffered from "a want of exactness which marks his habits of thought," and a lack of objectivity: "we see nowhere proof of a suspension of the judgment over disputed facts, . . . He seems not indeed to have the power of doubting."[50]

A little less painful review appeared in the Congregationalist *New Englander* in 1844. Noah Porter, at that time a prominent Congregational clergyman, thought it ironic that Parker called himself a Christian minister, for his thought seemed "more like the dogmas of a French or Hindoo deist, or mayhap the more refined religionism of a Persian Soofee, than the Christian theology of a Christian teacher." Parker's entire presentation was much too vague for Porter, who only wished "that Socrates could have the handling of him for an hour, and by questions drive him to say what he does or does not mean, and whether in some cases he means anything." Porter concluded that "the truly liberal mind sickens at the amount of nonsense that has been written vaguely about the Bible, under the name of spiritual interpretation. It is stunned and confused amid the Babel-like confusion and the wordy wars of modern exegetes."[51]

But to Parker's way of thinking the evangelicals had confused themselves. They had attempted to turn the "rationalization" of Christianity in the eighteenth century into the "verification" of Christianity in the nineteenth. The Baconian method of doing theology, Parker told the readers of the 1842 *Dial*, "begins by neglecting that half of man's nature which is primarily concerned with divine things." In an era characterized by the development of scientific positivism, evangelicals had already assumed an essentially positivistic stance. Baconianism could be applied "with eminent success to experimental science," said Parker, but it "recognizes scarcely the possibility of a theology, certainly of none but an historical theology. Positivistic critics tried to excise everything from Christian history that could not be scientifically explained, and evangelical defenders attempted to show that all parts of biblical theology are scientifically credible. Both sides were united, however, in insisting that the content of Christianity must in some sense be verifiable. To Parker, this kind of religion was something that "lives in the senses, not the soul." Interestingly enough, Parker cited Auguste Comte as "one of the most thorough Baconians of the present day," and noted that his method had arrived at "materialism in psychology, selfishness in ethics, and atheism in theology." Obviously, Baconian evangelicals were going in the same direction. Christianity, quite clearly, had to be rescued from its facts.[52]

However, American orthodoxy was a long way from seeing the need to be rescued from its facts. Many would never reject the "facts" of Christianity; they would rather relinquish the facts of science. Others faced a long, hopeless struggle that never ended, not even when Darwin made the task immeasurably more difficult in the 1860s. Americans wanted to *know* what they believed. For them science would always be better than metaphysics, reality would always be better than symbol. For those reasons, orthodoxy and literalism would always appear to be straighter answers than higher criticism and mythology.

5

Nature and Supernature

No controversy brought the nineteenth-century dialogue between science and religion into sharper focus than the great debates over miracles. No theological issue aroused more hard feelings, caused more dissension within churches, or forced more scientists to restate or reconsider their positions.

The reason is clear. In its broader sense the miracles controversy was at the heart of all the fundamental issues separating Protestant orthodoxy and science. Questions of biblical criticism were ultimately questions about the reality of miraculous events. The entire evangelical furor over Strauss and Parker can be reduced to a disagreement about the historicity of biblical miracles. The exciting scientific issues of the day—the age of the earth and the method of its creation, the unity of mankind, the developmental hypotheses—all forced people to take a position regarding the actuality of miraculous events. In the evangelical's eyes the geological uniformitarian, the evolutionist, the higher critic, and the empiricist sceptic were all men of the same mind: they denied the supernatural.

There were two kinds of miracles: biblical and nonbiblical. Biblical miracles were those miracles recorded in the Bible. Their historicity could be demonstrated in two ways. First, one could appeal to the *need* for such miracles; for example, the divinity of Christ was necessary because the world's savior had to be both God and man.[1] Secondly, one could simply cite the fact that accounts of miracles are contained in the infallible Bible, which was sufficient evidence for any evangelical.

Extrabiblical miracles, on the other hand, were not recorded in Scripture. Their defense rested entirely on their usefulness in explaining certain phenomena. Catastrophic geologists, for example, talked about large scale supernatural destructions of life on earth in order to explain the fossil record. Progressive creationists talked about creative acts not mentioned in the first three chapters of Genesis. Die-hard biblical literalists suggested miracles to solve the problems created by uncomfortable geologic evidence, as when Yale theologian Nathaniel Taylor suggested to Benjamin Silliman that God created the entire fossil record in a single act.[2] Men who denied the unity of the human race spoke about extrabiblical creations far away from the Garden of Eden in order to account for the diversity and distribution of species.

The controversy over biblical miracles was generally limited to religion and the biblical sciences. Although the primary issue was the historicity of biblical miracles, other questions also arose: Could the miracles be explained by natural causes? Do miracles really constitute a violation of the laws of nature, or might there be "natural laws" that man knows nothing about? Perhaps the most important of these questions involved the necessity of belief in miracles as part of Christianity's defense mechanism. For Unitarians and most evangelicals the historical fact of the miracles was the strongest proof of the truth of the Christian religion. Take them away and Christianity would become insupportable.

The controversy over extrabiblical miracles also had theological implications, but most of the issues were confined to the sciences. The most important questions concerned how far one could carry the presupposition of the uniformity of nature. Must the history and phenomena of the physical world be explained entirely in terms of natural causes, or are supernatural explanations sometimes appropriate?

Catastrophic geologists and progressive creationists generally answered "yes" to the last part of that question. Catastrophism was often an effort to give scientific explanations for the origin of the earth while preserving as much as possible the historical integrity of Genesis. Progressive catastrophism saw the earth developing through a series of stages (often six, to correspond with the six days of creation) separated from one another by some sort of cosmic catastrophe, such as a flood, earthquake, or glacier. Following each catastrophe, God created a new set of organisms on earth, generally a little more sophisticated than the previous set had been. This accounted for the increasing complexity of fossils as one moved up through geologic strata.[3]

In the first half of the nineteenth century, catastrophism was an essentially antiempirical position. It often suggested scientific explanations beyond the range of any known scientific observation. Implicit in catastrophism was a very close mixing of science and theology. Even the more sophisticated catastrophists who were not particularly interested in the infallibility of Genesis, such as Cuvier and Agassiz, could not rid their scientific paradigms of theological terms. In the 1850s Agassiz was still talking about "centres of creation" or "multiple creations," just as if "creation" were part of the scientific record of the world. He was still describing species as "ideas in the mind of God," just as if God's thoughts could be part of nature's empirical data.

Doubters of miracles appeared in America almost as early as in Europe and England. Revolutionary War hero Ethan Allen's *Reason the Only Oracle of Man* outlined a position that was fairly representative among radical deists. If we assume, argued Allen, that God created an absolutely perfect natural order, then any alteration of the course of nature ("miracles" by Allen's definition) would have the effect of making the universe less than perfect. This would be obviously inconsistent with the nature of God. On the other hand, if we assume that miracles are improving, or perfecting, the course of nature, then we must believe that the world was imperfect to begin with. That is also inconsistent with God's nature.

Having presented believers with this dilemma, Allen concluded that there is only one solution. God is perfect; the laws of nature were established by God and therefore they are perfect and never require any kind of "adjustment." Obviously, "to suppose that God should subvert his laws (which is the same as changing them) would be to suppose him to be mutable."[4]

That rationalistic argument against miracles may have convinced some radicals, but orthodox Americans refused to listen to such casuistry. They were much more threatened by David Hume, who had used some of orthodoxy's own tools to construct an *empirical* argument against miracles.

Hume stood as far away from Enlightenment deists as any Presbyterian evangelical. While Ethan Allen's rationalism ended in a rather well-defined theism, Hume's empirical method led him to a thorough scepticism. Rather than speculating about whether a perfect God could perform miracles, Hume examined the empirical grounds for belief in the miraculous. He noted first that all "evidence" of biblical miracles comes from testimony. The testimony of someone else, however, is always weaker than one's own sensory observation. This is so, said Hume, because everyone has experienced false testimony. Witnesses can be lying or mistaken. Our senses, however, almost always give us reliable information. Furthermore, since none of us has witnessed a miracle, we cannot confirm the testimony of witnesses who claim to have seen one. The implication was clear: for any given instance in which a witness claims to have seen a miracle, it is more probable that the witness is lying or mistaken than that a miracle has actually occurred. Hume concluded then that testimony can never establish the occurrence of any miracle.[5]

Evangelicals attacked every variety of disbelief in miracles, but no one drew as much fire as Hume. It was not because his argument was foolproof. On the contrary, the argument was bad, and men as disinclined toward philosophical reasoning as Timothy Dwight and Alexander Campbell became experts on its shortcomings. In the early nineteenth century, when "Hume" and "scepticism" were nearly synonymous, evangelicals could easily disprove the empirical argument against miracles, and destroying Hume in a philosophical argument was no small victory.

Samuel Stanhope Smith attacked Hume's argument in *A Comprehensive View of the Leading and Most Important Principles of Natural and Revealed Religion*, Smith's grand attempt to defend Christianity from all its critics. Smith found the miracles of Christ to be "attested by numerous witnesses of the soundest judgment and the most unsuspected integrity." This, he said, was reason enough to believe in their historicity. Furthermore, Hume's argument went much too far. Anyone who accepts Hume's conclusion would have to deny that the earth ever had a beginning (obviously a miraculous event). Rather, he would have to "embrace the philosophical absurdity of an eternal succession of mutable and perishing beings."

Smith's second response to Hume's argument was much more empirical. If what Hume said about the circumstances under which witnesses are to be believed were true, then men from one part of the world would never believe sojourners' reports of peculiar phenomena in other parts. Smith told the story of a king of tropical Siam who punished a Dutch navigator for telling him that in Holland "water became so hard during part of the year, that it bore horses and carriages upon its surface." Obviously, said Smith, man has become too sophisticated for that sort of thing. When a traveler tells us about some unusual phenomenon, we generally expect that he is telling the truth, even if we have not seen it ourselves. The same holds for witnesses' reports of miracles.[6]

Yale's Timothy Dwight also found Hume's argument "a mere mass of sophistry." Dwight's response to Hume showed more logical sophistication than Smith was able to muster. Suppose, suggested Dwight, that a "ferry-boat has crossed the ferry a thousand times without sinking." Reasoning from Hume that *"the same causes produce, in the same circumstances, the same effects,"* Dwight decided that everyone would fully expect that this ferry could make it safely to its destination any time it tried. Nevertheless, "the smallest, credible testimony will induce any man to believe that [the] ferry-boat has sunk; although it may before have crossed safely, and regularly, for many years."

No one would call the witness of this tragedy a liar, even though his story contradicted the "universal experience" of people who had been watching the ferry all their lives. The same ought to apply to those who claim to have witnessed miracles. Dwight believed that the ferry-boat illustration clearly proved the invalidity of Hume's argument.

But Dwight also disclosed a much more fundamental flaw in Hume's reasoning: "he, at first, uses the word *experience*, which is all important to this controversy, to denote . . . *the actual evidence of a Man's own senses*. In the progress of his Essay, he soon diverts it into a sense, entirely different; and means by it *the experience of all who have preceded us*. But of their experience we know nothing, except by Testimony; the very thing, which *Mr. Hume* professedly opposes what he calls Experience." During the argument, Hume had subtly shifted the meaning of "experience" from one's own personal experience to the universal experience of all mankind. How could Hume know that miracles are contrary to the universal experience of men? Obviously, noted Dwight, only one way: by listening to other men talking about their experiences. Hume did not pit "testimony" against "experience." He pitted testimony of one kind against testimony of another kind. But that could prove nothing.[7]

Dwight's response to Hume was literate, intricate, and effective, but, like many of Dwight's ideas, it was not his own.[8] Dwight had appropriated the response, including the ferry-boat story, from a Scottish Realist friend of Thomas Reid: George Campbell, Principal of Marischal College, and author of *A Dissertation on Miracles*.

Campbell had apparently been the first to discover the giant equivocation in Hume's argument. He noted that "in proposing his argument [Hume] would surely be understood to mean only *personal* experience; otherwise, his making testimony derive its light from an experience which [in turn] derives its light from testimony, would be introducing what logicians term a *circle of causes*." The first definition of "experience" will not get Hume to his conclusion; so "in whatever sense he uses the term *experience* in proposing his argument; in prosecuting it he with great dexterity shifts the sense." How can Hume know that miracles are contrary to the experience of all men everywhere? "Only I suppose by testimony, oral or written."[9]

Campbell's masterful essay provided evangelicals with all the ammunition they needed, and they used it against Hume every time the opportunity arose. For example, Bishop Charles M'Ilvaine of the Protestant Episcopal Church of Ohio did not even bother to read Hume. In his *Evidences of Christianity* he quoted the summary of Hume's argument which "is abridged in the *Encyclopedia Britannica*" and then added Campbell's response.[10] Generally, evangelicals of all kinds, from rather sophisticated Congregationals to Baptists and Campbellites, found it easy to be philosophers when refuting David Hume. These prepackaged refutations were popular throughout the first half of the century.[11]

Hume's argument against miracles incited evangelicals, but the increasingly influential German Transcendental philosophy had an even greater effect on Unitarians and some of the more elite conservatives at Andover. The rise of American Transcendentalism brought *both* sides of a new miracles controversy to America—to a great debate, not between Americans and the books of dead Europeans, but between two very lively groups of Masschusetts intellectuals.

Through their preoccupation with the rational defense of Christianity, the Unitarians created most of their own problems with miracles. Rationalistic apologists seized upon anything that looked reasonable and tried to convert it into a "justification" of Christianity. Inevitably, miracles became not just one of the phenomena of Christianity but an integral part of its defense mechanism. Orville Dewey, an Andover graduate who departed from the trinitarian fold around 1820 and became a Unitarian leader as pastor of New York City's Second Congregational Church, declared that miracles were the cornerstone of the Unitarian faith. His "Discourse on Miracles," first delivered as a Dudleian lecture in May 1836, attacked "the modern system of German Rationalism" and the "presumption against miracles" lurking in the very "bosom of science." Dewey wanted to prove that belief in miracles is "preliminary to the Argument for a Revelation": that is to say, one cannot have a divine revelation unless he believes in miracles. For Dewey this meant quite simply that one cannot have Christianity without miracles.

Miracles are to Christianity the "massive subterranean arches and columns of a huge building. We do not prize them so much for their own sake as for the building which they support; but pull them out and the building will certainly collapse." Dewey tried to show that every justification of Christianity by its best apologists depended on God's ability to work miracles. Did not the apologists argue that the Old Testament prophets spoke from God because so many of their prophecies came true? But is not prophecy itself a miracle? "Miracle," concluded Dewey, "holds its place in every honest explanation of the external evidences of Christianity."[12]

Like his evangelical peers, Dewey also attempted to refute Hume's argument against miracles. But from the beginning the argument over miracles between Unitarians and Transcendentalists was quite different than the argument between Hume and his critics. Evangelicals were usually concerned with the plausibility of miracles. Transcendentalists more generally debated their necessity. The Unitarians argued consistently that no one who doubted miracles could call himself Christian. The Transcendentalists vehemently answered that miracles were not part of the permanent values of Christianity but merely a mythical mechanism for bringing the Word to the people.

The following *Christian Examiner* contained an innovative response to Dewey's arguments from George Ripley, a brilliant graduate of the Harvard Divinity School who by age thirty-five had already been pastor of Boston's Purchase Street Church and Professor of Germanic languages at Harvard. In 1836 the young scholar, steeped in Swedenborg, Coleridge, and Cousin, and an active member of the growing Transcendental Club, was ready to make his own statement on miracles. Orville Dewey's vigorous defense of the orthodox position gave him the opportunity he needed.

Ripley's attack on miracles was relatively mild. He argued that they were not necessary to establish the truth of Christianity: "the revelation is not for the sake of the miracles, but the miracles for the sake of the revelation." Furthermore, said Ripley, the orthodox view of miracles is too dependent on an outdated theory of biblical inspiration. Rather than reject miracles and inspiration together, however, Ripley chose to Romanticize his view of inspiration. To him, as to Parker, the Bible became a "revelation of spiritual life and truth" rather than a history book. "Whoever believes the truth which it was the mission of Christ to announce, is entitled to the name of a disciple, whatever be the foundation on which he has been led to rest his faith."

Coming from an American Unitarian, Ripley's article was revolutionary. The meat of Parker's "Transient and Permanent" was already there: the meaning of religion lies not in historical fact but in ethical value. According to Ripley, Christ "ever enforced the paramount need of faith in his doctrine, which bore its own evidence on its face to those who would do his will; and . . . so far from requiring a faith in his miracles as the condition of receiving his word, he required a faith in his word as the condition of receiving his miracles."[13]

Nothing in Ripley's article suggested that he believed Christ's miracles were myths or fictions. But the view that the miracles had no apologetic value would not sit well with conservatives. Ripley was not suggesting merely that the grounds of Christian faith could not be established by miracle; he was arguing that faith has no empirical foundation. One had to accept the Word on its face, without the host of proofs, verifications, and rationalizations traditional Christianity had created to accompany it. Ripley, like other men of his movement, wanted to detach questions of religion and ethics from questions of history and verification. In the process he would put an end to the continual flow of scientific "defenses" of Christianity.

Andrews Norton was the first to respond to Ripley. He minced no words. In a November letter in the *Boston Daily Advertiser* he declared that those who subverted doctrines and were not settled in their own beliefs should not be permitted to publish, at least not until their articles "first go into the hands only of those who are capable of judging of their correctness." This was not even an attempt to refute Ripley but an insistence that heretical views be quashed without exposure, and this coming from a Unitarian tradition priding itself for its tolerance of wide-ranging rational inquiries.[14]

A religious party placed on the defensive often becomes "empirical," clinging tenaciously to approved doctrine and decrying the introduction of new "hypotheses." Ripley believed that Norton was doing exactly that, and he noted it in his reply.

"You," he wrote in an open letter, "are a disciple of the school which was founded by Locke. . . . For that philosophy I have no respect. I believe it to be superficial, irreligious, and false in its primary elements. The evils it has brought upon humanity, by denying the mind the power of perceiving spiritual truth, are great and lamentable."[15] Already in these early stages the miracles controversy was developing into a much broader argument over the relation of religion to science. Ripley believed that as long as Unitarianism clung to religious tenets based on verifiability it was doomed. Science would inevitably destroy the historical bases for those beliefs, and Unitarians would have nothing left to defend. Better now to cut the cord between religion and verification, while time remained.

The controversy sharpened when the reactions to William Henry Furness' *Remarks on the Four Gospels*, published earlier in that same year, began to come in. Furness, a scholarly man who spent nearly his whole life in the area around Philadelphia and Boston, had been a classmate of Emerson at Harvard. He graduated from the Divinity School in 1823 and became the minister of the Unitarian Church in Philadelphia. But his greatest interest was the German critics, particularly the New Testament scholars who were trying to reconstruct the life of Jesus.

Furness tried to be as subtle as Ripley had been in speaking about miracles. Rather than denying their historicity he tried to show that the whole question of verification was much more difficult than conservatives would have it. Like Dwight and other evangelicals, Furness noted that miracles are not contrary to human experience; they are simply *in addition to* experience. But from that point Furness moved in a different direction than Dwight. Miracles are outside of human experience, he said, because experience, "so far from possessing anything like completeness, is most imperfect." The universe is full of things that humans have never experienced. The division between natural and supernatural is a false dichotomy. Men have simply called phenomena within their experience "natural," while they have described anything outside human experience as "supernatural." God's activities are not to be distinguished in any such way. He does some things we know about, and some things we can never understand. "We stand but on the borders of the tremendous abyss of being. We have caught but a distant glimpse of its great author." Because we have limited knowledge of the manifold workings of the universe it is presumptuous for us to "pronounce an alleged fact a violation of its order."

Without denying that miracles occurred, Furness did deny that they were supernatural. Miracles are part of the natural order of the universe, but men do not yet know everything about that natural order. Nineteenth-century man perceives miracles in the same way that primitive man perceived the lightning. Until he understood the cause, he was forced to regard lightning as supernatural.[16]

But orthodox Unitarians could not tolerate that kind of rationale. It was precisely because the miracles *were* supernatural that they could be used to prove the validity of the Christian religion. To call miracles nothing more than currently unexplainable natural phenomena was to put them at the same level with the difficult problems of geology or physical anthropology. Those mysteries could certainly not be used as "proofs" of the validity of Christianity. On the contrary, they gave Christianity a great deal of difficulty. "Natural" explanation for miracles was no better than denying miracles altogether.

Support for Furness's position came, surprisingly enough, from the American West. In 1835 William G. Elliot, Ephraim Peabody, and James Freeman Clarke, a precocious graduate of the Harvard Divinity School, went to Cincinnati to establish a new journal designed to promote "Unitarian views of Christianity." Almost immediately the short-lived *Western Messenger* distinguished itself from the conservative *Christian Examiner* by siding with the young Transcendentalist movement. In June 1836, Samuel Osgood, another Harvard Divinity student who had decided to join the struggling Cincinnati group, contributed a "Word on Miracles" to the new journal. Osgood argued that it was extremely arrogant for anyone to object to miracles simply because they violate fixed laws of nature: "every age is revealing new laws of nature." Until all laws of nature have been discovered, no one can pronounce an alleged miracle impossible. The problem, said Osgood, is that men have taken the wrong definition of the word "miracle." Miracles might well be violations of "natural" law if we use the word "natural" in a narrow sense. But "nature" contains an additional, spiritual realm, about which men know very little. Those things that seem to go beyond natural laws might easily be in perfect conformity with the laws of the spiritual universe.[17]

William G. Elliot, one of the editors of the *Messenger*, agreed. Like Osgood, he wanted to maintain the historicity of the miracles but explain them a way other than as "violations" of the laws of nature. In his short essay "On Miracles, etc," Elliot argued that miracles, just as any other events, are the result of uniform causes; however, they are causes beyond ordinary sense perception.[18]

Unitarian conservatives were slow to arm themselves against this new interpretation, but when they did they had a great deal to say. Martin Luther Hurlbut, a Williams-educated Unitarian clergyman from Southampton, South Carolina, pointedly attacked Furness and the position he represented. Hurlbut insisted that Christianity consists "essentially, in its facts" and that too many liberals had attempted "to get rid of the question of miraculous agency." Men such as Furness, Elliot, and Clarke have spent too much time "philosophizing away the pecularities of the Gospel, and reducing it to a level with mere naturalism." For Hurlbut there could be no middle position on miracles. The miracles of Christ were either clear occasions when the arm of God ripped through the blanket of natural law or else there were no miracles at all: "if they are to be regarded as mere wonderful events,' wonderful because not understood, we can perceive no adequate reason for their having been wrought, no reason worthy of the wisdom of God or the respect of man." Hurlbut's point was clear. The "impossibility" of miracles makes them miraculous and gives them strong apologetic value. By Furness's definition, miracles are no more convincing than the tricks in a magician's bag: "we can conceive of nothing besides the display of power *strictly* miraculous, which would justify any human being in claiming the religious faith and homage of mankind."[19]

By the beginning of 1837 the argument over miracles had reached a stalemate. The publication of Emerson's *Nature* only publicized the deep and final schism in the Unitarian Church. Francis Bowen's attacks on the Transcendentalists in the *Christian Examiner* in 1837 revealed that the breach extended to such basics as a theory of knowledge, the nature of the human mind, and the being of man. German criticism and the integrity of the Bible had become American issues—if not because of Furness, certainly by the hand of Parker.[20]

It is difficult to imagine the speed with which the miracles controversy precipitated. What started out as a squabble over a few minor points ended only a year later as a rift so wide that it is difficult to believe that the Transcendentalists ever sprang from New England Unitarianism. The Norton-Ripley exchange over the "Latest Form of Infidelity" in 1839–40 was actually nothing more than a post-mortem.[21]

Christians have generally maintained that the universe is an orderly place. God would not create a disorganized world where events occur at random. To Calvin, Galileo, Newton, and Francis Bowen, "order" meant that the series of events that people observe are connected to one another in some sort of rational fashion. Events must be *caused*. "Order," "Natural Law," "Nature," "course of nature" were, in this respect, all synonyms. Miracles, however, violated the established order. They were effects with no apparent causes. The "course of nature" could not be seen in the parting of the Red Sea, the virgin birth, or the resurrection. Nineteenth-century evangelicals never seriously considered abandoning their belief in miracles. But many less orthodox Christians did question whether miracles were plausible in an ordered universe. More relevantly, they wondered how scientific explanation could be possible for one who allowed miracles into his system.

The orthodox had a ready answer. God, they said, created everything, not only the physical matter of which the earth is composed, but the order of nature as well. The Protestant paradigm of the universe contained three stages, with the physical world at the bottom, the "laws of nature" in the middle, and sovereign God at the top. The world is always beneath the law and must always conform to it. God, however, is above the law, and whenever he chooses he can manipulate things on earth as he pleases.

This paradigm solved many problems. It left the world working in an orderly fashion under "normal" conditions, always controlled by unchanging, predictible laws. At the same time it demonstrated that man could not work miracles. He is part of the physical world, the lowest stage, and is of his own power always restricted by natural law. Only God is above the law; miracles are for him alone. Thus within the paradigm confirmation of a miracle is clear and convincing evidence of the existence of God, something upon which orthodox apologetics relied heavily. It was the perfect Protestant world-view.

The most obvious question is: How do we know that God will not frequently and at random manipulate the world as it pleases Him, leaving people with lives full of special forces, divine powers, and unexplainable phenomena? He will not, replied Calvinists, because of his absolute constancy. He will not, replied more Arminian Christians, because of His great love. God could never be arbitrary. He voluntarily subjects himself to the law, even though He is not obliged to do so. The law runs the universe; God breaks in only to reveal Himself in unusual ways. He must have a special reason for every miracle, and to both Calvinists and Arminians, "reason" meant something that mortals could comprehend.

Debates over miracles generally became sophisticated philosophical endeavors like the ones described in this chapter. The debaters themselves were generally theologians and philosophers, for scientists could not always afford the time to become involved in such metaphysical struggles. But throughout the 1830s the metaphysical debate over supernatural activity was inching its way closer and closer to the natural sciences, especially geology and paleontology.

The debate between catastrophists and uniformitarians was not simply a debate between supernaturalists and antisupernaturalists. Cuvier actually conceived of catastrophist geology as a nonsupernatural alternative to the almost mythical geologic explanations of eighteenth-century theorists.[22] Sophisticated Cuvierians such as Louis Agassiz generally tried to steer away from supernatural explanation. In fact, Agassiz even made a half-hearted attempt to describe the "special creations" of his own theory as nonmiraculous, a fact Asa Gray thought marvelously inconsistent.[23]

However, many geologists who studied Cuvier saw in his theories an excellent mechanism for creating new syntheses of Genesis and the geological record. For example, William Buckland's *Vindiciae Geologicae: or, the Connexion of Geology with*

Religion Explained was designed in part to show that the facts of geology "are consistent with the accounts of the creation and deluge recorded in the Mosaic writings."[24] For America's Edward Hitchcock "Special Divine Interpositions in Nature" were not only an important part of geologic history, they were miracles as well. Hitchcock believed that the earth's past contained dozens of catastrophic deluges and sudden annihilations of entire species. But such events could be explained only as deviations "out of the ordinary course of nature." This kind of explanation, he told his readers, is "the essential idea in a miracle." Hitchcock's own synthesis of theology and geology was only one of several supernatural-catastrophic theories of the earth's birth and development.[25]

The question was simply how far science could be compromised. Catastrophist geologists wanted to be scientific, but at the same time they wanted to preserve a reverence for the Bible and for their own evangelical churches. Inevitably this path became a little too narrow for some scientists to walk. One anonymous but obviously orthodox reviewer of Bakewell's *Geology* found it a "palpable absurdity" that Benjamin Silliman, its editor, should "acknowledge the deluge to have been the result of a miracle, and in the same breath endeavour to account for it by the action of natural causes." The inconsistency was too glaring. "Why, in the name of common sense," he asked, "torture our brains in accounting by the known laws of nature, for an event which was confessedly the result of miraculous interposition, and of course, in direct opposition to the action of those laws?" The answer, like most answers to obvious questions, was simple—but it was too radical to be considered by many evangelicals. To give something a physical explanation was science; to give it a supernatural explanation was theology; but to attempt to do both at the same time was sheer nonsense. the "male-sana admixtio . . . which incurred the most thorough reprobation of Lord Bacon."[26]

Religious explanations would not do, nor would hybrid explanations. Inevitably Americans would have to face some kind of uniformitarian explanation. "If Buckland feared that without cataclysms there was no God," writes C. C. Gillispie, "Lyell was as fundamentally apprehensive lest, without uniformity, there be no science."[27] Epistemologically speaking, the latter

threat was much greater than the former. If we are able to observe physical processes, catalog our observations, and make
probability statements about the past or future, then science is
possible. On the other hand, if we cannot "project" natural
operations, then both natural history and scientific prediction
are impossible. Like Newton, uniformitarian geologist Sir
Charles Lyell knew that to say "I just pushed my apple from
the window and it fell' is no science. Science must say "Whenever I push my apple from the window it will fall," and such
statements simply cannot deal with any miraculous "interposition" that might occur.

Its implicit positivism prevented uniformitarianism's rapid
growth in America. Although uniformitarianism is not necessarily atheistic, the same point could be made about it that
would frequently be made about Darwinism: it is perfectly consistent with atheism. Uniformitarianism was unpopular not because it eliminated God from the picture, but because it forgot
to mention Him. That oversight went much further than the
mere substitution of thirty-three thousand years of sedimentation for the Right Arm of the Almighty. Just as uniformitarianism would not talk about supernatural causes, so it abhored
supernatural definitions. Agassiz's "definition" of *species* as "a
thought of the creator" was no more scientific to Charles Lyell
than a Norseman's definition of *thunder* as a "blow of Thor's
hammer." But Romantic Americans liked their science mixed
with a generous dose of religion. Ideal species, special creations,
universal deluges, and Towers of Babel would remain as part of
their theories for several more years.

The orthodox church had always regarded questions about
the creation of the world as completely within the scope of
theology. The simple fact that there were two "accounts"—the
scientific record and the biblical record—had always meant that
questions about the earth's origin and development were places
where parallel lines intersected. Uniformitarianism was saying
in effect that to speak about such intersections is nonsense:
theological language cannot be a part of meaningful scientific
dialogue. In terms of volume alone, this had the potential of
greatly reducing the number of legitimate theological questions.
Actually, the uniformitarian's quiet critique of theology went
much further than that: implicit in his world-view was the

idea that natural theology is impossible. When theological language is excised from scientific explanation, then scientific phenomena can no longer be used to make theological conclusions. This became much too obvious after the publication of *On the Origin of Species.*

Furthermore, uniformitarianism had the effect of weakening many of the statements about God that were not derived from natural theology. Biblical theologies devoted many pages to the doctrines of the "sovereignty of God" and God's "divine government." As positivism and uniformitarianism began to demand that every observable effect be explained by a natural cause, however, illustrations of God's government and watchfulness became much more difficult to maintain. In a world where natural causes prevailed and differential equations could be used to describe processes that had gone on for endless ages without being affected by any transcendental agent, the whole idea of a god watching over his creatures started to loose any referential meaning.

6

"Hewn and Measured Stones"

Americans of both the Enlightenment and Romantic eras were obsessed by the need for order. Even those who called themselves "empiricists" believed that the miscellaneous data the mind receives form part of a well-structured whole. This insistence on orderliness obliged philosophers to create elaborate world-views, designed to explain how all the parts of the universe fit together.

Intellectuals at the time of the American Revolution generally saw the universe as a well-oiled, stable, and unchanging clock ticking through eternity. This clock contained millions of moving parts, whirling about in accordance with preestablished laws and altogether in a beautifully harmonious unity. However, all the motion was circular. Parts did not change position with respect to one another; the machine did not change in its shape or operation. If some transcendental observer should peek into the worksroom at regular intervals he would always see the same thing: a great mechanism with all systems in order and no squeaky axles or worn-out parts.

Although this picture of the world was perfectly consistent with Jeffersonian deism, it could be made quite compatible with orthodox Protestantism as well. For deists the worksroom was unmanned; for the orthodox it had a staff of One.

Even before the beginning of the nineteenth century, however, other ideas were starting to compete with this mechanistic world-view. Nobody had any doubts about a world without squeaky axles and wearing parts; everyone agreed that the universe would not simply wear out or fall apart. It was the simple circular motion that became a subject of controversy. That unchanging mechanism, whirling constantly but always occupying the same position, lost its novelty after one had looked at it long enough. Something that changed once in a while—that had the capacity for growth and development— would be much more fascinating.

The seventeenth and early eighteenth centuries had been fascinated by mechanics and by intricate gadgets; their science was physics. The later eighteenth century was also fascinated by gadgets, but it became increasingly interested in more earthy sciences as well, first geology, then biology. That period cherished order, but it was as organic as it was mechanistic. It was as easy to imagine a well-ordered universe as an organism as it was to see it as a whirring gadget. Organisms also contained many moving parts, and the operation of those parts was every bit as orderly and harmonious as were the movements of the components of a great clock. But the organism had one capacity the machine did not have: it could change. It could be born an infant and become a juvenile and then an adult. Its extremities could develop at various rates. More importantly, however, an organism could have two parts: a mind and a body. It could have a consciousness, even a self-consciousness. It could reflect on itself. It could respond to situations. It was sufficiently complex to satisfy any philosopher's demand for profound and sublime subject matter.

Throughout the early nineteenth century this organic world-view competed with the mechanistic view for the position of basic scientific paradigm. By the 1820s and 1830s it was increasing rapidly in popularity. Eventually it won out and replaced mechanism until it was itself superseded by the naturalism of the 1870s. Throughout the first half of the century, however, there was a giant struggle between mechanism and organism. Philosophers were forced to opt for one or the other or else come up with some rational compromise.

For the orthodox, however, organism contained even more liabilities than mechanism. While mechanism opened the way to deism, organism seemed eager to become pantheism, especially for those who carried the organic analogy so far as to assign their universe a self-consciousness. In addition, the idea of organic cosmic development at least *implied* uncertainty, or an open-ended universe; and uncertainty seemed very inconsistent with the idea of a sovereign, predestining God. Finally, the idea that the universe *has* a mind led much too easily to the idea that the universe *is* a mind. The organic view of nature became idealism so often that evangelicals frequently equated the two, and of course they could look at German Protestants like Kant, Fichte, Schelling, and Hegel as examples of such a subtle transformation. Idealism—at least the absolute idealism of these Romantic philosophers—was not merely consistent with pantheism; it was pantheism. That was a line no orthodox Protestant would cross.

This organic transformation was a symptom of the gradual secularization of the dominant world-view. Cosmic explanation before the Newtonian revolution had been loaded with theological terms. It was quite proper for Edwards to talk about God as the "cause" of natural phenomena, especially of particular, unusual phenomena such as the Noachian flood, the redemption, or the second coming. Deism was conceived by its founders as an attempt to naturalize this kind of theological explanation. The well-oiled mechanical universe of the deists internalized cause-effect relationships; geologic change and theories of motion could be explained as part of the Order of Nature, without reference to the hand of the divine. At the same time, however, God was always somewhere in the picture. The universe, like the universe of John Calvin, still consisted of two very distinct parts, one natural and one divine.

The organic view of nature took the secularization process a step further. Like the deist, the Romantic could assign natural causes to natural events, but he could provide "natural" answers to metaphysical questions as well. His pantheism meant that he could look for the answers to questions about First Cause, cosmology, or purposiveness *within* nature. Deism had internalized the explanation of natural phenomena by ceasing to use "God" as the subject of scientific statements. Romanticism internalized philosophical explanation through a parallel process. The pantheistic Romantic did not merely move Christianity's God who transcends all nature into the natural order. He eliminated that particular God from all consideration. When the Romantic talked about "god" he was talking about something entirely different, something that was not the First Cause of nature but was identical with Nature, whose personality and identity were equivalent with the motion and change of the universe. That god had very little in common with the God of Christian orthodoxy.

On a September day in 1831, on the small campus of Rhode Island's Brown University, a young man named Francis Wayland stood before some of his colleagues and students to read an important lecture. He began with an apology for what he feared would be the excessive abstraction of his address, a discourse on the "Philosophy of Analogy." His theme was obvious from the beginning. He was a Lockean and he was interested in the problems of gaining scientific knowledge. Man, he said, "commences his existence entirely destitute of knowledge." However, he is "so constituted, that knowledge must inevitably result from the elements of which his intellectual character is composed, and the circumstances under which those elements are placed."[1] Most of his audience had heard that dozens of times before, but they did not begin to doze yet. Better things were promised. "The first step in the progress of knowledge is the observation of facts," Wayland continued; "that is, that *certain things exist,* and that certain changes are taking place in them." Furthermore, "these changes, or, as they are technically called, phenomena, do not take place at random, but in the order of a succession, at first, dimly, but, by close inspection, more clearly, seen." The knowledge of these successions "forms the first conception of a law of nature."

In 1831 Francis Wayland was thirty-five years old and already for four years had been president of Brown University, a center for American Baptist intellectuals. Educated at Union and Andover, once a student of Moses Stuart, Wayland was steeped in Locke, Scottish Realism, and American Protestant orthodoxy. All of these things became the inputs of a book he was beginning to write: *The Elements of Moral Science.*[2]

But on this day Francis Wayland was interested in neither ethics nor theology. He wanted to talk about science. All the events that we observe, said Wayland, are connected to one another by "laws of succession," such as the laws of motion. "By knowing the laws which govern any particular class of objects, we preclude the necessity of innumerable experiments and are enabled to predict, under given circumstances, what . . . will be the certain result."

But, continued Wayland, "laws of succession" themselves exist in relationships with one another. These relationships are laws *"more general"* than the laws of nature that they contain. For example, "the laws by which the attraction of magnetism, and that of electricity operate, have also [in addition to the law of gravity] been discovered, and these laws are found to coincide, and hence we derive a *general law* of attraction, applying to gravity, magnetism, electricity, and probably to all kinds of attraction throughout the universe." Furthermore, "these *general laws* may be subject to others yet more general." So Wayland began building a pyramid of blocks as perfectly formed as those of any Pharaoh's stonecutter. A "general law" could explain and predict everything below it. But that general law was itself a part of an even more general law. At the top, of course, was a single law explaining every phenomenon in the universe. All things in nature point to this single, universal law.

For the time being Wayland was not interested in the point of the pyramid. That was for the theologians. He was more fascinated by the blocks of which it was constructed. "The work of an intelligent and moral being must bear, in all its lineaments, the traces of the character of its Author." That is, diverse aspects of nature are similar in one respect: all of them contain evidence indicating that they were created by one designer. "Suppose," Wayland continued, that "I should present before you one of the paintings of Raphael, and, covering by far the greater part of it with a screen, ask you to proceed with the work and designate where the next lines should be drawn." Only trained experts, reasoned Wayland, would even bother to try, but *it could be done*; and the person to do it would be one "who is most thoroughly acquainted with the character of the Author," who has "observed, with the greatest accuracy, the manner in which that character is displayed, in that portion of the system which he has condescended to reveal to us." That man who knows most thoroughly the workings of the artist's mind will be able to draw in the unknown lines.

Wayland's lecture was a call for gifted men, learned in science and philosophy, to develop a "philosophy of analogy"—to fill in the missing lines precisely as the careful student of Raphael could do. This new method would occupy an equal position with deduction and induction. It would begin with the specific facts of the physical world and end with a complete and perfect cosmology, a single "general law" that could be applied to every event in the universe. "Just in proportion as the science of analogy is perfected, will the useless intellectual labor of the human race be diminished."[3]

Natural theologians had been using the method of analogy for centuries. Since the time of Plato philosophers had speculated that the best way to gain knowledge about God's activities was to compare them with "similar" activities the philosophers themselves could observe.[4] But Wayland was suggesting an analogical method for science, not for theology. He was hoping that clever philosophers could discover analogies between the facts of one science and the facts of another. In this way scientists could develop a mechanism for organizing and mapping all the facts of nature.

There was real urgency in Wayland's call for a great philosopher who could devise a new analogical method. In 1830 science was being deluged with a hailstorm of miscellaneous facts. Geologists, botanists and zoologists, anatomists, and chemists were straining the Baconian method by filling innumerable notebooks with unclassified and unstructured data. In many cases the result of all this data gathering was a disaster for the early-century Realists who were its chief advocates. Rather than revealing a perfectly systematic universe filled with natural classes, levels, groups, and sets, the large number of facts was making data organization impossible, at least under the existing systems.

The result was not the end of rational world-views. On the contrary, the belief in a structured universe was so deeply ingrained in nineteenth-century thinking that philosophers and scientists looked all the harder for natural systems. The fact that existing systems were being threatened was the cause of the great preoccupation with system building, which characterizes the nineteenth century. The chief issues in mineralogy, botany, chemistry, and zoology revolved around the acceptability and development of new classification systems. The great names of American science—Dana, Torrey, Silliman, Gray, Agassiz—were deeply concerned with proper system building and data sorting.[5]

Many of these men were like the system builders of the eighteenth century in one respect: they had a firm commitment to, almost a reverence for, mathematics as the key to the underlying structure of the universe. Only with the help of mathematics could a philosopher create elaborate world-pictures or establish coherent relationships between natural phenomena. Until the time of Descartes, Leibniz, and Newton, mathematics had been developed primarily as a tool of astronomers and navigators. Later the development of analytic geometry and the calculus created for mathematics an important new role in the description of motion. Then it became an increasingly important tool of the physical scientist. By the beginning of the nineteenth century, mathematics had become sufficiently sophisticated that the time seemed ripe for more integrated views of the universe. Between 1800 and 1805 the Marquis De Laplace produced his massive five-volume *Traité dé Mécanique Céleste* as an attempt to integrate all motion, from the tiny atoms to the largest star. An impressive set of books, filled with complex equations describing the laws of nature, the *Celestial Mechanics* convinced many people that mathematics could in fact provide a unified explanation for everything that happens. Laplace's American translater brought these new revelations to an excited English-speaking audience.

Nathaniel Bowditch of Boston was primarily a navigator, secondly an astronomer. Born in Salem in 1773, Bowditch learned mathematics as a young man and devoted his life to developing its practical use. His *Practical Navigator* was generally considered the best guide any skipper could carry with him on the seas.[6] But Bowditch was fascinated by bigger questions, particularly fascinated by the *Mécanique Céleste*. In 1815 he resolved to update, translate, and publish it together with his own commentary. Those books came out between 1829 and 1839. With them Bowditch established a reputation for himself as one of the dozen or so living men who knew the mathematical keys to the universe—a man for whom the motions of the waters of the seas and the layers of air were part of the same universal system regulating planetary movement and the arcs of falling objects.[7]

Bowditch himself was not a metaphysician—not nearly so much as Laplace had been. But metaphysics was implicit on every page of his edition of the *Celestial Mechanics*. Benjamin Peirce, Harvard mathematician, believed there was nothing mathematics could not explain. "When we consider, that mathematics treats of all forms and motions," he wrote in an 1839 review of Bowditch's translation, "when we find the sweetest tones and the brightest colors, the lightning and the rainbow, heat and cold, and the very winds and waves subject to the strictest laws of motion . . ., we must concede that the ocean upon which the mathematician has launched his ship, is as unbounded as the material universe."[8]

To Peirce the entire system of Laplace was a vast teleological argument—clear proof of a thoughtful, purposive creation by a wise and moral God. For example, Laplace had proved that the universe is gradually running down. "The constant resistance of the ether or the light which pervades all space, small though it be, must at length destroy the motions of the planets, and cause them to fall into the sun," Peirce deduced from Laplace's work. But the disconcerting idea that the universe would someday die did not lead Peirce away from his faith in divine providence. On the contrary, "that there is such a sure principle of destruction in our world, affords an irresistible proof, that the system cannot have existed in its present form beyond a certain time; but it must have had a beginning, a creation, and a Creator." The grand view of Laplace "bears upon its front the stamp of truth and of divinity."[9]

Peirce's review of Laplace was only the beginning of a long career of explaining the mathematics of the universe. Borrowing heavily from German *Naturphilosophie*, Peirce became an

American pioneer in phyllotaxy, the study of the arrangements of leaves and nodes on the stems of plants. In a paper he gave before the 1849 meeting of the American Association for the Advancement of Science, Peirce revealed his discovery that the ratios of the successive distances between nodes on some stems "are approximate expressions of the relative times of rotation of the successive planets of the solar system." To Peirce this was convincing evidence that "the object of geometry in all its measuring and computing, is to ascertain with exactness the plan of the great Geometer, to penetrate the veil of material forms, and to disclose the thoughts which lie beneath them."[10] By 1849, however, Peirce had become sufficiently idealistic and his scientific listeners sufficiently sceptical that some, particularly his colleague Asa Gray, took issue with his ideas.[11]

But Peirce's presentation did impress the laymen and some of the more idealistic scientists. Agassiz's protegé and future Harvard president Thomas Hill was fascinated by Peirce's discoveries. "The study of abstract law" leads us "to a perception of the great thoughts of God," wrote Hill in a review of the AAAS meeting. Hill found Peirce's arguments "so forcible" that they required lengthy analysis, a task he was more than eager to perform, announcing that "there is hidden in the surd itself (the square root of five) some infinite and inexpressible beauty, of which we shall learn more and more, as we become more and more conversant with the thoughts of the Creator."[12]

Beyond Peirce and Hill this kind of mathematical metaphysics was carried on *ad nauseam* and *ad absurdam*. Even hard-core Realist journals like Andover's *Bibliotheca Sacra* published such articles as "On the Idea of an Infinite Series, as Applicable to Natural Theology." Here Boston journalist and Congregational clergyman Joseph Tracy speculated about nature and God, wondering if it was not sacrilegious to speak of a room "four yards square and four yards high" as "containing sixty-four cubic yards of God." Actually, Tracy's thesis was that the existence of infinite series of repeating decimals (such as $15/111 = .135135135135 \ldots$) provides an analogical foundation for understanding the workings of God's mind. Orthodox theology insists that God is both eternal and unchanging, but it is impossible for men to imagine an eternal succession of unchanging thoughts—unless they look at the clear example of the infinitely repeating decimal! Tracy was no mathematician; he did not even know that the square root of two is an irrational number. But that did not prevent him from using mathematics for the most elevated of all activities. For mathematics as mathematics one had to be an expert; for mathematics as natural theology any beginner's knowledge would do.[13]

But mathematics was not the only cosmic glue. Already in 1834 an American reviewer of London geographer Mary Somerville's *On the Connexion of the Physical Sciences* praised its talented author for showing that the "progress of science" is distinguished "for a tendency to simplify the laws of nature, and so unite the detached branches by general principles.[14] But Somerville found analogies in nature that the mathematics of the day could not hope to explain, such as animals capable of producing the same electricity as that which comes from the Leyden Jar. The notion that one needs more than mere numbers to explain how everything fits together led Americans to seek a "law of unity" as a universal cosmic principle.

Perhaps no one was more aware of the omnipresence of a law of unity or more eager to satisfy Francis Wayland's request for a brilliant scientific theorist than Harvard natural historian Thaddeus William Harris. Men must cease regarding the universe as an "accidental combination of isolated thoughts of God" and view it instead as *"one thought of God*, an organic whole,"* wrote Harris. The "Law of Unity" demands that men learn "that all the observations of all the naturalists in all ages seem only to have elucidated this truth, that *creation is one*; different phenomena, different combinations, different planes, but the same identical law." Scientists must realize that "every thing in its place has a certain analogy to every thing else in its place." The "work of science is to trace this clew through all modifications."

But the extent to which Harris used the analogical method in order to map out the Law of Unity approached absurdity. The Law of Unity explains the wonderful similarities between the blood of man and the sap of trees; in addition, "the same law bids both stand erect; the same law distributes among both the mysterious relations of sex. Each breathes the same atmosphere. . . . We might continue the analogies. What are arms and legs but branches and liberated roots? muscles and tendons bind both; the skin renews itself as the bark does; and in a cross section of a bone no one can fail to notice the woody structure. . . . These coincidences are not accidental nor partial; if followed up, they lead us into one rigid, universal law of unity in variety."

"Look at the skeleton of a leaf," he continued, "and you see a miniature tree; nay, according to a recent theorist, a miniature of the generic tree to which the leaf belongs."[15] That hypothesis came, not from Harris, but from Goethe, the great German poet and scientist. It was no accident that Harris should look to Germany for an idea. For some years already, especially since the arrival of Agassiz in the United States, the influence of post-Kantian German Romanticism had been developing rapidly in American scientific thinking.

Naturphilosophie could not have developed without Immanuel Kant. The *Critique of Pure Reason* had left the world divided into two parts: a phenomenon, which contains all the things that man can see and know; and a noumenon, something "beyond" the phenomenon. Kant frequently called things that exist beyond our perception "things-in-themselves" and tried to show that men could have no scientific knowledge of them. But Kant had some problems at this point. According to some of his followers, the claim that men can know nothing about the "thing-in-itself" is itself a knowledge statement about such things.

Johann Gottlieb Fichte, a protege of Kant who did most of his writing at the beginning of the nineteenth century, was convinced that Kant had given an inadequate explanation of the thing-in-itself. On the one hand Kant had shown that men can make no knowledge claims about the thing-in-itself, can never even assert its existence or nonexistence; on the other hand, Kant wanted to retain the concept of the thing-in-itself as a defining or limiting notion—as a mechanism for describing the boundaries of human knowledge (as, for example, in the statement, "man can know everything *about* an object but he cannot know the object itself."). To Fichte, this claim was fatally inconsistent: one could not retain the *concept* of an object in his system while claiming that there can be no knowledge about that object. To Fichte there was only one proper solution: the entire idea of the thing-in-itself had to be eliminated.

Getting rid of the thing-in-itself was more easily said than done, but Fichte, Schelling, Goethe, Hegel, and a host of other German philosophers of the early nineteenth century attempted it anyway. To all these representatives of German idealism, doing away with the thing-in-itself meant doing away with one thing: the idea of the *object*. Beginning with Aristotle's description of the process by which men obtain knowledge, philosophers had seen the world as containing an absolute dualism: perceiving subjects on one side, perceived objects on the other. Kant's strictures on knowledge about the thing-in-itself were in fact an assertion that one cannot say anything about the "object." Properties can exist as ideas in a perceiver's mind, but objects themselves are always beyond his grasp. To Fichte and Schelling this meant that all of the knowable world is "subject." Since only a mind can be a subject (for only a mind can perform the act of perception), it follows that all the universe is mind. This could not mean, of course, that all of the universe is one's own perceiving mind. That position implied solipsism. No, Fichte asserted, the universe is a trans-individual mind—a universal containing all individual minds as subsets of itself. He called this the universal "ego" and asserted that all philosophical systems must begin with it. The universe is a great mind. Everything that happens in it is equivalent to the thinking of its thoughts.

Fichte's paradigm solved several philosophical problems. Most obviously, it eliminated the need for speculation about the nature of the thing-in-itself. However, it also explained away many of the unpleasant dualisms that had always plagued western philosophy. It was no longer necessary to divide the world into a knowable, empirical part and another unknowable, mysterious part. No longer was it necessary that one part of the world be thought of as nature and another part as "non-nature" or "supernature." Metaphysicians no longer had a "beyond" about which to speculate.

But all this did not make philosophy simple. On the contrary, German idealism substituted one kind of metaphysics for another, and in many ways the new metaphysics was far more complex than the old dualisms. Instead of a transcendent, unobservable God (an "object"), the new philosophy had to deal with a "cosmic self-consciousness." The idea of the thing-in-itself was certainly no more problematic than the concept of the world as pure subject. To understand metaphysics as the study of the "beyond" was no harder than to believe it was the "human mind's reflective awareness of its own spontaneous formative activity."[16]

Two of the most important words in the vocabulary of German idealism were "unity" and "order." Although British empiricism (including Scottish Realism) had a strong commitment to an orderly world, it nevertheless viewed the world as a collection of objects. "Design" was confined to similarities between separate objects, or else it referred to a structure that could be superimposed on those objects. The idealist notion of Kosmos as "universal subject," however, implied a much more intrinsic unity. The whole universe as infinite subject is of a single piece; change in one aspect is always coordinated with all other aspects. In this respect German idealism demanded that natural science have a specific nonempirical content. According to Newton, science can be used to *describe* phenomena but it cannot *explain* them. But in Schelling's opinion true science must do both of these things. Moreover, the explanations of natural forces cannot be "deduced" from the data alone; they must be constructed from the first principles of the idealist philosophy. Schelling would agree with Wayland that one should be able to begin with simple observations and from them deduce all the laws of the universe.

The aspect of natural science most directly affected by this world-view was taxonomy. The issue between German idealists and extreme Baconians was not the *data* of science but rather the "links" between the data. Both idealists and realists believed that science demanded an orderly arrangement of data. However, empiricists such as Asa Gray tried to view such arrangements as little more than conveniences. For them classification involved nothing more than the selection of a few obvious reference traits. To say that a large number of species shared a certain characteristic was to make absolutely no statement about any absolute unity in which they might have a place. In this respect, consistent empiricists were nominalists: "these things look alike, so I shall name them this."[17]

Idealists, on the other hand, saw connections between objects as part of the structure of the universal mind. The "connections" themselves are part of the discernible form of the universe, and it is the scientists' task to discover the "form" of the universe just as much as the "matter." However, as Schelling often pointed out, one needs to observe the phenomena most carefully and in great detail before his mind can generate correct thoughts about their underlying unity. It was precisely for this reason that so many idealistic scientists could be such careful "empiricists." Careful study of nature's objects served as a basis for the discovery of its forms, and knowledge of the forms became the basis for correct taxonomy.[18] Baron Georges Cuvier's classification of animals was based on this presupposition. Cuvier suggested in 1812 that the rather arbitrary Linnean classification be replaced by something more "natural." He divided the animal kingdom into four "archetypes"—mollusks, radiates, articulates, and vertebrates—each of which contained the most basic units of taxonomic identity. Each archetype, he said, was present since the beginning of the world and depended on "supernatural inspiration" for its existence. There was no genetic connection between them. Cuvier described Nature's "archetectonic modelling of her objects" only after extensive examination of individual fossils. This careful field work gave Cuvier his famous ability to reconstruct entire skeletons from a single fossilized bone-fragment. This was exactly the kind of creativity that Wayland was looking for—the ability of the careful student to fill in the unknown lines of that covered Raphael.[19]

Louis Agassiz, Cuvier's greatest student, introduced these ideas to Americans. His early scientific career had already made Agassiz a leader in the development of idealistic science. When he immigrated to the United States in the late forties he gave America its first chance to participate actively in the creation of a scientific model for natural history. One of Agassiz's first intellectual contributions as an American went to the *Christian Examiner* and was not about glaciers or fossil fish or any of the other subjects upon which he had built his European reputation. It was an essay on metaphysics. "Contemplations of God in the Kosmos" so thoroughly intertwined science with theology that it may as well have been written by one of the Unitarian ministers who were the most frequent contributors to the *Examiner*.

Believing that geology had proven conclusively "that all organized beings have been created at particular times, and have not, according to the theory of the atheist, an eternal, self-sustaining existence," Agassiz thought he could throw some light on the "relations between the Creator and his works."[20] He was particularly concerned with one popular scientific heresy: transmutationalism, the idea that each species of animal or plant had descended from some simpler, "lower" species. Agassiz believed the idea was preposterous. Each species, after all, is a "specific thought" of the creator. Each is the "product of direct creative acts, independent of each other." Obviously, said Agassiz, the living world shows far too much structure to be the result of any kind of "developmental" process. Rather, creation is "a drama, the plan of which was complete in the mind of its author before the first scene was written out."[21]

Like Cuvier before him, Agassiz had taken issue with one aspect of the prevailing *Naturphilosophie*: its cosmic evolutionism. Some idealist naturalists, such as Lorenz Oken, had in effect "mobilized" the great hierarchy of organisms, describing one as a "higher" development from another. Oken had hypothesized that, as part of the maturation process, higher animals pass through stages "corresponding to the permanent constitution of the lower classes." Thus, individual organisms represent "different degrees of development of a few primitive types." This evolutionary process, said Oken, even applied to man himself.[22]

Cuvier and Agassiz combated this evolutionary theory with their own carefully structured hypothesis: progressionism, the idea that all organisms were *immediate* creations of God, not the end-products of some developmental process. However, all creations were not simultaneous. During each new geologic epoch, God created a new set of species to replace a previous set that had died off or been destroyed. Each new creation consisted of organisms more sophisticated than those in the previous creation. Progressionism allowed Cuvier and Agassiz to do two things. First, they could explain the fact that as one moves upward through the geologic strata he finds increasingly complex organisms. Secondly, they could maintain their belief that each individual species is a direct creation of God himself, not a product of development.

The fullest development of Agassiz's idealistic science did not come until he produced his *Essay on Classification*, part of an extensive *Contributions to the Natural History of the United States*.[23] In his *Essay*, Agassiz tried to redefine the purpose of a classification system. He conceded that classification systems "have to this day been considered generally as the expression of man's understanding of natural objects, and not as [parts of] a system devised by the Supreme Intelligence and manifested in these objects." Contrary to this, Agassiz believed that the "relations and proportions which exist throughout the animal and vegetable world have an intellectual, and ideal connection in the mind of the Creator," which "matured in his thought, before it was manifested in tangible forms." Agassiz strained his creativity to show that classification must be based on ideal principles. For example, he argued that "useless" organs (such as "whale's teeth" or the breasts of male mammals) exist "not for the performance of a function, but with reference to a plan.[24] In order to demonstrate that organisms are representatives of ideal types, Agassiz cited some of the same evidence that Darwinian evolutionists would use only a few years later to support natural selection. For example, evolutionists regarded the blind eyes of *Amblyopsis Spelaeus*, the fish from Kentucky's Mammoth Cave, as evidence of degeneration through lack of use. Agassiz was convinced, however, that the blind eye was one of "a combination of structural characters as that fish has in common with all other fishes." The fact that the blindfish cannot see is irrelevant. What is important is that in its ideal structure the fish has an eye.

In this way Agassiz developed his own method of analogy. The archetypal taxonomy of Cuvier, he said, is "homological," that is, it is based on "relationships arising from identity of structure without reference to function." However, science also recognizes relations of "analogy," which are "based upon similarity of function, without reference to structure." This was a new distinction. Wayland would have used "analogy" to describe both, although he undoubtedly associated his own "analogy" most closely with Agassiz's "homology." For Agassiz, homology was a much stronger part of analogical method than analogy. Homology enabled the scientist to see that the same creative mind designed the wing of the bird and the foreleg of the horse. These two organs are structurally similar and the evidence of unity is convincing. On the other hand, the relationship between the wing of a bird and the wing of a fly is merely analogical. Although these two organs perform the same function, they have very different structures. For Agassiz the underlying, metaphysical unity of the world was essentially homological, related mainly to structure.[25]

Agassiz had been raised on the Continent and had studied with the great masters of German Transcendentalism. His reviewer for the *American Journal of Science*, however, was thoroughly American. Born and raised in rural New York, educated by Benjamin Silliman at Yale, a veteran of the great United States Exploration Expedition led by Commander Wilkes, James Dwight Dana represented the best of what was American in the science of the 1840s and 1850s.

Dana's admiration for Agassiz was effusive. Agassiz had "borne science to a higher level than it had before attained, and given a force and direction to thought which will insure rapid progress towards perfection.["26] Dana's only strong criticism of Agassiz's ideas about species was that Agassiz denied that the "laws of the sexes or hybridity" provide "an unfailing criterion of specific identity." Although Agassiz never said so explicitly, he was reluctant to use any easily observable criterion, such as the ability to propagate, to distinguish species. After all, the actual criteria for determining which individuals constitute a single species are *ideal*. Dana argued that although the primary criteria are ideal, mutual fertility is still a distinguishing feature.[27]

Dana's own very dogmatic "Thoughts on Species" had been read before the AAAS meeting in Montreal, August 1857. That paper, considered so important that it was published simultaneously by *Bibliotheca Sacra* and The *American Journal of Science*, showed even more than Agassiz's work how well science could be mixed with Romantic metaphysics. The purpose of science, suggested Dana, is to "harmonize" the thoughts of nature, and in pursuit of this there are two proper methods: first, "investigation of individual objects in nature"; and secondly, "reasoning from central principles to the circumferential." If the latter method was not clear to Dana's readers when he first mentioned it, it would be all too clear before he finished his essay.

Dana's definition of *species* was no more empirical than Agassiz's: "a *species* corresponds to *a specific amount or condition of concentered force, defined in the act or law of creation.*" Dana agreed with Agassiz that the true nature of species is not to be found in "the resulting groups" (the individuals themselves) but in "the idea or potential element which is at the basis of every individual or group." This idealistic notion became an essential premise of Dana's argument for the permanence of species—an argument in which he made extensive use of the analogical method.

Dana took his analogies from inorganic nature. "Do we . . .

find oxygen blending by indefinite shadings with hydrogen or with any other element?" he rhetorically asked his readers. Obviously not. It is never the case that the weight of oxygen in water is "usually 8, but at times 8 and a fraction. . . . Far from this, the number is as fixed as the universe."[28] This stability is true of all of nature; numbers "definite in value and defiant of all destroying powers" characterize nature "from its basement to its topstone." God has put this great "temple" together "of hewn and measured stones . . . ," so whatever is true for inorganic nature "is necessarily the law for all nature." Then Dana's analogy became broad and direct: "the units of the inorganic world, are the weighed [chemical] elements and the definite compounds or their molecules. The units of the organic are *species*."[29] The conclusion was obvious: "were these units capable of blending with one another indefinitely, they would no longer be units, and species could not be recognized."

Dana's method of analogy was built on his grand perception of the unity of science. It allowed the natural philosopher to use research in inorganic chemistry to make conclusions in botany and zoology. Dana was only doing what Wayland had suggested twenty-five years earlier. He was studying a small piece of that giant but unknown Raphael and trying to recreate the whole. In the principle of fixity he had discovered one of the "general laws" of the universe. As John Harris, a London theologian whose work was much more popular in America than in England, put it, "if the whole creation is to be, in some sense, an analogue of the Divine nature (and in no other way can it manifest God), then every separate portion of it must be similarly related to every other part, otherwise the *whole* will not resemble Him."[30] One should easily be able to apply knowledge taken from physics and astronomy to the question of species, and Dana attempted exactly that when he discussed variation within species. Individuals vary, he argued, because they exist in varying sets of relationships. "The planets have their orbits modified by other bodies in space through their changing relations to those bodies." Likewise, "a substance, as oxygen or iron, varies in temperature and state of expansion from the presence of a body of different temperature." Again, for Dana the conclusion was obvious: "a species in the organic kingdom is subject to variations, and upon the same principle." Just as the expanding and contracting iron is always iron, so the different variations of the common canine are all dogs.

Dana ended his paper with some attention to a much older scientific problem. He was aware that the chief opposition to his views on species and his faith in analogical reasoning would come from nominalists such as Asa Gray, who were arguing that science must be less concerned with metaphysics. Dana tried to compromise. "One system of philosophy," he said about the nominalists, "argues that [the] result of induction is nothing but a notion of the mind, and that species are but an imaginary product of logic." Dana found this incomprehensible. "Another system infers," however, "that species are realities, and the general or type idea has, in some sense a *real* existence." Although Dana obviously found this view attractive, he was troubled enough about the nonempirical nature of this claim to look for a mediating position. A third school, he concluded, "admits that species are essentially realities in nature, but claims that the general idea exists only as a result of logical induction." Here was the perfect harmony of empirical and transcendent that Romantic science was looking for. A scientist begins with nature, discovers evidence of unity and purpose, and creates a ruling principle; then he applies the principle back to nature itself. Science, as Dana saw it, bounced its facts off a metaphysical mirror before it formed its conclusions. In the process it multiplied a hundredfold the discoveries that the tiniest observation could yield.

The result of this method, argued Dana, would be ideas of the natural world as fixed and clear as the elements of mathematics. All the knowledge about any species should fit into a mathematical formula and supply the individuals of that species with a numerical definition. "Could we put in mathematical terms the precise law . . . which is the basis of the species iron . . . , this mathematical expression would stand as a representative of the species; and we might use it in calculations, precisely as we can use any mathematical term." One could do the same thing, argued Dana, with organic species and substitute the formula "as an expression for the species."[31]

The science of men like Agassiz and Dana was popular among laymen. The idea of science as endless sorting of data was not very intoxicating to the nonscientist. He wanted a science that could arrange and organize the multivarious aspects of the universe. Agassiz's metaphysics eventually saved his career. After 1859, when he began to lose his hold on the scientific community, he was still able to make a successful appeal to interested lay persons all over the country. The *fact* that he rejected Darwin did not explain his continuing popularity; Americans could hear any number of sermons from evangelical ministers who denied evolution. But Agassiz could excite them with clear, sophisticated, and ultimately quite reassuring explanations of the harmony of nature. The lyceum circuit enabled Agassiz to end his years with a faithful, if somewhat less literate, group of followers.[32]

Agassiz had been interested in the scientific education of the nonscientist long before 1859. His influence had been most instrumental in obtaining the works of Scottish popularizer Hugh Miller for American publishers. Miller, a preacher turned science writer, did little science himself; rather he read widely in the important books of geology and paleontology until he came to two conclusions: first, nature is orderly and shows clear evidence of an ideal structure; secondly, the evolutionary hypothesis is absurd. Miller found it quite easy to weave an argument that demonstrated both of these things at once. First he showed that according to the theories of the Lamarckian evolutionists one should find progressively refined forms as he goes up through successive geological layers. Thus Lamarckians made a great deal of the "fact" that the lower Silurian rocks contain no fossil fish, but only primitive crustacea and mollusca. However, Miller, quite correctly, found all kinds of fish there, most notably the noble *Asterolepis*. Not only was *Asterolepis* present among the earliest fossils, argued Miller, but it was one of the most highly developed of all fish. In fact, later fossils show a marked degeneration. That discovery led Miller to suggest that creation is not evolving at all but may in fact be degenerating. At the same time, however, his elaborate discussions of the structure of *Asterolepis* were an intricate teleological proof of divine direction in nature.[33]

However, the well-ordered, mathematically precise world of Miller, Agassiz, and Dana was soon to be replaced by the open-ended, imprecise, and chance-filled world of Charles Darwin. Darwin's command of the evidence was so thorough that after a long, agonizing struggle even Dana would become a convert, with such qualifications as were necessary for an orthodox theist, of course.[34] Dana's struggle underlines one of the most important statements about the scientific reception of evolution. It was not so much the facts themselves that gave all the trouble, but the entirely new way of looking at nature, which Darwin's method entailed. Wayland, Dana, and Darwin all believed that they were "empiricists." Darwin, however, gave that word an entirely new meaning. To him the "severest inductive method" of American Realism was no more empirical than the speculative philosophy of Fichte or Cuvier. For a Protestant American scientist, trained in natural theology and analogical method, Darwin's brand of empiricism was more futuristic than his most speculative imagination.

7

A Theory of the Earth

The first natural science to threaten American Protestantism was geology. Since the middle of the eighteenth century, Europeans had been writing earth histories that conflicted with the biblical account of the world's creation. The geological debate did not mature, however, until the nineteenth century.

The debate certainly had not matured sufficiently to be a threat to Presbyterian Divine Samuel Miller in 1803. Educated at the College of New Jersey during its intellectual heyday, caught up completely in the ideals of the Scottish Enlightenment, and as thorough a Common-Sense Realist as one could find anywhere, Miller was evangelicalism's best copy of the Renaissance man. He had decided to use the turn of the century as an excuse to share his perspectives on all human knowledge with the rest of the literate world. *A Brief Retrospect of the Eighteenth Century* was an American equivalent of the great French Encyclopedias. Wideranging, wordy, almost monomaniac in its glorification of Bacon, and stuffed with every conceivable evangelical prejudice, the *Brief Retrospect* became to two generations of Princeton students a quick-and-ready summary of everything they would need to know in order to pass their final exams.

No intellectual, including the evangelical variety, could hope to pass himself off as educated without a thorough knowledge of the sciences. Science was nature's display of God's greatness. "Every sober and well-directed inquiry into the natural history of man, and of the globe we inhabit," wrote Miller, confident that he had all the answers, "has been found to corroborate the . . . important events recorded in the sacred volume. . . . Never was there a period . . . in which so much light and evidence in favour of Revelation were drawn from the inquiries of philosophy."[1]

Miller believed that the entire history of geology supported him. To be sure, early speculators had produced a number of unbiblical theories about the formation of the globe. De Maillet's *Telliamed*, John Whitehurst's *An Inquiry into the Original State and Formation of the Earth*, and James Hutton's *Theory of the Earth* all had one thing in common: they compromised biblical revelation in order to arrive at satisfactory natural explanations of the earth's development.

But times had changed, and in 1803 Miller believed he had *true* geology entirely on his side. As the eighteenth century had progressed it had become obvious that the more threatening theories of the earth were not holding up. For example, many of the theorists, noted Miller, had speculated that there was not sufficient water in the world to allow for any *"possibility of a general Deluge."* However, "further progress in mathematical and physical knowledge has since shown, that the different seas and oceans contain at least *forty-eight* times more water than they were supposed to do, and much more than enough for the extent ascribed to the deluge in the sacred history."

Further, said Miller, the geologists of the middle eighteenth century had often suggested that the history of the earth required much more than the 6000 years granted by the Pentateuch. "Early in the century, and, indeed, until within a few years, several geological phenomena were considered, by superficial inquirers, as indicating that the creation of the globe we inhabit was an event much more remote than the sacred history represents it." But, assured Miller, this fallacy was the result of nothing more than the primitive state of the science at the time. "The investigations of the latest and most accurate philosophers have afforded proof little short of demonstration, that the earth, at least in its present form, cannot have existed longer than appears from the Mosaic account; the absolute falsehood of many positive assertions, and specious inferences, hostile to the scripture chronology, has been evinced."[2]

Miller had a unique perspective on the earth sciences. The beginning of the nineteenth century was in one sense a watershed in the development of geology. Before that time most theories of the earth were based more on speculation than on actual analysis of data.[3] However, the science was rapidly becoming empirical. Miller was in effect looking back on one hundred years of speculative geology (with notable exceptions, such as Hutton's *Theory of the Earth*) and looking forward to one hundred years of scientific growth. Like any good Scottish Realist he was convinced that the transition from rationalism to empiricism could do nothing but good for the cause of Christian orthodoxy. As soon as geologists gave up their hypotheses and began to look at the true facts of the universe, geology would become another of the many ways in which the truth of divine revelation would be displayed to the world.

Miller did his work too early to have any perspective on the great controversies developing in European geology. By 1803 Wernerian and Huttonian schools were already well formed, but Miller's preoccupation with the "Mosaic record" prevented him from looking for such irrelevant distinctions. The examples of antiscriptural, "speculative" geology that Miller cited were by pre-Wernerians, Wernerians, or by Hutton himself—all acknowledged indiscriminately.[4]

Miller's faith in geology as a way to God proved ultimately to be as ill-founded as any belief Protestant orthodoxy developed. But American evangelicals would not recognize the full implications of the new science for some time. In the second decade of the nineteenth century, when Werner's theories were widely publicized in America by Silliman and Amos Eaton, most evangelicals realized that the absolute literalness of scripture was going to have to be compromised. In general, however, Werner's theories and data showed a marvelous consistency with the Mosaic record; and they should have—most Wernerians had that in mind all along.[5] Not until true Huttonians and uniformitarians became prominent did evangelicals begin to worry that geology might not be as valuable for Christianity as Miller had prophesied.

Abraham Gottlob Werner, professor of mineralogy at the University of Freiberg, had fathered a marvelous harmony of geologic knowledge and the biblical record. At one time, postulated Werner, the whole of our present earth was under water. All of the matter comprising the earth's surface was suspended in this tremendous bath. Eventually the less soluble material precipitated and the earth began to form in five distinct stages. First the "primitive" rocks (granite, gneiss, porphyry); next, "transition" rocks (slate, shale). This second stage included the creation of the first fish. In the third epoch the waters began to evaporate and dry land appeared in a few small areas. Mammals were created in this period, and "secondary" rocks (limestone, sandstone, chalk, basalt) began to precipitate. Massive disturbances in the fourth epoch caused the deposition of alluvial rocks, clay, sand, and pebbles. Finally, after the proportion of dry land to water was much as it is today, the violent fifth stage began. Mighty volcanoes erupted, depositing lava and giving the earth its present rough, irregular contours.[6]

Obviously, evangelicals could find endless parallels between Werner's paradigm and the Genesis record. They could easily translate the Wernerian history into six days of creation, and even more easily account for the Noachian deluge. These possibilities gave evangelical colleges and scientists a strong motive for engaging in geological research and point out one of the most positive results of Scottish evangelicalism in America: its belief that geology could be an aid to natural theology inspired colleges to invest in the material and faculty to teach the earth sciences. Had geology appeared as an open threat to Christianity in 1815, as it did in the 1850s, places like Princeton, Amherst, and Yale would have been much slower to spend money in its pursuit.

America's first important geologist was a Scotsman. It was to William Maclure's advantage that he was wealthy and that he had been trained by Werner himself. When he immigrated to the United States in 1796 he had both the independence and the expertise to pursue his great task: the first complete geological map of the United States.[7]

Without sounding heterodox, Maclure managed to take his theories far beyond those of his teacher Werner. Although he adopted the Wernerian classification system, he tried to avoid the issues of cosmology that choice implied.[8] He was particularly noncommittal about the age of the earth, which was the biggest battle developing between scientists and evangelicals. "I am equally ignorant of the relative periods of time, in which those modifications and changes may have taken place," Maclure told his readers. "These speculations are beyond my range, and pass the limits of my inquiries." Geology must be thoroughly descriptive and avoid such broad, cosmological questions.[9]

Unfortunately, many Americans were asking precisely the questions that Maclure wanted to avoid. Although Vulcanism, the theory of James Hutton, the "fire-king," would not be widely known in America until 1820, Maclure no doubt realized that it presented a potential threat to biblical orthodoxy. Such matters were better left undiscussed.

James Hutton was also a Scotsman. Unlike Maclure, however, he had found Werner's theory to be so different from the facts that it was unfit as a geologic paradigm. Hutton's own *Theory of the Earth* (1785) presented a radically different, devastatingly unbiblical, picture of the earth's development. Hutton was determined to explain the history of the earth without reference to supernatural activity. He found no evidence of a universal flood, no sign of the watery origin described by Werner, and furthermore, he told his readers, "no vestige of a beginning,—no prospect of an end."[10] He tried to describe past events entirely on the basis of processes he could observe in operation. According to Hutton's theory the earth's crust contained two kinds of rock. Most of the underlying structure was of "igneous" origin— molten rock blown up from a superhot core and left on the surface to harden and settle. First came a long period of cooling. Then an epoch of weathering, flooding, and erosion left deposits of sedimentary, or aqueous, rock, topsoil, or sand. Hutton needed no supernatural activity to explain the present configuration of the earth's surface. He had sufficient evidence that the intense heat of the earth's core could produce immense pressures causing volcanic eruptions, earthquakes, and even local deluges. However, this whole process required many more than the 6,000 years the Mosaic record allowed.[11]

Hutton's threatening ideas did not become popular until the

1820s. Hutton's own literary style was so obscure that his *Theory* lay practically unread until it was popularized by John Playfair in 1802.[12] Even then, however, most geologists chose to reject Hutton's ideas as too radical and used instead the rather simple Wernerian classification system and the concomitant theories about geologic formation. Of the two most popular American geologists of the twenties, one, Amos Eaton, was a thoroughgoing Wernerian; the other, Benjamin Silliman, tried to create a synthesis of his own, but during his early career he was generally most sympathetic with Werner's views.

Amos Eaton was among the most colorful of a long list of colorful American scientists. Born in New York in 1776 and educated at Williams College, Eaton embarked on a promising career as a lawyer in 1800. However, in 1811 he was convicted of forgery on a trumped-up charge and sentenced to life in prison. Pardoned by Governor De Witt Clinton in 1815, Eaton decided to change his occupation. He went to Yale to study with Silliman, then a young professor of mineralogy and chemistry.[13]

Already by 1818 Eaton was ready to publish. In *Conjectures Respecting the Formation of the Earth* he speculated that at one time the earth was composed of water mixed with various solid materials to form a thick paste. Slowly the solid material in this "globular mass of mortar" began to precipitate toward the center, leaving the water on the surface. Like Werner, Eaton believed the strata were formed because different kinds of solid material precipitated at different rates. After "primitive rocks" had settled, elementary marine plants and animals were created, and later the fish. Only after precipitation was complete and small amounts of dry land began to appear were vertebrates and land plants created. Eaton believed that his scheme coordinated perfectly with the plan of creation outlined in Genesis, although he admitted that the "days" of creation were probably periods of thousands of years.[14]

Silliman thought his student had done an admirable job. He reviewed the *Conjectures* in the *American Journal of Science*, citing it as "creditable to the author's industry and discernment, and as bearing every mark of verisimilitude."[15]

Silliman himself was not so hasty with a theory of geologic development. Although he had more experience in geology than Eaton, he was not to make his own rather extensive conjectures until late in the twenties. Teaching geology, chemistry, and mineralogy at Yale was a time-consuming task, and Silliman exhausted most of his energies there. His most pressing problem was the lack of a satisfactory text, and he did not even have time to prepare one of those himself. Finally in 1829 he chose to bring out a modified American edition of Englishman Robert Bakewell's *Introduction to Geology*. To this Silliman appended his own views on geological development, the creation, and the deluge. This edition of Bakewell's *Geology*, published together with Silliman's own *Outline of the Course of Geological Lectures Given in Yale College*, became the standard geology text in America for many years.

Although Silliman held many Wernerian views, he selected the text of a convinced Huttonian. Robert Bakewell found Werner's world, with all the perfectly-formed strata surrounding the globe "in different layers like the coats of an onion," too simplistic to conform to the actual geological evidence. Werner's theory was simply "not confirmed by experience to the extent which these geologists contend for."[16] Bakewell found Werner especially unconvincing with respect to the origin of volcanoes. Werner's paradigm had forced him to suggest that even basaltic rocks were not of igneous origin but had precipitated from a water-base solution. "It is scarcely possible for the human mind to invent a system more repugnant to existing facts," wrote Bakewell. Obviously, "Mr. Werner, and most if not all of his disciples" had simply "never visited active volcanoes, and seem disposed to close their eyes upon their existence."[17]

In spite of his differences with Werner, Bakewell was forced by the state of the science at the time to adopt Werner's method of classifying rocks and minerals. However, he spent over one hundred pages of his *Geology* explaining why Werner's system was really unsuitable and trying to make satisfactory modifications. The result was something of a hodgepodge of Wernerian and Huttonian ideas, containing many unanswered questions and almost as many conjectures as Werner's original work. But it was probably the best text available in the 1820s. And it was vastly superior to most geology books in one respect: it did not attempt any conclusions about the relation between geology and Genesis.[18] Like Hutton, Bakewell attempted to do science without regard either to Genesis or to the demands of the orthodox Church. This made some of his more religious readers unhappy, but it promised his *Geology* a much longer life than many of the transitory reconciliations of science and religion that were constantly going to press.

However, such a "secularized" text was not what Silliman wanted. He used it in its English edition for a few years but finally decided that its scope had to be broadened. In 1829 he came out with his own "enlarged" edition, complete with the appendix that tried to make geologic history consistent with the Mosaic accounts of the creation and the Noachian flood.[19]

But Silliman did much more in his appended *Outline* than merely discuss the compatibility of Genesis and geology. He took geology back twenty-five years by opting for Wernerian positions where Bakewell had rejected them. "If Werner attributed too much to [aqueous] causes," wrote Silliman, then might others, like Bakewell, be in "danger, at this day, of vibrating to the opposite extreme?" Silliman admitted that Werner's views were in eclipse; but "without being his blind admirer, I may be permitted to ask, who has done more for geology, and who has done it better?"[20] Silliman himself, of course, was "neither Wernerian nor Huttonian, Neptunian nor Plutonist; but simply a student of facts."

It was nothing short of remarkable where "the facts" led him. "Geology declares," wrote Silliman confidently, "that the original, or at least early state of the surface of the planet, was that of a watery abyss; and the book of Genesis . . . reveals the same fact." Out of that aqueous solution precipitated, just as Werner had described, the "primitive rocks": granite, gneiss, and mica slate. These, said Silliman, are obviously the oldest of the earth's rocks. Because their precipitation corresponds to the first creation day, they do not contain any fossils. The second step in the creation process was the appearance of dry land. Eventually enough material settled so that high peaks began to protrude from the water. Then "it became possible, that vegetables should begin to exist, because they had now a place and soil on which to grow." So far, geology and Genesis were in perfect harmony.

By 1829 geologists had generally agreed that the crystalline structure of the "primitive rocks" could not have resulted from the precipitation process that Werner and now Silliman described. Silliman's own difficulties were exacerbated because he was unable to explain the reason for the differences between primitive rocks and the higher "transition rocks" that marked his next geologic epoch. He was forced to suggest that "primitive" granite and "transition" limestone were formed by identical processes—a suggestion absurd enough to make one suspect that Silliman had not spent any more time looking at rocks than Werner had studying volcanoes.[21]

In Silliman's paradigm the transitional rocks contain the fossil remnants of the first "organized beings" and mark the beginning of a second geological epoch. During this period the earth was in a transition from watery abyss to a balanced surface of land and sea. This epoch contained the third and fourth creation days. "The creation of the vegetable and animal races appears to have gone on progressively with the deposition of the mineral strata and masses. . . . The only point that admits of discussion is, as to the amount of time employed."[22]

Through this process Silliman was developing an explanation for Genesis 1 that was to become very common among defenders of biblical orthodoxy. The "long day" theory, so popular during the nineteenth century, suggested that the Genesis account is literal scientific history in every respect except as to the length of the creative days. This position eventually satisfied many of the more flexible evangelicals, because philologists could easily find Old Testament uses of the Hebrew word for day ("*yom*") that did not imply twenty-four hour periods. Silliman no doubt had more to do than any other American with the popularization of this view. In 1829 he appeared quite satisfied that this combination of Wernerian geology and directed biblical scholarship could do the job.[23]

With the description of the transition rocks, Silliman finished laying the groundwork for his analysis of geology in terms of Genesis 1. Having established that the fossil record extends from the transitional rocks up through the secondary, sedimentary rocks, Silliman had only to find evidence of a universal deluge. He found evidence so clear that he divided the tertiary in terms of Noah's flood. "The *diluvial*," or lower tertiary, "embraces what is conceived to belong to the deluge"; the upper tertiary or "*alluvial* is now restricted to the deposits, chiefly mechanical, arising from agencies still in operation, and which have been always active, such as the weather, floods, rain, frost, electricity, &c, &c."[24]

Although Silliman believed that "the immediate cause of the deluge was the will of the deity," he nevertheless thought it important that the flood be explained by natural causes. He hypothesized that "in a sphere of eight thousand miles in diameter, it would appear in no way extraordinary that many cavities exist, which collectively, or even singly, may well contain much more than all our oceans, seas, and other superficial waters." In order to cover the "highest mountains," as Genesis suggests, "no more water would be required than is sufficient to occupy a cavity whose cubical contents are equal to about 1/265 part of the globe." Alexander von Humboldt had already discovered that volcanoes are able to spurt lava at elevations as high as 18,000 feet. Since the specific gravity of lava is about three, such a force would be sufficient to push water out to a depth of fifty-four thousand feet. "This would cover the Himmaleh mountains," with enough left over to account "for the depth, from the surface of the earth, of the cavity where the power might be exerted."

Silliman's matter-of-fact explanation made it all sound disarmingly plausible. So plausible that Silliman suggested that "we need not the history [the Bible] in order to prove the occurrence of an universal deluge. This is sufficiently proved, by the vestiges left upon the globe." Of course, the whole idea was plausible only if related to a thoroughly Wernerian paradigm for geologic history. Even then it would be difficult to explain why such massive pockets of water should exist under the earth's surface.[25]

In the same months that Silliman was preparing his first edition of Bakewell, Charles Lyell was penning his massive *Principles of Geology*, which convincingly argued that no large-scale deluge had ever played a significant part in the earth's geologic development. By the time Silliman brought out the second American edition of Bakewell in 1833, both he and Bakewell had had a chance to study the first volume of Lyell's *Geology*.[26] But Silliman's views remained unchanged. He omitted his *Outline* but substituted a long essay on the "Consistency of Geology with Sacred History," complete with a chart illustrating the "Coincidences between the Order of Events as Described in Genesis, and that unfolded by Geological Investigation." Silliman's analysis led him to conclude once again that "geology contradicts nothing contained in the scripture account of the creation; on the contrary, it confirms the order of time and requires only that the time should be sufficiently extended to render it physically possible—without calling in the aid of miracles in a case where natural successions are sufficient to account for the facts."[27]

In 1833 only a trained, up-to-date geologist could find the holes in Silliman's theories. The fact that the years 1829–34 correspond roughly to the peak of Silliman's professional popularity and influence indicates that not many such men could be found in the United States.[28] Silliman's work was forming young scientific minds whose chief education had been in the classics, philosophy, history, and the interpretation of the Bible. Silliman's ideas were as beautiful to his students as they were repulsive to more uniformitarian geologists. The publication of his edition of Bakewell precipitated a small crisis in American scientific education. Throughout the 1830s, the Silliman text was virtually the only one available for use in American classrooms. Regardless of Bakewell's competence, no one could study geology without exposure to Silliman's religious ideas. In orthodox, clergy-controlled New England colleges, that may have been fine; but in the liberal enclaves of the South it was unconscionable.[29]

No one felt more abused by Silliman's monopoly of the publishing market than Thomas Cooper of South Carolina. Once a protegé of Thomas Jefferson and nearly appointed to a faculty position at the University of Virginia, more often between jobs than in them, Judge Cooper was an absolutely sincere materialist and liberal—thoroughly committed to his cause and willing to suffer any amount of abuse for the sake of the truth. In spite of these disadvantages, however, Cooper was way ahead of Silliman in at least one respect: he kept up with his geology.

In the early 1830s Cooper, at that time President of South Carolina College, was facing one of his life's many crises. He had been selected for his office in 1829, and already in 1831 the Trustees had to deal with a broadly-supported resolution demanding his removal. Cooper was charged by the constituency with infidelity, anticlerical activities, and with teaching the falsity of the Pentateuch. During the course of his bid to keep his office, Cooper wrote a number of pamphlets defending his views. One of these was a full-scale attack on Silliman's edition of Bakewell's *Geology.*

"The addition of your Syllabus to Bakewell's Geology, has given rise to this essay," wrote Cooper in the preface to *The Connection Between Geology and the Pentateuch: in a Letter to Professor Silliman.* "When *you* came out in full theological garb, an orthodox Wernerian, I was compelled to obviate the difficulties which you had offered to the consideration of my class, and take up the gauntlet which you had thrown on my table. My theories and my geological reputation were in jeopardy with my young men."[30]

Unfortunately Cooper was beseiged from all sides, much more for his materialism and ideas about revelation than for his views on geology. As a result he did not attempt to focus on the geological issues, where he stood at least a chance of being convincing. Instead he turned his letter to Silliman into an attack on the integrity of the Pentateuch—an attack that no doubt further alienated Cooper from his orthodox constituency.

He *had* common ground with Silliman. Back in the mid-twenties, when the only public university lectures on geology in the United States were his and Silliman's, both geologists had selected Bakewell's *Introduction to Geology* as the best text available. Cooper admitted that Silliman had done the American scientific community a favor by publishing an American edition. But why had he encumbered it with "a full syllabus of his own lectures on Geology, founded on the Mosaic account of the formation of the earth and of the Deluge, as being delivered under the authority of Divine inspiration?" This syllabus, continued Cooper, contained "positions which no well informed Geologist of Europe or this country would now sanction, and which no well informed Theologian, of the present day, would venture to support." There is "hardly a single Divine of reputation in Europe, who now believes that the book of Genesis . . . was written by Moses, or by any one else, under the influence of divine inspiration." Cooper felt that he had no choice: "as the geological doctrines I complain of, have been published by

Dr. S. as being based on the dictates of a divinely inspired writer, Moses, I must defend myself as well as I can, by shewing that the books called the Pentateuch, commencing with Genesis and ending with Deuteronomy, were not in fact written by Moses."[31]

Cooper's theological views, together with his complete lack of tact, virtually guaranteed that his work would alienate rather than educate his audience. Nevertheless, his *Essay* was as fine a piece of higher criticism as any American writer had produced. His argument was simple: the best way to destroy the credibility of the Mosaic cosmogony was to destroy the credibility of the entire Pentateuch. Cooper analyzed the language and anachronisms of the Pentateuch, concluding that it had to have been written at a period much later than that which tradition assigned it, and that its cosmogony was "unworthy of the countenance of any intelligent being." Cooper had nothing but contempt for Silliman's efforts to harmonize Genesis 1 and Wernerian geology: "all these strange assertions, which the geologists who live at a distance from New-Haven, will read with utter astonishment as doctrines advanced from a Professor's chair in the year 1829, are founded not on any geological or chemical fact . . . , but on the account in the first chapter of Genesis." As to Wernerian geology itself, "we know as a chemical fact, and the Professor ought to know it too, that the quantity of water contained in the surface of the globe is not capable of holding in solution one hundreth part of the mineral substances that compose the crust of the earth." Professor Silliman has thus "laid down as the very basis of his geological lectures, a supposed fact, not improbable, but impossible."[32]

Cooper was acquitted of the charges against him, but not because the trustees of South Carolina College agreed with his views. He held his presidency because he had once been an outstanding trial lawyer and was able to convince his jury that his personal beliefs were irrelevant to his capacities as president. His views would not be popular in America for at least twenty more years, and Cooper was a lonely prophet until his death in 1839. As geology slipped further and further beyond any possible harmonization with Genesis, Americans tried all the more valiantly to prove that the two accounts were quite reconcilable after all.[33] The work of another of Silliman's students, Edward Hitchcock, epitomized American attempts to harmonize geology and revelation in the second quarter of the century.

Hitchcock had studied Congregational orthodoxy and Silliman's science at Yale in the early twenties. Having graduated with a thorough knowledge of both natural theology and the earth sciences, Hitchcock promised to do as much as any American to unify geology and religion. In 1835, as professor of chemistry and natural history at Amherst, he began a series of articles on geology and Christianity in Andover's *Biblical Repository*. Here he hoped to show "that the student of natural theology will find the records of geology no unfruitful source of evidence as to the existence, perfections and plans of Jehovah." Hitchcock's early essays were rather extreme cases of analogical reasoning, but he did claim to find straightforward evidence "of direct and repeated acts of creative power" in the earth's geologic history. In spite of the fact that Hutton had found "no vestige of a beginning" in his geologic theory, Hitchcock managed to make Vulcanism an aide-de-camp of divine creationism. Huttonian geology, said Hitchcock, postulated that the earth had once been a superhot ball of molten rock and metal. Since we know that cooling must occur at a relatively steady rate, it follows that the earth could not have an eternal existence. That would imply that it had been "infinitely hot" at one time; or else that it had existed indefinitely without any heat loss. Both of these suggestions were clearly contrary to the laws of nature. "Hence we reasonably infer, that our planet had a beginning." Obviously, it could not create itself.[34]

Hitchcock was even more influenced by French paleontologist Georges Cuvier than he was by Hutton. In 1812 Cuvier had published his own ideas about the origin of the earth. Cuvier's work was translated into English and published in 1813 by Robert Jameson, one of Werner's most faithful disciples and Silliman's former teacher. Jameson's edition of Cuvier's *Essay on the Theory of the Earth* came to America when Samuel Latham Mitchill republished it in New York in 1818, together with his own *Observations on the Geology of North America*.[35]

Cuvier differed from Hutton in one dramatic respect: while Hutton attempted to trace the history of the earth strictly in terms of processes still in operation, Cuvier was certain that this was impossible.[36] In Cuvier's thinking, the relatively mild processes of erosion, drift, and climatic variation could not possibly account for the geological scars on the earth's surface. "The march of nature [has been] changed," he told his readers, "and none of the agents that she now employs were sufficient for the production of her ancient works." Cuvier believed that the chief instrument of geological change was the sudden, cataclysmic rushing of waters caused when pressure inside the earth forced bulges, quakes, and other violent changes of topography. Cuvier thought these inundations had occurred dozens of times in restricted regions; but they had occurred on a global scale at least twice. He suggested that at some point prior to the creation of man, subterranean disturbances had so violently disrupted the earth's crust that the seas completely evacuated their beds and flooded the continents. Essentially, water and land exchanged places. This first catastrophe destroyed all existing life and completed the formation of all the geologic strata below the alluvium. For this reason the fossils found in these strata were almost universally extinct. After this first worldwide catastrophe, God introduced new varieties of life—the same organisms, including man, as are living today. Then, said Cuvier, at some point not long ago, the great catastrophe occurred again, only this time in reverse. The seas again flowed into the dry land and their evacuated beds formed new continents: "if there is any circumstance thoroughly established in geology, it is, that the crust of our globe has been subjected to a great and sudden revolution, the epoch of which cannot be dated much farther back than five or six thousand years ago," he wrote. This most recent catastrophe "buried all the countries which were before inhabited by men" and "laid dry the bed of the ocean, which now forms all the countries at present inhabited." Fortunately, a "small number of individuals of men and other animals that escaped from the effects of the great revolution, have since propagated and spread over the lands newly laid dry."[37] Without specifically mentioning the Bible as part of his geologic theory, Cuvier made it implicitly clear that his geology could easily be harmonized with Genesis.[38] The six days of creation were quite clearly God's reconstruction of the earth in the wake of the first universal deluge. This creation took place *after* the geologic substructure of the earth's surface had been established. The second great catastrophe was none other than the Noachian flood. The sedimentation that had occurred since that time contained the fossils of species still in existence.

Like Cuvier, Hitchcock believed that catastrophist progressionism was the best theory for explaining the fossilized remains in the geologic strata. However, where Cuvier had been implicit, Hitchcock was explicit: he saw each geologic catastrophe and each progressionist creation of new organisms as a special, supernatural act, a proof of God's existence and providence.[39] Hitchcock saw at least some catastrophes operating in reverse, so to speak, of Cuvier's catastrophes. Instead of suggesting sudden cataclysms that destroyed part of the earth's surface, Hitchcock borrowed a Huttonian idea that the cooling of the earth brought about steady changes in climate. Many organisms were unable to adapt rapidly enough to these changes, and as a result entire species became extinct. After nature had allowed most of the organisms in an area to die off, God intervened suddenly and miraculously to create a new set of species, properly designed for the region's new climate. Thus some catastrophes were constructive, not destructive, operations. This "production of new forms of animal and vegetable life" in the wake of each catastrophe, said Hitchcock, "must be regarded . . . as the highest and most astonishing exercise of creative power."[40]

Although Hitchcock introduced his readers to Cuvier's rather consistently biblical theory of the earth's development, he used his articles to present orthodox nonscientists with several challenging hypotheses: that the earth was perhaps three hundred thousand years old; that its geologic formation demanded a vast period of time; most questionable of all, that different species of plants and animals were created in widely separated places and times. As Hitchcock introduced each of these heresies, he assured his readers that he was still using geology to present evidence of God's design.

Hitchcock also tried to analyze some geological models for the earth's creation. He suggested several theories that might be acceptable to both geologist and evangelical. One of these was "that the fossiliferous rocks with all the petrifactions which they contain, were created just as we find them, in a moment of time, and were not the result of a slow process of deposition and consolidation." Hitchcock's chief objection to this was that "it is opposed to all the known analogies of nature." Hitchcock felt obliged to make the same kind of faith claim that Lyell made in reference to miraculous intervention: science will simply not allow such reasoning. Furthermore, Christianity would be harmed by it, for "it must be a weak cause that resorts to such a mode of vindication."

The most popular theories about Genesis were the various long-day theories, one of which Silliman supported. Hitchcock discussed some variations. Perhaps "the earth occupied a longer time in its diurnal revolution at first than it does at present." Hitchcock rejected this for lack of evidence. A more plausible theory was that the creation periods were times "of indefinite length, instead of 24 hours." Hitchcock acknowledged that several people held this view, but he rejected it without explanation. The most sophisticated Genesis theory supposed "the inspired account to be a pictorial representation of the successive production of the different parts of creation, having truth for its foundation, yet not to be regarded as literally and exactly true." Hitchcock found a number of scientists who supported this view and admitted that on the surface it appeared quite plausible. However, it presupposed "that Moses' description of the creation is metaphorical," that it is "poetry instead of history." Hitchcock was not quite ready to go that far.

Hitchcock also rejected some other theories: that perhaps "Adam . . . lived in Paradise for an indefinite period previous to his fall; and that then geological changes were going forward," or that "the fossiliferous rocks were deposited by the deluge of Noah." He believed that these theories were supported by neither geology nor revelation.

Finally Hitchcock returned to Cuvier. Throughout the history of Bible interpretation, the second verse of Genesis had fascinated scholars. The first verse states that "in the beginning God created heaven and earth." The second says that "the earth was without form and void." The third verse begins the account of the six creative days. Perhaps, Hitchcock suggested, the first chapter of Genesis contains two creation accounts: one in the first verse, then an intervening "void," and finally a second, six-day creation explained in much greater detail. Before this intervening void, "numerous races of animals might have been created and destroyed, which Moses does not describe; because they had little more connection with our present races than the organized beings on other planets, if such there be."[41] Genesis could be saying exactly what Cuvier implied: the entire geologic history of the earth, together with all the fossils of extinct organisms, belongs to the first creation. When that creation was destroyed (by Cuvier's first universal catastrophe), then God began a new creation. He created the present world order—including extant plants, animals, and man—six thousand years ago and all in a space of six days.[42] Hitchcock believed that this theory of creation was perfectly compatible with both biblical and geological evidence.[43]

Hitchcock's "re-creation" theory elicited a quick rebuttal from Moses Stuart, who found the Amherst professor's ideas to be without any biblical foundation. Although he knew nothing of geology, Stuart claimed to know a great deal about philology, and he said that there was no way the "without form and void" of Genesis 1:2 could be describing a state in which the organisms now fossilized might have developed.[44]

In general, however, open-minded Protestants saw a great deal of promise in Hitchcock's attempts, even if they did not agree with the particular explanation he chose. The reviewer of an American edition of William Buckland's *Geology Considered with Reference to Natural Theology* found the re-creation theory a little hypothetical, but plausible provided that a little more evidence could be found.[45]

Presbyterian clergyman Matthew Boyd Hope reviewed the American edition of John Pye Smith's *On the Relation Between the Holy Scriptures and some Parts of Geological Science* and declared that the long-day theory had "had its day." As English clergyman-geologist Adam Sedgwick had pointed out, said Hope, "vegetables were created on the third day, and animals not until the fifth." Therefore, according to the long-day theory "about one third of the fossiliferous rocks, reckoning upwards, ought to contain only vegetables; whereas, in the lowest group nothing but animal remains has yet been found."[46] The latest and most certain theory, said Hope, is "that God created the world in the beginning, without fixing the date of the beginning; and that passing, in silence, an unknown period of its history, during which the extinct animals and plants found in the rocks might have lived and died, he describes only the present creation, which took place in six literal days, less than 6,000 years ago." Hope paraphrased this "latest" theory entirely from Hitchcock's own *Elementary Geology*, which had been published a year earlier.[47]

John Pye Smith, however, had carried Hitchcock's re-creation theory a step further than Hope was willing to go. Smith had suggested that the six-day creation account referred only to the immediate area of the Garden of Eden; that Genesis 1:1 referred to a "beginning" and to an entire "heaven and earth," but that verse three referred to a time hundreds of thousands of years later and to the preparation of only a small part of the earth for the creation of man. Hope found this theory "purely hypothetical, and not an inference from geological facts" and "very likely to compromise the authority of revelation." He dismissed it as "undeserving of criticism." However, in the same year liberal Unitarian Rufus P. Stebbins saw a great deal of promise in Smith's novel thesis. Stebbins took support for Smith's view from, of all people, Moses Stuart, who had frequently argued that the Bible was not designed to "teach the Hebrews astronomy or geology." It followed that it could not teach geography either.[48] Ten years later Hitchcock himself gave Pye Smith's theory reluctant approval in his *The Religion of Geology*. "Without professing to adopt fully this view . . . , I cannot but remark, that it explains one or two difficulties," wrote Hitchcock. The first of these problems was to conceive "how the inferior animals could have been distributed to their present places of residence from a single centre of creation without a miracle." Secondly, Smith's theory explained why many of the fossil relics of the first creation were of extant species. If God had destroyed all living things in order to begin a new creation, then he must have re-created identical species (a view Agassiz was to adopt). However, by Smith's view, God needed to destroy only the living forms in the area around the Garden of Eden. Hitchcock found this argument quite powerful, although he suspected that it was not "essential to a satisfactory reconciliation of geology and revelation."[49]

Bible scholars were obviously on the defensive. Geologists were insisting that Genesis was not accurate if it referred to the entire earth throughout its geologic history. The theologians responded by searching for a mechanism for narrowing the range of Genesis 1. Hitchcock's suggestion that the creation story referred only to the most recent geological epoch was the first step in this limitation. John Pye Smith's geographical limitation of Genesis 1 to the Fertile Crescent came next.

By this point, however, the fabrication level was pretty high. The attempts to give Genesis 1 some kind of literal meaning that would satisfy geologists had caused interpretations of that chapter to become increasingly complex, gradually more offensive to the Protestant principle that any layman should be able to read and understand the Word of God. When Rufus Stebbins reviewed Hitchcock's *Religion of Geology* ten years later, he pushed the point even farther. According to the creation account, light had not been created until after the long, intervening void. But what about all those organisms of an earlier period? "Were these animals and fishes furnished with eyes millions of ages before light was created?" asked Stebbins.[50]

Stebbins's objection uncovered the fundamental absurdity of all of these elaborate harmonization efforts. John Pye Smith, Silliman, and Hitchcock were all trying to preserve in some way a "literal" Genesis. But each was forced to twist or deny the most obvious meanings of that passage's words. To be sure, Hitchcock had tried to answer Stebbins's objection long before it had been voiced. He explained in great detail that the phrase "let there be light" did not refer to the *creation* of light at all, but merely to its first appearance on the re-created earth. Eventually, however, someone would raise a new, far-fetched objection. Hitchcock's or some other evangelical's only response would be to create a new, equally far-fetched, explanation.

In 1837 Hitchcock temporarily abandoned his concern with the creation and focused his attention on the Great Deluge. "The Historical and Geological Deluges Compared" stretched through three volumes and across 135 pages of the *American Biblical Repository*. Hitchcock surveyed a number of ancient deluge epics and concluded that all of them could be traced to the original Mosaic account of the flood, although "not one can compare for a moment in verisimilitude with the Mosaic."[51] Hitchcock believed that the pagan accounts of the deluge were less reliable because they had been "conveyed down to the present time through the various winding and muddy currents of tradition, semi-barbarism, and false religion," while the Mosaic account had been kept pure in the inspired Word.

Since Hitchcock's re-creation theory held that all geological strata had been created long before the Noachian deluge, it followed that "it is unreasonable to look for any . . . evidence [of a universal flood] in the regular strata of the Globe. We must, therefore, confine our attention solely to the surface."[52] For his proof, Hitchcock relied heavily on data he had collected for the Massachusetts Geological Survey, 1830–33, as well as the observations of other geologists. Hitchcock had found that "bowlders and diluvial gravel are found almost uniformly in a southerly direction from the rocks from which they have been detached" and that there were a large number of "scratches and grooves, having a direction nearly north and south, upon the ledges of rocks that have never been moved, and of vallies having the same direction, worn out in the softer strata."[53] These data indicated to Hitchcock that a large, south-flowing mass of water had passed over the globe at some point in its recent geological history.

Hitchcock relied heavily on an argument provided by *Bridgewater Treatise* author William Buckland. Buckland had found caves in Yorkshire containing the bones of extinct "tropical animals" buried under diluvial mud. He had concluded that the caves had once been the abode of hyenas that had carried animals inside for food A subsequent inundation had covered the victims' bones with the mud. Heavy stalagnation resting on the mud indicated that this deluge had occurred many ages before. Further, since all the buried bones belonged to extinct animals, Buckland concluded that England before this deluge had been populated with a completely different set of species than at present. First to Buckland, now to Hitchcock, this seemed conclusive, independent geologic evidence of a great inundation and repopulation of the earth.[54]

One problem that had plagued Bible interpreters for many years was the universality of the flood. Obviously, said Hitchcock, the ark was not large enough to hold the hundreds of thousands of species of land animals. However, the Genesis account seems to imply that the flood was universal. Hitchcock decided that the flood was universal as to man; that is, it covered every part of the earth that was populated with the human race. It did not necessarily cover those parts of the earth containing only animals. However, both Genesis and geology agreed that the flood was "very extensive, if not universal."

Hitchcock's last question was in some ways the most crucial to his geological-religious paradigm: could any "natural causes . . . have produced the deluge"? Generally, said Hitchcock, scientists are not at liberty "to superadd to natural agencies a miraculous energy where the former is sufficient to accomplish his purposes." Some "paroxysm of internal power" could easily have raised the beds of the former oceans, causing them to spill their contents onto what had previously been dry land. Hitchcock believed he had ample evidence that "our present continents once constituted the bottom of the ocean" and that "different parts of the same continent, were elevated above the water at different epochs." The tremendous volcanic activity necessary to cause such an upheaval, suggested Hitchcock, would also produce enough "aqueous vapor" to create the forty-day rain described by Genesis.[55]

Having said this, Hitchcock appeared confident in 1838 that "the Mosaic account of the deluge stands forth fairly and fully vindicated from all collision with the facts of science." In fact, "a presumption is hence derived in favor of the Mosaic account."

Hitchcock had a long, successful career studying Genesis and geology. By 1851 his work had carried him to the presidency of Amherst. His views, however, changed very little. *The Religion of Geology and its Connected Sciences*, his most ambitious synthesis of religion and science, employed long outdated arguments "for the Divine benevolence" and strained analogies revealing the "Divine plan" in nature. His argument for design was essentially the reverse of the argument Darwin was beginning to develop for natural selection. Man's environment was obviously planned for him, argued Hitchcock. Tillable land and water were distributed perfectly; the climate was optimal; metallic ores were readily available near the surface. All of these things indicated to Hitchcock that God had designed the earth with man in mind. While Darwin saw man as a product of his environment, Hitchcock saw the environment as the result of a divine analysis of man's needs. Either argument taken in any absolute sense is more metaphysical than scientific. However,

Hitchcock presented his argument in the most theological, absolute form possible; Darwin presented his merely as a scientific mechanism.

Inevitably, as geology became more sophisticated and as its findings made a literal interpretation of Genesis less plausible, evangelical Americans became sceptical of the whole harmonization effort. The harmonies themselves were becoming too complicated and reactionary. A crisis that would mushroom with the publication of *On the Origin of Species* emerged in the early 1850s with a spate of books suggesting that either science or religion must relinquish some of its territory. Evangelical critics began to take one of two positions: they rejected geology altogether as inconsistent with Christian truth; or they rejected the geology of the 1840s and 1850s in favor of an earlier, usually Wernerian, geology.[56]

In 1851 Eleazor Lord, an Andover trained conservative businessman from New York City and an amateur scientist, produced *The Epoch of Creation, the Scripture Doctrine Contrasted with the Geological Theory*. The title itself is important. It would not have occurred to Silliman or Hitchcock to "contrast" Scripture and geology. Lord did not want to attack all of science, not even all of geology. He tried to show merely that the geologists of his day were using bad science. Modern geology had exceeded its bounds, argued Lord, by attempting to analyze supernatural as well as natural phenomena. "The work of creation was necessarily a supernatural work," Lord said. Therefore, "all reasoning from the general laws of nature, which in their operation were subsequent to the work of creation, is . . . irrelevant in explanation of the Mosaic account."[57] Lord, in effect, pointed back to that original, absurd inconsistency: harmonizers invariably tried to give natural phenomena both natural and supernatural explanations. But that was bad science. Geology must discern what things have natural causes and deal exclusively with them; religion must decide which things are supernatural and deal solely with them.

Of course, when that distinction has been made, then one must follow it through and direct his questions either to science or to religion. Lord decided that "questions respecting the origin and epoch of the creation" were clearly not scientific questions. "The geologist, in his inquiries, is restricted to physical phenomena as seen under the operation of physical causes . . . to the exclusion of everything supernatural." Therefore, "if . . . a scientific geologist . . . ascribes the facts which he discovers to a supernatural cause—a cause not within his observation—he passes out of his own field of inquiry into that of revelation; out of the province of science into that of theology."[58]

In spite of his basically antiscientific position, Lord had made an incisive criticism of Romantic scientists. He found them too concerned with cosmology, with big, ultimate questions, rather than with the simple recording and cataloging of phenomena. He believed that the doctrine of analogy was far-fetched, particularly when it was used in respect to events that are not analogous to anything, such as the creation of the earth. Add to this Lord's attack on science's unhealthy liaison with theology, and one sees Lord as an unwilling prophet of the kind of "closed universe" science more characteristic of the end of the century. Invariably, however, Lord's critics failed to take notice of his philosophical insights. Rather, they looked at his geology, which, as one reviewer noted, "belongs to an earlier period." Knowing that, he discarded Lord's work as inconsequential.[59]

However, Lord's call did not go entirely unanswered. A number of evangelicals, growing increasingly uneasy about the willingness of their peers to allow science to dictate their religious beliefs, decided to be heard. The more conservative among them were gradually losing their faith in science's ability to provide a satisfactory account of the origin of the world. Increasingly they came to agree with the late Moses Stuart that such questions were biblical and not scientific.

The most competent defense of an exclusively exegetical interpretation of Genesis was Presbyterian Taylor Lewis' *Six Days of Creation*. Lewis, professor of Oriental Languages at Presbyterian Union College, actually developed an interpretation of Genesis 1 that was very similar to Silliman's "long-day" theory. It was the way in which he arrived at his conclusions that made moderate evangelical scientists so defensive and prompted James Dwight Dana to write a series of outraged responses.

Lewis thought it a "wretched self-deception" that evangelicals should claim to have "a belief grounded on the Scriptures, which after all rests for its main support on Buckland, or Lyell, or Hugh Miller."[60] A Christian must never sacrifice his belief in revelation; "he must hold that the record in Genesis is a true account of the matters and facts therein set forth. . . . If the twenty-four hour hypothesis is the one, and the only one, that comes from a faithful and exact exegesis of the Sacred Words, he must accept it in spite of any difficulties of science."

Lewis also had something to say about philology. Well-meaning evangelicals too often put "modern notions on very ancient language. They have not realized that the language of the Old Testament is "phenomenal," not scientific. That is, it pertains to "those last phenomena or *appearances* through which these remote energies finally manifest themselves directly to the senses, and which are . . . the same for all ages and all men— never varying like the language of science or philosophy."[61] To believe that Moses wrote Genesis with nineteenth-century geology in mind was absurd. Therefore, when geologists try to act as Revelation's guide "we can get along very well without [them]; our intellectual and moral dignity would not [be] impaired had no such science ever existed."[62]

The radical idea that religion and geology cannot be harmonized angered Dana much more than Lewis's conclusions about the method of creation. Dana had actually picked up *The Six Days of Creation* hoping to enjoy it, for he had heard that it supported a long-day theory similar to his own.[63] The bitter controversy that followed was more a matter of attitude toward science than to the details of interpretation. Before the fight was over each man had called the other "infidel"; each had abused the other's method; each had suggested that the other's position was thoroughly destructive of Christianity.[64]

Dana was convinced that Lewis's position represented a dead-end for Protestant science. But Lewis was not the extreme. The extreme was so far beyond Lewis that Dana did not even bother to reply to it. New York City engineer Thomas A. Davies, for example, found the attempts at geological harmony to be completely hypothetical and therefore contrary to sound, Christian principles. "The geologist, is a man of science," argued Davies, "so long as he develops and classifies *facts*." However, "when he *assumes facts*, and assigns actions to the *creator* based upon these assumptions, we have taken the liberty to call him a 'theorist.' " But exactly what is fact and what is theory? Davies voiced what may be the most extreme Baconian hypothesis ever uttered: the geologist finds fossils that "are mainly in the form of or have a strong resemblance to those of living animals and plants. But the theorist here takes up the fact, and places blood, bones, life, and fibre of wood, into these stones or imprints, none of which does he find there." In other words, to say that fossils are "rocks" is legitimate science. To say that they are the remains of once-living animals—no matter how obvious the resemblance—is pure "hypothesis." It would be very easy for a sculptor to cut fossils from quartz, noted Davies; "why could not the *creator* have as well made [the fossil] in its present form, as the surrounding rock, or any of the more intricate and beautiful forms of crystallization?"[65]

Having pushed science into this corner, Davies went on to create his own view of the earth's creation, supported exclusively by biblical revelation. As one might expect, it contained a six thousand-year-old earth and a six-day creation, a universal flood, and a complete disregard for every contrary theory of geology.

But the sword could cut both ways. For every evangelical reactionary who rejected some part of science, there was a liberal who took the opposite route. When Unitarian Rufus Stebbins had laid bare the inconsistencies in Hitchcock's harmonization efforts, he sat back to weigh the alternatives.[66] He had shown that elaborate syntheses of Genesis and geology would not work, but he appeared not to relish his victory. "What can be adopted in [their] place," he asked, "and still maintain the inspiration of the first part of Genesis?" Stebbins could find only one answer: nothing. The absolute historicity of Genesis 1 would have to go. Perhaps, he suggested, Moses simply compiled a large number of oral or written traditions about creation. Inspiration could lie in the fact that he "has correctly given them," even though "he has not vouched for their truth." Those were strong words coming from a Unitarian tradition whose Christian liberalism had always stood solidly on biblical literalness. But they were words that would appear more frequently in the 1850s and 1860s, not merely in the pamphlets of infidels, but in the respectable journals of Church-going American Protestants.

While religious critics were surveying the damage geology had done, however, geologists themselves were acquiring a radically different interest. Even the most orthodox state legislators were more excited about the market value of the coal and minerals upon which they were standing than they were about how they had developed and how long they had been there. As religious a scientist as Edward Hitchcock could conduct a state survey of Massachusetts and omit from his report any speculation about the great deluge. Hitchcock's thoroughly descriptive survey of Massachusetts in 1830–32 set the pace for a long list of others.[67] Slowly at first, then more rapidly, the emphasis in geological curricula began to change from cosmology to description. Geology, quite simply, meant money in state treasuries—new industry, new taxes, a higher standard of living. If geology was a liability to religion, it was nevertheless a tremendous asset to the economy.

In the second half of the century most theologians and scientists tried to leave Genesis alone and go on to more relevant things. Of course there would always be others—Christianity's orthodox extremists and science's outcasts or outsiders—to pick up where Silliman and Hitchcock had left off. Generally, however, they have added little to the old arguments. They have added nothing to our understanding of science or religion.

8

The Chosen Land

Religious Americans were almost as fascinated by Palestine and Egypt as they were by their own land. Those faraway countries, with a strange climate, an alien culture, and buried artifacts older than the ruins of Rome, were as important to many evangelicals as their own church buildings. The places described by the Bible awed them, and they were equally awed by the men who had been there. Every clergyman yearned to visit the Holy Lands and tell his congregation about them. Three years at Princeton Seminary provided one kind of education, but a visit to Jerusalem provided another, equally important.

Scholarly American Protestants naturally believed that by studying Palestine they could authenticate the Bible. By the 1830s Americans were beginning to recognize that one of the most important aspects of science is history. Enlightenment physicists had focused their attention on the laws of nature, but Romantic geologists were more interested in changes within nature. The results of this new emphasis were making some Christians uncomfortable. It was not only that geology made the earth appear very old; it was that Christianity by comparison seemed very young. According to the Bible, God's salvation plan, from promise to fulfillment, began with Adam's fall. It occupied the whole of history. But as Hutton and Lyell made the earth appear older, God's plan became proportionately shorter. For the critics like Edward Gibbon who had suggested that the world is "ancient" but Christianity merely "modern," Palestine provided startling evidence to the contrary. To the Western Christian a journey to Palestine was a telescope with which he could bring the remotest places into his viewing room. The Holy Lands explorer moved not only through space but through time as well—and when he arrived he found his discoveries immensely satisfying. Perhaps the world was old, but Palestine was ancient too. Perhaps things changed more quickly than the average orthodox Christian cared to have them change, but they did not change that quickly everywhere. Things in the Holy Lands still appeared very much as the Bible described them. To go there was not to discover conclusive evidence that the Bible was infallible, but it *was* sufficient to demonstrate that the Bible was not an elaborate hoax.

However, orthodox Protestants had more compelling reasons for examining the Holy Lands. Christianity's critics had raised difficult questions about the Bible's historicity, and committed scholars were duty-bound to answer them. Gibbon's shattering *Decline and Fall of the Roman Empire* alleged that the Bible grossly overstated Palestine's importance in world history. It was a "territory scarcely superior to Wales, either in fertility or extent," he wrote, and its impact must be evaluated accordingly.[1] In 1786 radical French historian Constantin Francois Volney said that Palestine was a wilderness and always had been. There was no "land flowing with milk and honey" nor any ancient splendor of Solomon's Temple. The Old Testament accounts of these were massive fabrications, designed to create a Jewish mythology like Homer's tales of the early Greeks.[2]

Evangelicals could not rescue the Bible from such attacks simply by studying theology or philology. They had to see the biblical sites themselves. They had to dig out and sift through the evidence that would show how mistaken Gibbon and Volney had been. The development of a scientific American archeology would not occur until the last half of the nineteenth century. Not until 1880 would bona fide Yankee diggers lead their own scientific expeditions to Palestine, more intent on reconstructing ancient cultures than in proving the inspiration of the Bible. The observations taken during the first half of the century were generally random and unscientific—collections of travels, diaries, and inspirational writings. Only a few authors called their reports "researches," "investigations," or even "expeditions"; most travelers were so taken with the fact that *they* were actually *there* that they neglected the more painstaking observations that might have made their work more useful. Nevertheless, in different ways and to mixed degrees they did produce the beginnings of a scientific look at Near-Eastern land and culture.

While higher and lower criticism were concerned primarily with *how* things happened, biblical researchers in Palestine were more interested in *where* and *when* biblical events had occurred. Most American researchers simply assumed that the Bible history was truthful. The problem was to put these events into a meaningful historical context.

Biblical geography was orthodoxy's best offense. Even if the authors of the Bible did not have their numbers and years straight, they were thoroughly familiar with the land about which they wrote. In addition, two thousand years of Church tradition in the Holy Lands had "identified" virtually every important biblical site. The clergyman with the most rudimentary education could make his once-in-a-lifetime journey and "discover" for himself the site of Christ's crucifixion, of Solomon's Temple, or of the place where Moses had parted the waters of the Red Sea. As a result, most American books about the Holy Lands were concerned with the description of sites.

Problems of chronology were more complex and required a higher degree of expertise. In addition, the Bible appeared to be most vulnerable on these points. The dating of the Noachian flood, the sojourn of Abraham, or the Exodus was problematic, to say the least. Already by 1800 theologians knew that they could not discover the date of the Exodus simply by adding up the genealogies of the Old Testament. First they had to deal with internal problems: conflicting genealogies, earlier Hebrew texts, and texts in tranlation that allowed many more years than the Masoretic. By 1825 biblical chronology was beseiged by external attackers as well: philologists, geologists, and historians all faulted the chronology of the Old Testament.

Nevertheless, evangelicals in antebellum America generally believed that the study of the lands around Palestine would be of great value for Christianity. In theory one could find two kinds of "evidences" in the Holy Lands. First, one could search for dramatic, positive verification of some important Bible incident. Should an exploring team actually discover Noah's ark or Christ's cross, that find would certainly put an end to everyone's doubts about the veracity of the Bible or the truth of Christianity. But such discoveries were seldom made and they were very difficult to verify. By 1800 the Catholic Church in Palestine had already collected enough pieces of Christ's cross to fill Noah's ark. This kind of searching was generally restricted to orthodoxy's extremists or to people whose interest in icons far exceeded their commitment to scientific investigation.

The real value in the study of the Holy Lands was less explicit. It lay not so much in exciting discoveries proving that the Bible was true, as in the more routine finds demonstrating that it was not false. "Could it have happened the way the Bible says it happened?" was on the minds of most Bible explorers. Could the Children of Israel have walked from Heliopolis to the Red Sea in two days, as Exodus describes? Were there such people as the Chaldees, and were they as wealthy and as cultured as the Old Testament implies?[3]

These interests resulted in the development of a science called "biblical studies" or "biblical researches." Biblical researches was a mixture of archeology, historiography, geography, cartography, textual criticism, and some primitive anthropology. Its leading practitioners were invariably generalists—men who had an acquaintance with all these areas but who were not experts in any of them. Biblical researches, however, was a scholarly field in America, and it produced outstanding men. At least one of them, Andover's Edward Robinson, acquired an international reputation.

The chief inspiration for biblical research was German textual criticism. Most of the biblical critics were philologists, but their conclusions far exceeded the bounds of philology. For example, philological considerations may have led several German critics to conclude that Abraham was not an individual but a type.

However, that statement was itself an historical assertion, to be studied not only by looking at the text of Genesis but also by digging into the history, archeology, and geology of Old Testament lands. Invariably, textual critics and biblical researchers came to very different conclusions about the Bible's historical basis. Biblical researchers were excited tremendously when their work showed that all the prophecies of Isaiah about King Cyrus had really come true. This seemed to be certain confirmation of part of the Old Testament. At the same time, however, the evidence carried higher critics in the opposite direction. The fact that the Isaiac prophecies about King Cyrus were both accurate and detailed indicated that they had actually been written *after* the "prophesied" events had occurred. This suggested to higher critics that Isaiah was written by two authors, separated by three hundred years. *That* conclusion was not nearly as supportive of Old Testament infallibility.[4]

At the beginning of the century, Americans had virtually no first-hand knowledge of the lands around Palestine. Except for the oral descriptions of a few missionaries, they had to rely on the explorations and diaries of Europeans. The best of these included Francois Chateaubriand's *Itinéraire de Paris à Jérusalem*, and Alphonse de Lamartine's *Souvenirs, Impressions, et Paysages, Pendant un Voyage en Orient. . . .*[5] Both Frenchmen wrote lively accounts of their journeys, but neither made particularly accurate observations. Germans such as natural historian Gotthilf Neinreich von Schubert and Johannes Burckhardt were only slightly more helpful. Burckhardt did some of the earliest geographical work in Palestine, discovering the site of Petra and mapping parts of the Dead Sea and the Sinai Penninsula. Much of his work, however, was highly speculative. British work in Palestine before 1835 was generally superficial.[6]

In 1819 Henry Dearborn became the first American to write a full length study of the Near East. He had never been there. Dearborn drew his material completely from foreign sources, often copying freely.[7] In the same year, Edward Everett saw part of the East while he was on his own world tour, but he did not leave an account of his journey.[8] Perhaps the first written description by an American traveler was Nathaniel Parker Willis's *Pencillings by the Way*. Willis, who was a graduate of Yale, imagined himself quite a dandy and playboy. His book was an entertaining but generally insipid guide to the kind of fun a care-free young bachelor can have while on a Mediterranean cruise.[9]

No American recorded his Holy Land observations with any precision until John Lloyd Stephens wrote his *Incidents of Travel in Egypt, Arabia Petrea, and the Holy Land* in 1837. Stephens, who would become famous with his discovery of the Mayan culture, achieved considerable success with his Holy Land travels. Within two years his book sold over twenty-one thousand copies and earned its author twenty-five thousand dollars—enough to finance his later expeditions to Central and South America.[10]

Generally, however, American travelogues of the Middle East were not the scholarly answers to deistic or historical critics that evangelicals wanted. More scholarly work would not appear until the late 1830s and 1840s. Then a diverse group of European and American evangelicals began answering the allegations of Gibbon, Volney, and the higher critics. E. W. Hengstenberg's *Egypt and the Books of Moses* provided, according to its American reviewer, "weighty evidence" in favor of the Pentateuch. A British evangelical, William Osburn, wrote *Ancient Egypt, her Testimony to the Truth of the Bible.* Osburn's book was not as scholarly as Hengstenberg's, but it was just as useful for confirming evangelical presuppositions. Americans wrote several of their own Bible Lands books. Among the most popular were Francis Hawks, *The Monuments of Egypt*, and William Maclure Thomson's best seller *The Land and the Book.* But the one work that outshone all the others, both the American and the foreign, was written by a softspoken, orthodox Congregationalist named Edward Robinson. Almost singlehandedly Robinson gave Biblical researches scientific respectability.[11]

Robinson was the son of a Congregational minister from Connecticut and a graduate of Hamilton College. He first became interested in biblical studies when he was a student at Andover Seminary. There he quickly became Moses Stuart's best and most favored assistant. Although he eventually acquired an international reputation far exceeding Stuart's, he remained firmly in the orthodox mold into which his teacher had cast him. In 1823 Robinson became Hebrew instructor at Andover and began working with Stuart on a useful Hebrew text. In 1826 he gave up his Andover position for studies in Germany. There he developed a consuming interest in biblical criticism and on-site studies.

Robinson returned to America a convinced advocate of biblical archeology and exploration. Two times in his career, in 1831 and again in 1843, he founded journals devoted exclusively to biblical research. Each time, however, the market failed to support such specialized periodicals. Both the *American Biblical Repository* and *Bibliotheca Sacra* became all-purpose religious quarterlies shortly after their first issue.

Robinson's greatest interest was geography. By locating the sites where biblical events had occurred, he hoped to throw some light on the way they had happened and in the process confirm the authenticity of Scripture. "On the Exodus of the Israelites out of Egypt, and their Wanderings in the Desert," printed with a carefully worked out map, was one of Robinson's earliest efforts in geographical scholarship. Here Robinson attempted to take a piece of *"terra incognita"*—a land unknown to western scholars—and trace out its geography, at the same time making pertinent illustrations "of that part of Holy Writ, which is more particularly connected with these districts." Robinson identified and located on his map the biblical "Land of Goshen," where the Israelites had lived during their enslavement. He also found the land of the Philistines, the Egyptian city of "Rameses" from which the Israelites began their Exodus journey, and the Exodus route itself.

An old question of scientific method came to haunt Robinson, just as it had dozens of other evangelical scientists. Biblical studies had been conceived as a method for illustrating and confirming the truth of biblical accounts, which suggested that the area of Palestine should be treated as the given data, and that the verity of the Bible should be the "variable" to be determined. Good method would prescribe that one begin with the data and arrive at conclusions about the variable—not vice-versa. Robinson, however, was quick to violate procedure when his purposes demanded it. He concluded that the ancient city of Rameses must have been Heroöpolis and not Heliopolis, the traditionally considered site of the ancient city. Heliopolis, which was near Cairo, was much too far from the Red Sea, and "it would have been impossible for such a company [the departing Israelites] to have travelled the distance of one hundred miles in three days."[12]

In the same manner, Robinson identified the place where the Israelites crossed the Red Sea as the present location of Suez, simply because that was the point at which a "natural" explanation of the parting of the waters was most plausible. The parting, said Robinson, was "not a direct suspension of, or interference with the laws of nature," but rather "an extraordinary, a miraculous adaption of those laws, to produce a given result."[13] At Suez the sea was sufficiently narrow that "a strong north east wind, acting here upon the ebb tide . . . would necessarily have had the effect to drive the waters out of the small arm of the sea . . . and leave the shallower portions in the narrow part dry."

By 1840 Robinson had had the chance to visit all these sites personally and verify his earlier work. In "The Land of Goshen, and the Exodus of the Israelites" he reaffirmed nearly all his earlier conclusions: that the land of Goshen and the ancient city of Rameses were not near Cairo but were east of the Nile Delta, in the part of Egypt closest to Palestine; and that the Israelites must have crossed the Red Sea near Suez.[14] At the same time, Robinson acquired a new interest—the circumstances of the destruction of Sodom and Gomorrah. Although the site of the ancient cities that God had destroyed by "fire and brimstone" during the time of Abraham had been fairly clearly established, no one had succeeded in finding a satisfactory natural explanation for their destruction. Like most Congregational evangelicals of his time, Robinson believed that the destruction of Sodom and Gomorrah could be simultaneously natural and supernatural— that God purposely intervened in the course of nature to bring the catastrophe about, but that he employed "natural" means to do it. When Robinson and his party found evidence that the strata below Sodom contained a great deal of asphalt and bituminous coal, Robinson was convinced that he had found the answer. He suggested that "the Lord, by means of lightning or fire from heaven, caused the strata of bitumen to be set on fire, which then burnt with a fury sufficient to destroy the cities, consume the strata forming the fertile surface of the valley, and thus in parts sink its level." This, he reasoned, would account for the fact that most of the site was now under the waters of the Dead Sea. Since Robinson made no claim as a geologist he wrote Leopold von Buch in Berlin to see if his bitumen theory was plausible. Von Buch found the theory quite plausible, but suggested that volcanic activity rather than lightning would make a more satisfactory explanation for the ignition of the coal.[15]

In the following number of the *Repository*, Charles A. Lee, a former professor of materia medica and medical jurisprudence at the University of New York, confirmed Robinson's hypothesis. Relying heavily on the geologies and travels of others, Lee tried to establish that the site of Sodom was directly over a volcanic crater, filled with "subterranean fires, ready to be fanned into an out-bursting flame, by the avenging breath of the Almighty." Furthermore, Lee had the clearest explanation for the site's subsequent inundation: "in consequence of the internal combustion of the bituminous materials, the whole plain sunk, causing the Jordan . . . to pour . . . into the volcanic crater, which had swallowed up the cities, and thus form a stagnant lake." Lee believed his theory accounted for the Dead Sea itself, as well as the destruction of the two wicked cities.[16]

The most important scientific work to come out of Robinson's expedition to Palestine was his massive, three-volume *Biblical Researches in Palestine, Mount Sinai and Arabia Petrea*, published in 1841.[17] Robinson's *Researches* was a masterwork, important enough to influence two generations of American and European archeologists.[18] As a rule, scholars before Robinson had been observant but not particularly critical. In their eagerness to see as much as possible they had generally not taken the time to question the information they were given. Evangelicals in particular were programmed to look for evidence that would verify the truth of the Bible and not for geographical problems that would inspire doubts. To most of them the Holy Lands were completely bizarre. The way of life, the relative backwardness of the people, the mixtures of religion, and the geography itself were sufficiently unfamiliar that few ministers or even professors had sufficient expertise to be critical. Paid Arabian and Turkish guides knew from centuries of experience how to take advantage of this situation. They easily "located" Golgotha, Christ's sepulcher, and Rebecca's well, and pointed them out to the awed visitors. Not until John Lloyd Stephens published his *Incidents of Travel* in 1837 had any American indicated scepticism about the accuracy of the Holy Lands tours. Stephens had expressed some doubts about the ease with which the Empress Helena, the mother of Constantine, had located Christ's cross, drawn it out "from the bottom of a dark pit," and scattered its pieces for the benefit of Christians everywhere. "It may be that the earnest piety of the empress sometimes deceived her," he mused.[19] But Stephens was not generally suspicious of the sites as identified by the guides. Instead he was enraged by the extent to which the Church had commercialized the shrines built over the hallowed spots. He usually accepted as genuine not only the sites of famous biblical events but of some non-biblical ones as well. In front of the Greek Chapel of the Cross in Jerusalem he saw an "unintelligible machine" which he was told was "the stone on which our Saviour was placed when put in the stocks." Frankly, he told his readers, "I had never heard of this incident in the story of man's redemption." However, "the Christians in Jerusalem have a great deal more of such knowledge than they gain from the Bible." Knowing that, he had no difficulty accepting the stone as genuine.[20]

Robinson, however, was not quite so gullible. He was determined to doubt everything he could, even the acknowledged locations of the most significant sites. He chose as a traveling companion Eli Smith, an American missionary serving in Lebanon and a master linguist. Smith's knowledge of Hebrew and Aramaic proved invaluable in the identification of sites. Only with Smith's help was Robinson able to cut through two thousand years of inaccurate Church tradition in Palestine. In the process he discovered a much more reliable tradition—the fact that the native Arab-speaking population still used daily many of the ancient place names employed in the Bible.[21] Armed with "an ordinary surveyor's and two pocket compasses, a thermometer, telescopes, and measuring tapes," Robinson and Smith journeyed from Greece to Egypt and Syria, and finally to Palestine, Lebanon, and the greater area around the Dead Sea and the Jordan Valley. Robinson saw it as one of his most important tasks to create a map of the Holy Lands more accurate than any before.

Robinson's researches led him to conclude that the guides had incorrectly identified sites as important as Christ's crucifixion and interment. His lengthy historical argument, supported by all the available archeological evidence, demonstrated rather clearly that the crucifixion and burial sites identified by the tour guides were inside the boundaries of the original city of Jerusalem. Since the Bible mentioned several times that the crucifixion site was "without the gate of the ancient city,"

Robinson concluded that the guides were in error and that all search for the actual site would "probably . . . only be in vain."[22] By similar methods Robinson dealt with several other alleged biblical sites: Modin, the ancient city of the Maccabees; the spot on Mount Sinai where Moses received the Ten Commandments directly from God; and the remains of the Jewish temple.[23]

Robinson's quest for an accurate map of the Bible lands led him to many of the Near East's less habitable regions. Near Suez his group nearly fainted for lack of water, but the Arabian guides managed to find a few natural cisterns in the rocks. The water was briny and "smacked of camel's dung," but the thirsty Americans drank it anyway. Repeatedly abandoned by their paid guides, frequently caught in the middle of skirmishes between rival Sheiks, and often fooled by unscrupulous merchants, Robinson and his party kept the presence of mind to perform their duties. Even by the standards of twentieth-century archeology, they did a remarkable job.[24]

Most Americans instantly recognized the value of Robinson's accomplishment. Unitarian minister George Edward Ellis thought only a mastermind could identify sites in spite of powerful local tradition to the contrary, although he admitted that Smith's knowledge of Arabic was undoubtedly the single most valuable tool the party had.[25] Episcopal minister Charles Hall, an avid follower of biblical researches, thought Robinson's work a "treasury" of valuable new information. He concluded that "no single expedition has ever contributed so large an amount of materials for the rectification of Scripture geography."[26]

More conservative evangelicals, however, suggested that perhaps Robinson's sword was too sharp. Joseph Alexander, professor of Oriental literature at Princeton Seminary, found the work "utterly unsuited for mere popular effect." Robinson obviously had "very little taste for the beauties of scenery, and no peculiar talent for describing them."[27] William Maclure Thomson, who accompanied Robinson on his second journey to Palestine in 1852, had nothing but respect for Robinson's ability as "the greatest master of measuring tape in the world." But he could not abide Robinson's cool objectivity. The author of *The Land and the Book* was inspired beyond control when he saw the Church of the Holy Sepulchre. Unlike Robinson, he found the shrine erected on this "most interesting half acre on the face of the earth" to be completely convincing. He protested that the site's genuineness was accepted by "all but a few learned men." The critical scholars' lust for knowledge had completely misguided them: "the reputed sepulchre of the Son of God is no place for soulless criticism, calm, cold, and hard as the rock itself."[28] Reverential worship was much too important to allow a few difficult facts to get into the way. By 1860 Thomson's literate but inaccurate book had sold more copies than any American work except *Uncle Tom's Cabin*.

Biblical researches inevitably discovered more technical and ambitious tasks. Shortly after Robinson had completed his pioneering work in Palestine, an Englishman, Austen Henry Layard, began excavations in Assyria. He published his findings in 1850 as *Ninevah and its Remains*, and in 1853 in *Discoveries Among the Ruins of Ninevah and Babylon*.[29] Layard was not particularly concerned with the verification of the Bible. Many Americans were happy to learn, however, that most of his discoveries did appear to confirm certain parts of the Old Testament. Young, Yale-trained clergyman Leonard Bacon found that the Assyrian monuments uncovered by Layard gave "the strongest confirmation" to the Old Testament account of Assyria's conquest of Israel in 676 B.C. Furthermore, Layard had discovered evidence that Israel had been paying tribute to the King of Assyria for more than one hundred years before the invasion.[30]

The Rev. Thomas Laurie, a missionary in the Middle East who reviewed Layard's work for the *Bibliotheca Sacra*, went even further. He used translations of cuneiform inscriptions to show how closely Assyrian history paralleled the Old Testament. In 1846 Sir Henry Rawlinson had published the first successful translation of the inscription of Darius I on the Behistun Mountain. The inscription, an Assyrian counterpart to the Rosetta Stone, had been written in both Persian and cuneiform characters. By 1857 a large number of clay tablets, inscriptions on temple walls, and even on statues had been translated. Laurie attempted to make a detailed comparison of these with the Old Testament history. He found no instance where inscriptions contradicted biblical history, but several where they confirmed it. The most exciting find was a long statement by Sennacherib, the Assyrian king who had warred constantly against an anti-Assyrian coalition led by Egypt and containing the Kingdom of Judah. Other inscriptions confirmed the tradition that Sennacherib was indeed assassinated by his own sons in 681 B.C., as narrated in 2 Kings 19:37. These discoveries led Laurie to conclude that the study of Assyrian archeology would inaugurate a "new era in our knowledge of the Past" and certainly confirm the Bible as the true word of God.[31]

Although the Old Testament may have been accurate with respect to geography, its system of dating was hopelessly contradictory and misleading. When Jean Francois Champollion deciphered the Rosetta Stone in 1822 he provided early Egyptologists with the means for answering a number of chronological questions insofar as Egypt itself was concerned. Rather than confirming the Bible, however, the new discoveries raised a number of questions about the relationship between Egyptian and Old Testament history.

The hieroglyphic system fascinated Edward Robinson. He devoted an entire article to explaining it to American evangelicals, optimistically suggesting that the discovery would lay all of Egypt's darkest secrets open to scholars.[32] From the beginning, however, the translation of Egyptian inscriptions was to create problems for believers in an inspired Bible. First of all, there was no mention of the Israelites, a people who must have numbered more than four million, who were responsible for the construction of entire cities, and who finally broke away from Egypt after a devastating series of plagues. The Egyptians never said a word about them. Secondly, it was beginning to appear that Egyptian civilization had begun before the date orthodox Protestants had assigned to the great flood.[33]

Robinson was not about to change the biblical date of the flood, at least not very much. By using the Samaritan text of the Old Testament, he was able to move the deluge back to 2943 B.C. By even more extreme calculations he was able to suggest an "outer limit" at 3155 B.C. That date would put the flood approximately one thousand years earlier than Archbishop Ussher's chronology had put it. Then, by an elaborate analysis of Egyptian astronomy and chronometry, Robinson concluded that the reign of King Menes and the rise of Egyptian civilization must have occurred around 2890 B.C. This, he suggested, "will leave a space of time . . . sufficient to allow for the emigration of Ham [Noah's son], with his son Misraim, into Egypt." Robinson even suggested that Misraim, the son of Ham mentioned in the Old Testament account, and Menes, the first king of Egypt, were the same person; or perhaps that Menes was "even Ham himself."[34] A year later, however, he decided that Menes was really Anamin, the grandson of Ham.[35]

By 1827 scholars building on Champollion's work had carefully reconstructed the succession of Egyptian dynasties—enough to make Robinson declare with confidence that the Israelites had lived in Egypt during the nineteenth dynasty. The Exodus, he said, occurred shortly before the reign of the sixth king of that dynasty, Rameses VI, or Sesostris.[36] He dated the Exodus at 1495 B.C. Furthermore, Robinson noted that one of the kings who occupied the Egyptian throne during the period of enslavement was Ousirei, a monarch whose sepulchre had been thoroughly explored. Upon his sarcophagus was "sculptured a procession representing a few individuals of four different races. . . . One of these groups is so characterized by the features which we still call Jewish, that they are at once recognisable as representing individuals of the race of Jacob." Furthermore, "they are represented as captives or bondsmen." To Robinson this was magnificent proof of "the bondage of the Israelites in Egypt," and provided "a most striking corroboration of the sacred history of that event."[37]

The most elaborate harmony of Egyptian and biblical chronology by an American was worked out by Episcopal clergyman Alonzo Bowen Chapin in 1836. Chapin himself apparently did no on-site work, but he did try to systematize and augment the work of others. His three contributions to the *Quarterly Christian Spectator* were a detailed but highly speculative narrative of Egyptian and Jewish civilization since the beginning of recorded history. Chapin explained the captivity of the Israelites by noting that during the period immediately preceding their enslavement, the Hyksos held the Egyptian throne.[38] The Hyksos, or Shepherd-kings, conquered Egypt about 2082 B.C. Because Abraham and his family were also shepherds, the two groups got along well. However, shortly before the death of Joseph, around 1798 B.C., the Hyksos were run out of the country. The fact that the Israelites had been good friends with the Hyksos caused the new Pharaohs to hate and enslave them. Building on these points of agreement, Chapin devised a detailed harmony of Egyptian and Old Testament history, complete with a large table comparing the two chronologies. As far as Chapin was concerned, Egyptologists posed no problem for believers in the historical accuracy of the Old Testament.[39]

Not everyone, however, had Chapin's imagination or his enthusiasm for harmonizing secular history and the Bible. George Gliddon, the American Consul at Cairo, was undoubtedly America's most thorough and scientific Egyptologist during the 1840s. His *Ancient Egypt* attempted to cut through some of the speculation and artificialities of the biblical researchers.[40] Although Gliddon professed a superficial respect for the Bible, he believed it to be confused and full of errors in the matter of ancient Egyptian history. He found the chronology of the Septuagint to be closer to the archeological data than the Masoretic Hebrew, but he believed that even the Septuagint was short by more than one thousand years. Gliddon himself divided Egyptian history into four periods: the Ante-monumental, the Pyramidal, the period of the Hyksos, and the positive historical period. The earliest of these periods, said Gliddon, began long before the earliest possible biblical date of the flood.

But Gliddon was as good a politician as he was an Egyptologist. He refused to commit himself in any great detail on the question of Old Testament credibility. His silence frustrated his reviewers to no end. One of them had concluded from his own research that there were three kinds of Egyptologists: Christians, Neologists, and infidels. The Christians were usually American or British; the Neologists were generally German; and the infidels, French. But Gliddon had him puzzled. "At one time he seemed to be a Christian; at another, a Neologist; at another, an Infidel." Occasionally Gliddon "admitted principles derived from Holy-writ" but he was also frequently brought to "the moon-struck madness of German Theories, or to the dark gropings of infidel France." Actually, the reviewer was more disturbed by Gliddon's geology than by his historiography. Gliddon spoke too frequently of oceans that had covered the Eastern hemisphere for "incalculable centuries"; or of alluvial deposits that determined that the Nile was more than 7,000 years old. All of this led the reviewer, with some reluctance, to declare the book heretical. "Whatever Mr. Gliddon may have gained by his intercourse with the learned in Europe, he certainly has not improved his Christianity."[41]

But bigger shocks were to come. Although an Egyptian chronology that stood in direct opposition against Old Testament chronology was not to be designed by an American, it was predicted and popularized by one. Josiah Clark Nott, a radical southerner from Mobile, trained as a physician at the University of Pennsylvania, a competent anatomist, and a lifelong antagonist of the organized church, had developed quite an interest in early man. In December of 1848 he delivered a pair of lectures from the Chair of Political Economy at the University of Louisiana.[42] For some, Nott's lectures were a milestone in early physical anthropology; for others, however, they were but another contribution to the collected infidelity of the age.

At the time Nott gave his two lectures, Germany's great Egyptologist Karl Richard Lepsius had not yet published his dramatic *Chronologie der Aegypter*.[43] But Nott was familiar with his work, and from his own communications with Gliddon (who knew Lepsius) Nott had a good idea of what Lepsius would say. Nott himself began by doing what Thomas Cooper, Thomas Paine, and Theodore Parker had all been obliged to do—he attacked the inspiration of the Old Testament. Although he was not a formally trained biblical scholar, Nott did read the critics. From Eichhorn, De Wette, and Strauss he concluded that the Pentateuch must have been written long after the date assigned to Moses, "and probably about the time of the captivity." This was enough to convince Nott that the chronology of the Pentateuch was thoroughly unreliable, especially when there were much better chronologies available. Nott found his chronology in the monuments of Egypt—"the mummied skulls" proving that "Egypt was old, populous and civilized, one thousand years before God made his covenant with Abraham." By the time Abraham visited Egypt, said Nott, it already had "seven or eight millions of inhabitants" and "the pyramids were built." His conclusion was direct enough: "the chronology of Egypt, even for some centuries beyond Abraham, is no longer a matter of speculation, while that of Genesis vanishes before it." Gliddon had written Nott that Lepsius's book, when it came out, would most certainly prove that recorded Egyptian history went back to 3900 B.C., long before the Noachian flood, and by Ussher's calculations only one hundred years after the creation.[44]

When Lepsius's *Chronologie* did come out, a little later that same year, it did everything Nott said it would do and more. Lepsius agreed with the higher critics in abandoning the chronology of the Old Testament, although he generally did so for different reasons. As Nott had predicted, Lepsius produced proof that even the Septuagint chronology was not long enough to account for all the history of ancient Egypt. Nott reviewed Lepsius's book in 1850, taking the opportunity to attack Moses Stuart and several other American evangelicals for their outdated views of Scripture, particularly for the idea that the "Bible must stand or fall *as a* whole." Nott demanded that scholars "cut the natural history of man loose from the Bible." For him, this meant cutting historiography loose from natural theology.[45]

Nott relished "parson skinning" so much that he could never pass up the opportunity to put a pretentious clergyman in his place. He could not resist mocking the "Reverend Doctor Howe." George Howe, Andover-educated professor of biblical literature at Georgia's Columbia Seminary, had suggested that in a period of 130 years, Adam and Eve could have produced two hundred thousand descendants.[46] Nott laughingly pointed out the absurdities in that hypothesis. He loved to rub salt in festering evangelical wounds. He dwelt for long paragraphs on his proofs that the Pentateuch was unreliable, uninspired, and historically false. Like Thomas Cooper, Nott invariably turned his essays on science into long attacks on the credibility of the Bible. Also like Cooper, he frequently "set up" his opponents, ascribing to them the most conservative or outdated theories when in fact many of them had already reached compromise positions. Of course, there was always a hyperorthodox preacher to be found someplace, ready to be murdered and mutilated.[47]

Nott also ridiculed the attempts of evangelicals like Francis Hawks to show that Egyptian and Hebrew chronologies actually tended to confirm each other. Most such attempts, he noted, were built on the presumption that Old Testament men lived to be several hundred years old. That was the only way evangelicals could explain why ten Hebrew generations, from the deluge until the time of Abraham, must be made to correspond with twelve Egyptian dynasties. "We *know*," said Nott, that the

Hebrew's "contemporaries, in Egypt, lived no longer than generations of modern times; and no one will contend for differences of longevity between Jews and Egyptians." Nor could the evangelicals escape by citing an old argument: that the Bible was not intended to teach science. We can only judge what it intends to teach, Nott said, gleefully quoting Moses Stuart, "*by its language.*" And in this case, unlike the first chapter of Genesis, the language is obvious. The fifth, tenth, and eleventh chapters of Genesis "give us, in plain language, *genealogies* and *chronology*, without qualification. [They teach] *genealogies* and *chronology*, as clearly as language can speak, which are manifestly wrong."[48]

The evangelical battle against chronology was hopeless from the beginning. Even Gliddon and Nott eventually lost interest and began to attack Protestant orthodoxy on another front. By the early 1850s, both had developed a compelling fascination with physical anthropology and had decided to collaborate on a study of the origin and races of men. That work was more than a denial of things as superficial as the dates of the Old Testament patriarchs. *Types of Mankind* gnawed at one of the pillars of the Christian faith—the nature of man himself.

9

The Unity of Man

Americans were committed in two ways to the unity of the human race. The Jeffersonian tradition placed a great emphasis on man's essential oneness. Although deists did not believe that the Bible was inspired and infallible revelation from God, they *did* believe in a primordial "Adam and Eve," specially created and different from all other creatures.

Evangelical Protestants, however, had an even stronger vested interest in the unity of humanity. Some Protestants conceded that Christianity could survive scientific attacks on the infallibility and historicity of the Bible. By the 1830s, many evangelicals were admitting that the Holy Scripture could be supported without an absolutely literal interpretation of every word. But the unity of origin of the human race was a different matter. Other abandoned or challenged doctrines of orthodoxy were part of the "evidences" of the truth of the Christian system, but the oneness of man was a fundamental part of the system itself. "For by one man sin entered the world, and death by sin," the Apostle Paul had written, "so also by one man shall all be made alive."[1] To deny that all men descended from a single set of parents was to destroy one of the most important parts of the plan of salvation. Virtually every ten-year-old evangelical child knew that sin began with the disobedience of Adam and Eve. For older evangelicals, Original Sin was an "inherited characteristic," passed from Adam to all his progeny in the same way as blue eyes, flat feet, or diabetes. The only difference was that everybody had Original Sin, because, as the Bible clearly said, everyone had descended from the first great sinner.

Henry Bronson stated the doctrine as clearly as anyone. A physician and historian who would someday be a medical professor at Yale, young Bronson was called upon in 1831 to review a book written by one of the heretics—Charles Caldwell's *Thoughts on the Original Unity of the Human Race*. "The *evening* and *morning* referred to by Moses, may have constituted a longer period than our present day of twenty-four hours," admitted Bronson, "but we must abandon the whole record, if we hesitate to admit, that . . . a single pair was created, that their children peopled the earth, that all mankind with the exception of a single family were destroyed by a deluge and that from this family 'were the nations divided in the earth.' "[2] Writing twenty years later, Princeton professor of rhetoric Matthew Boyd Hope was just as blunt: "we have no warrant for offering the salvation of the Bible to any but the race of whom it is the genuine history."[3]

If evangelicals were going to yield to the scientists, it would not be on the question of human origins. Other apparently heterodox theories split the evangelical church and finally won many of the orthodox as converts. But in the case of the unity of man there was no such inevitability—the evidence always seemed to point both ways.

Protestant solidarity undoubtedly accounted for Samuel George Morton's reluctance to commit himself on the unity question. Morton, a brilliant and affable Philadelphia physician and anatomist, had developed an obsession with crania. He collected everything he could find—first animals, then the different races and tribes of men. A quiet, gentle homebody, more interested in his medical practice and his hobby than in making any dramatic scientific announcements, Morton was nevertheless destined to be involved in controversy. In the early 1820s he began publishing the results of his studies.

By carefully measuring various skulls Morton found that he was easily able to identify the tribe to which a particular head belonged. That was so because there were obvious, permanent differences in cranial types. Morton publicized his findings in a way sufficiently undramatic that few evangelicals would become excited by what he himself had to say. But some of his findings were unambiguous: there were great differences between the crania of widely separated races, such as the Negro and the Caucasian. Furthermore, three-thousand-year-old crania taken from the tombs of Egypt, which contained both Negroes and Caucasians, showed these differences just as dramatically as the crania of the present day. Since the flood was only four thousand years in history, Morton concluded that the diversity of cranial types "must have been effected in at most a thousand years." This finding led Morton to disagree with Samuel Stanhope Smith, who had argued that the "varieties of complexion and figure" in the human species were the result of adaptation to new climates.[4] Rather, said Morton, "each race was adapted from the beginning to its peculiar local destination," and this adaptation was "independent of external causes."[5]

Morton's most controversial suggestion came in his book on the skulls of American Indians, *Crania Americana*. After a long study of physical measurements together with anthropology and migration patterns, Morton concluded that "the American race differs essentially from all others, not excepting the Mongolian."[6] This quietly-stated finding challenged long-standing scientific and religious theories that American Indians were Asians who had once migrated to the Americas, either by boat or else via a land-bridge that no longer existed. Morton was implying that the Indians of North America had no connection with the children of Noah—that they were not even descendants of Adam and Eve.

Morton did not carry his argument to its logical end. Inevitably, however, those who accepted his reasoning, that each race was adapted "from the beginning" to its immediate environment and that this adaptation was independent of external causes, would accept a final, more dramatic conclusion: each race had been created specifically for the area it now inhabits. There had been as many creations as there are races of men.

Obviously, the members of both sides of the controversy were theists. The issue was not whether or not there had been a supernatural creation, but *how many* of them. In fact, the charges of excessive supernaturalism inevitably fell on the heterodox advocates of multiple creations. Morton, Gliddon, Agassiz, even Josiah Nott, were at least nominally religious. Each believed that his own particular scientific theory could be harmonized with the Christian faith. Furthermore, they were all catastrophists: they all believed that supernatural explanation could be a useful part of science.

But to the evangelicals, the polygenesists may as well have been Voltaire or David Hume. Agassiz was the champion of orthodoxy against uniformitarianism and the evolutionary hypothesis, and evangelicals quoted him freely. But he risked his reputation with them when he advocated multiple, extrabiblical creations. Nott, a self-proclaimed parson-hater from the beginning, was scorned by conservative and moderate Protestants alike.

Evangelicals themselves had to walk a rather narrow path between a crossfire of heresies. Most orthodox Protestants were committed to Smith's original thesis of 1787: that climatic adaptation is quite adequate to explain varieties of color and form. But they stopped short of evolution. This put them in a difficult position. Emphasize the fixity and permanence of species too much, and one invites the heresy of multiple creation. On the other hand, too much trust in the notion that organisms could adapt to climatic conditions and pass these adaptations on to their offspring led to the equally heretical developmental hypothesis. Evangelicals who combatted one heresy nearly always felt obliged to assure their readers that they were not advocates of the other.

The orthodox defenders of the unity of the race invariably supported one of two broad positions. At the evangelical extreme was a significant number of crusaders who believed that all scientific investigation of the question was improper and anti-Christian. One must find his answer in the Bible and nowhere else. For example, in 1850 Matthew Boyd Hope was almost as critical of John Bachman, a scientific defender of the orthodox position, as he was of the enemy. Bachman had chosen the right side but the wrong battleground. He had tried to answer the theories of Morton and his followers by means of scientific analysis of the nature of species. The nature of man's origin, said Hope, "is not simply a question of interpretation. It enters into the heart of the very object for which the scriptures were given." When the Bible touches "incidentally" on a scientific question, such as the age of the earth, there might be some room for compromise. But the case of human origins is altogether different. The Bible does not touch on that incidentally; it is at the very heart of scriptural history. Once the Christian realizes that, said Hope, then he knows that he must rely on the Bible alone for his answer.

Hope conceded that nature and scripture are equally reliable data sources. From that it would follow that a thorough analysis of any question must include the study of both science and the Bible. However, in those cases when the Bible is much more detailed in its historical presentation than nature is in its empirical evidence, then the answer must come from the Bible. For example, the scientific decision as to whether the China goose and the common goose are of the same species rests on "a slight anatomical difference in the structure of the larynx." In this case the anatomical evidence is all that is available and the decision must rest on it. "But supposing we had a clear, unquestioned and continuous history, established by an indefinite amount of evidence, of the origin of these different varieties from a single stock?" The small bit of anatomical evidence would surely not "compel us to set aside that history as false." By analogy, the supposition that the races of men are different species rests on differences no greater than those between the two varieties of geese, but the Bible contains clear and unbroken evidence of their unity. Unity is, in this case, the logical conclusion.[7]

Furthermore, the biblical evidence was direct, while the scientific evidence was only indirect. Most 1840s definitions of *species* implied unity of origin; however, species were identified and catalogued on the basis of anatomical characteristics. As a result, taxonomists were using criteria for determining species that were very different from the criteria established by definition. "Unity of origin" or "common parenthood" was, quite simply, unverifiable. Botanists and zoologists depended implicitly on some kind of linking argument, such as "similarity of structure implies unity of origin."[8] But that statement was itself unverifiable and highly debatable. Other attempts at a definition of *species*, like Agassiz's "idea in the mind of God," or Morton's "primordial organic form," were even more difficult to use in any empirical situation.

This lack of clarity was a real boon to orthodoxy. Rather than seeing a united scientific front opposed to a literal Bible, as was the case in geology, the orthodox saw only isolated heretical scientists unable to agree among themselves about what constitutes species, about how separate species can be identified, or about how organisms adapt. Alonzo Chapin found it most presumptuous of Agassiz to use "Science teaches" at the beginning of his heterodox statements about man. It was quite plain that "science" did not know what it taught. "One [heretical scientist] holds that the proof which establishes identity of race in the domestic animals, establishes it in regard to man. Another denies this, and declares that there must have been at least three *original centers of creation*." Chapin was obviously entertaining himself. Other scientists, he mused, "suppose *five*, some *seven, eight*, and even *eleven*." If anyone wanted the correct answer to the problem, science should be the last place to look.[9]

The conservative evangelicals who did use the Bible alone to resolve the question of human origins believed that several incidents in the book of Genesis might satisfactorily explain racial differences. The first of these was the "Mark of Cain." After Cain killed his brother Abel, God put a Mark on his forehead and sent him away from the rest of his family. Was it not possible, suggested some Protestants, that the "Mark" refers symbolically to the fact that Cain would become father of the inferior races? A second and much more believable account of racial origins grew out of the Tower of Babel incident described in Genesis eleven. In order to make sure that men would populate the entire earth and not congregate in one small area, God confused their language. Many evangelicals in the early nineteenth century believed that the Tower of Babel incident explained the origin of human language differences, but some believed that the story explained differences in physical characteristics as well. If God could do one, he could certainly do the other.

The most popular biblical explanation of racial differences, however, came from the story of Noah's curse upon Canaan. After the flood Noah, no doubt relaxing after a difficult voyage, drank himself into a sleepy stupor. His second son, Ham, found him lying naked and inebriated in his tent. He ridiculed his father and told Noah's other two sons, Shem and Japheth, about his indiscretion. Shem and Japheth judiciously covered their father's naked body. When Noah awakened and learned of Ham's disrespect he cursed Ham's son Canaan, prophesying that "a slave of slaves shall he be to his brother."[10] A long Christian tradition developed that blackness was the primary result of Canaan's curse. By the nineteenth century, many evangelicals believed that the descendants of Canaan had migrated to Ethiopia, and that the black men of Africa constituted the greater portion of accursed Canaanites. For example, one southern writer tried to convince his readers that Canaan should be "identified with the Ethiopian" and that because of his curse the black man is inferior in virtually every respect to the Caucasian. The writer absolutely rejected any claim that Africans were a "distinct species": "such a conclusion cannot be correct and the Bible be true." However, he agreed fully with Morton that the Caucasian and African are permanently distinct. "The nerves of the spinal marrow, and the abdominal viscera, being more voluminous than in other races, and the brain being ten percent less in volume and in weight," the black man is necessarily "more under the influence of his instincts, appetites, and *animality* than other races of men." But one did not need either climatic adaptation or multiple creation to believe that. The answer was plain to anyone who would bother to read the book of Genesis.[11]

Many moderate evangelicals, however, believed that scientific evidence was as important as biblical evidence in explaining and defending the unity of man. John Bachman, Josiah Nott's most formidable opponent, tried to answer Nott's arguments completely in the scientific arena.[12] At the same time, theologians who were interested in science tried to show that the Bible's statements could easily be harmonized with the latest scientific discoveries.

While John Bachman's work was the most elaborate scientific defense of the evangelical position, Thomas Smyth's *The Unity of the Human Races* was the most sophisticated combination of theological and scientific arguments. Smyth, an Irish-born Presbyterian whose family immigrated to the United States in the late 1820s, had been able to get an education at Princeton College and Seminary. By 1850 he was a respected minister in Charleston, South Carolina. Like Bachman, Smyth believed that the strongest enemy was Josiah Clark Nott. Smith had Nott's theories most specifically in mind when he wrote his study. Smyth's chief liability was that he was not a scientist. As a result, he drew several of his scientific illustrations from the works of older scientists, many of which were outdated or in disrepute by 1850.

The Rev. Smyth was one of the few evangelicals who believed that the questions of "unity of species" and "unity of origin" were not identical. This distinction had come about mostly as a result of Agassiz, whose "centres of creation" theory suggested that identical species were the products of different creations in separate geographical areas. To Agassiz the *species* question and the *origin* question had "almost no connection with each other," in spite of the fact that evangelicals constantly "confounded" them. Smyth agreed with Agassiz. He believed that most of the scientific evidence pertained to the "species" or "type" questions and could therefore not be strictly applied to questions of genealogy. Smyth conceded that if one should prove conclusively that all men were of the same species, heterodox scientists could still assert that they were of distinct origins. Bachman's scientific approach to the question generally ignored the distinction between origin and type. Because Bachman had been interested in showing that all of the human race were of the same species, he merely assumed that they all came from the same parent stock. After all, the prevailing "empirical" definitions of the term all linked *species* closely with the idea of a common parent stock. Only Agassiz's more idealistic notion, which allowed for separate creations of the same species, separated the type question and the origins question.[13]

Evangelicals, however, were not satisfied by the belief that all men were merely of the same species; they had to believe that all men were descended from the same parents as well. Smyth suggested that the *species* question was "a question of scientific observation and induction." However, "the question of origin" could be "determined only by the evidence of Scripture, history, tradition." While Bachman had addressed himself chiefly to the species question, Smyth was more interested in the problem of origins.[14]

Smyth's theological defense of unity was as good a collection of biblical quotations as any evangelical could assemble. He argued that it was clearly intrinsic to Christian orthodoxy that God had made all the nations of the earth from "one blood," which obviously implied that all men were of the same family. Smyth thereupon launched into a lengthy Old Testament exegesis designed to show that the Bible could not be read, as Agassiz had suggested, as an account of only one fragment of the human race. To do that, he concluded, would be to say that only the descendants of Adam were fallen and sinful. Furthermore, the promise of salvation is extended only to those whom the Bible describes explicitly—those who are literally of "one blood" with Adam and who are figuratively of "one blood" with Christ.

Most orthodox clergymen were immensely relieved by Smyth's work. English theologian and self-taught geologist John Pye Smith found the arguments convincing, although it was apparent that the writer had been "hurried and distressed." As a result much of his scientific evidence appeared "either uninformed or careless."[15] James McCosh, a Scottish Presbyterian minister who would move to the United States in 1868, believed that Smyth's book was "well written and well reasoned"—certainly a satisfactory answer to orthodoxy's opponents.[16]

The lecturers on the evidences of Christianity at the University of Virginia also addressed the unity question. The Rev. Thomas V. Moore, pastor of the Presbyterian Church in Richmond and a self-trained naturalist, discussed the alleged discrepancies between biblical and scientific evidence. Most of Moore's lecture was highly derivative. He borrowed heavily from John Bachman and came to virtually identical conclusions about the unity of man. Like Bachman and most other evangelicals, Moore believed in limited adaptation. Two great things are characteristic of nature, he said: "one is the great flexibility and adaptability of the law of resemblance within certain limits; the other is, the rigid, inflexible permanence of the law beyond these limits."

Then Moore rather adroitly launched into the problem of supernaturalism and scientific explanation. The position of the evangelical extremists, who tried to explain racial differences on the basis of the Bible alone, was essentially unfalsifiable. It was rejected by more moderate Protestants, but not because it could not explain the given data. On the contrary, it performed that task remarkably well. The Curse theories and the Tower of Babel explanation were unsatisfactory simply because they lay outside the boundaries of scientific investigation. They relied much too heavily on divine tampering with natural processes. By the 1850s, most moderate evangelicals were rejecting excessively supernatural explanations in geology. Moore was saying the same thing about physical anthropology. The multiple origins advocates, however, were also relying heavily on supernaturalism. Moore noted that Agassiz's "centres of creation" theory and Gliddon's multiple origins theory both depended on a number of separate, divine creations. But that suggestion was certainly just as supernaturalistic and no more scientific than the Tower of Babel theory. Furthermore, the Curse of Canaan and the Tower of Babel hypotheses at least were based on miracles recounted in the Bible. Agassiz and his friends were suggesting miracles the Bible did not even mention.

The advocates of diversity were clearly at a scientific disadvantage. According to Moore, the theory of climatic adaptation was the "least supernatural" of all theories respecting the development of early man. Moore conceded that the adaptation theory might involve a limited amount of supernaturalism; for example, perhaps at one time organisms adapted more rapidly than they do today. However, the adaptation theory in any case was not as supernaturalistic as the theories of the evangelical extremists. In turn, however, the extremist theories were themselves not as supernaturalistic as the multiple origins theory, which required several divine interventions. Having made this point, Moore created a new version of Ockham's Razor as an empirical principle: "If we must assert an interposition of divine power, as our opponents contend, the rules of hypothesis require us not to assume a higher cause of interposition if a lower is sufficient to explain the effect." To Moore, the Tower of Babel explanation certainly demanded a "lower" level of divine interposition than the multiple origins hypothesis; but the climatic adaptation theory could succeed with a "lower" level still. The last theory was clearly the most empirical of the three, and therefore the most plausible.[17]

The important word in Moore's principle, however, was "sufficient." Agassiz, Morton, Gliddon, and Nott denied that climatic adaptation was "sufficient to explain the effect." Moore disagreed, and he spent most of his lecture trying to establish that climatic adaptation could indeed explain the result adequately. However, even if the adaptation theory were disproved, he said, that would not justify the multiple origins position. He had his opponents both ways. Ultimately, the excessive supernaturalism in Agassiz's position proved to be its undoing—particularly in the 1860s and 1870s, when many scientists found Darwin's theory the least supernaturalistic and the most scientific of all explanations.

Most orthodox Christians knew very little about anatomy or paleontology. When Nott and Agassiz attacked the unity of the human race they had to rely on a few specialists like John Bachman to speak in their behalf. But a large number of Protestants were familiar with another, somewhat less technical field: comparative philology. Most clergymen and many educated laymen had studied at least one of the biblical languages. For some of them, an introduction to Greek or Hebrew became the starting point for an impressive expertise in linguistic science.

In the eighteenth century, deists had reasoned that one way to prove the unity of mankind was by showing that all the world's languages point back to a single source. By 1800 most philologists believed that the languages of Europe and Asia had a common base. The problem areas were the more mysterious continents, particularly Africa and the New World. Since American philosophers had the American Indians close at hand, they naturally studied New World languages. Thomas Jefferson argued in *Notes on the State of Virginia* that Indian languages were mutually related and very similar to the languages of Eastern Asia.[18] A few years later one of Jefferson's friends, Benjamin Smith Barton, reached a more specific conclusion. Barton, a Philadelphia physician and botanist, was also a charter member of the American Philosophical Society. In 1803 the Society decided to make the study of American Indians one of its most important objectives. Barton wrote a paper in which he compared Indian languages to several Asian languages. He concluded that the American Indians were really Persians who had long ago left their homes.[19]

Evangelicals agreed with Jefferson and Barton that philology could demonstrate the unity of man. However, orthodox Protestants had a radically different view of human language itself. Deists generally believed that language was a product of man's reason, a creation of his own mind. As a result, Enlightenment thinkers explained the diversification of languages in purely natural terms: as a function of cultural complexity, of communication or the lack of it, or simply as the product of the diverging cultures of growing nations. Evangelicals, however, believed that language was a gift from God—divinely created and developed as a tool for humans. Although they might use natural explanations for linguistic development, they generally emphasized supernatural explanations as well, such as the incident at the Tower of Babel. Most evangelicals did not believe that God radically changed human language at that time, but rather that he simply modified it enough so that different families could no longer communicate with one another. Thus the languages sounded different, even though they shared many common roots and structures. Since this single incident accounted for both man's linguistic diversity and his geographical dispersion, evangelicals believed that scholars could trace the wanderings of ancient man by looking back into the post-Babel development of his language. Both man's movements and his speech should point back to the Fertile Crescent, and in general philology seemed to show exactly that.

The implications of the opposing position were relatively clear. Both Agassiz's "centres of creation" theory and Gliddon's and Nott's theories of separate creations implied that separate races had developed independently of one another. According to Agassiz, the American Indian was unique to America; therefore his language should have no more than a few coincidental points in common with the languages of Europe and Asia. Nott's idea that the American Indians or the Africans were distinct species carried the same corollary. However, by the middle of the nineteenth century, evangelicals had plenty of evidence to attack the multiple-origins advocates on this point.

Naturally polygenesists tried to explain away the underlying similarities in the world's languages. Agassiz himself suggested that the "analogy of the sounds" as well as of the structures of various languages derived exclusively from the "similarity in the organs of speech," which causes men to produce "naturally the same sound." Men's sounds are similar, said Agassiz, in exactly the same way that the brayings of asses and the barkings of different dogs are similar. Furthermore, some groups, notably the American Indians, are able to utter sounds that outsiders are completely unable to duplicate, even after extensive practice. To Agassiz this suggested more than simple developmental differences in languages. It revealed a basic difference in the structure of vocal organs, even though these organs are, on the whole, quite similar. Thus men's languages differ "in the same proportions as their organs of speech are variously modified.[20]

The most elaborate attempt in an American work to explain linguistic similarities in this way was contained in Gliddon's and Nott's *Indigenous Races of the Earth*. In 1854 these advocates of human diversity had attempted to publish a final word on the subject. They collected evidence of their own, commissioned several articles from noted American and European scientists, and published a massive, ponderous book, *Types of Mankind*, dedicated to the late Samuel George Morton. The book contained little new science but was designed to summarize and sharpen all the existing arguments in favor of multiple origins. Its immediate success and the uproar that followed inspired the co-authors to assemble a sequel, *Indigenous Races of the Earth*, published in 1857.[21] It was a cluttered book, filled with color pictures of monkeys and savages, maps that located the world's discrete races, and dozens of drawings of Morton's crania. Since they had overlooked the language issue in 1854, Nott and Gliddon were determined that it would be given adequate coverage in *Indigenous Races*. They commissioned Alfred Maury, the librarian of the French Imperial Institute and an expert linguist, to prepare an extensive analysis of the arguments from philology.

Like Agassiz, Maury believed that comparative philologists had generally failed to distinguish "that which belongs to the very constitution of speech" from that "which appertains to such or to such another given form of utterance." The development of a language follows laws that are as fixed, Maury explained, as the laws of physics. Early man "endeavored to imitate everything that surrounded him." Tribes in no way related to one another would naturally use similar sounds to describe the same object or process.

Nevertheless, even Maury admitted that more than coincidental similarities existed between groups of languages covering vast portions of the globe, such as all of Europe including Turkey and the Balkans, all of the Orient, and all of Australasia. He acknowledged that African and Oriental languages contained many similarities to one another, but he was able to account for these with historical incidents, such as the early Phoenician conquests of northern Africa, and of the Arabs in Ethiopia. The American languages gave Maury the most difficulty, and his treatment of them was noticeably brief. The only hypothesis he attacked was that significant similarities existed between Indian and African languages. He found these to be purely coincidental. Strangely enough, he did not even deal with the much more formidable suggestion—that American languages had been derived from Asian bases.

Maury's conclusions about the origins of language harmonized neatly with Agassiz's theory of the origins of the human races. Maury found two discrete language bases serving the "white" race: the Indo-European and the Semitic; two serving the "yellow" races: the monosyllabic family and the Ougro-Tartar. He believed the African tongues to be indigenous to the black races of the African continent, and that the Australian languages were confined to Australasia. Finally, he concluded that the American Indians spoke languages unique to the New World. Within each of these great linguistic families was a vast complex of common roots and structures; however, there was little more than coincidental or historically explainable correspondence *between* the families. Maury's article was the most elaborate and sophisticated statement of the multiple-creation position, and it was the argument that evangelical philologists were most eager to destroy.[22]

Most of the philological evidence gathered in the first half of the nineteenth century favored the evangelicals. They did not have to rely exclusively on the sketchy researches of Barton and Jefferson. More complete and much more scientific studies had been made in England. In 1813 James Cowles Prichard, a British physician and amateur ethnologist, had argued convincingly that all the world's languages had developed from a common source.[23] Furthermore, Prichard suggested that the heaviest burden of proof was clearly on those who doubted man's unity; their premise was that no relationships existed between the various language families. The defenders of unity had only to affirm that there indeed were some relationships. For Prichard that seemed to be a simple task. He believed that those who denied the unity of language usually studied languages in a superficial manner. They invariably argued from the mere fact that languages sounded so different. Prichard published tables to show that languages as dissimilar as the German and the Syrian, the German and the Mongolian, or the Greek and the Chinese, actually had many common roots. In 1823 the German philologist Julius Klaproth suggested that these similarities in roots showed that the "idioms of nations" had been "allied by physical structure and historical traditions." Furthermore, said Klaproth, this alliance was definitely "from antediluvian times." Klaproth then speculated that floods before the Noachian deluge forced people to separate and develop different languages. That argument inevitably degenerated into an absurd mixture of Genesis and secular history. But Klaproth's point was clear to Prichard, who incorporated it into later editions of his work: men had a common tongue at exactly the same time that, according to Agassiz, they were developing in ignorance of one another.[24]

Prichard went on to identify two kinds of linguistic relationships. The first was a relation between languages that have "no connexion in their vocabularies" but have "a remarkable and extensive analogy in the laws of their grammatical construction." Secondly were those groups of languages having "little or no resemblance in grammative structure, but an extensive correspondence in the vocabularies." Prichard also identified some language pairs as similar in both vocabulary and structure, and some as similar in neither. His analysis and taxonomy of languages told him two things. First, the fact that languages were related at all indicated that they had come from a common source. Secondly, the fact that many of the relationships were very weak, pertaining only to vocabulary but not to structure, or vice-versa, revealed that the relationships were very ancient.

Prichard made one additional suggestion: "the number and diversity of languages is nearly in proportion to the barbarism of nations." That is, while civilized nations tended to have unified, nationally-understood languages, barbarians generally had tribal, locally-understood tongues. This, said Prichard, revealed that the primitive state of mankind was civilized and not savage. Gradually, as people became more savage and war-like, and as communications between them broke down, the languages of different nations became increasingly unlike one another. This supported the evangelical belief that man had been created civilized, but had gradually "fallen" into barbarism.[25]

Nicholas Cardinal Wiseman combined the work of Prichard and other philologists into *Twelve Lectures*, which he delivered in London in 1835. Wiseman's *Lectures* became a very popular work of natural theology in America. Wiseman developed the thesis that most evangelicals would argue in the 1840s and 1850s: "that mankind descended from one family—spoke but one language; that, in consequence of their being united in a design which accorded not with the views of Providence, the Almighty confounded their speech." However, this confusion "consisted, not so much in the abolition of the common tongue, as in the introduction of such a variety of modifications in it as would suffice to effect the dispersion of the human race."

Wiseman began his book with a sketch of the development of comparative philology. Throughout the eighteenth century, he wrote, researchers had believed that languages were unlike one another and could not have come from a common source. To "a religious observer," philology had "the appearance of a study daily receding from sound doctrine." However, by the turn of the century "a ray of light was penetrating into the chaos of materials thrown together by collectors." As a result of philologists' more careful attention to the roots of European words, "it was clearly demonstrated that one speech . . . pervaded a considerable portion of Europe and Asia" and united a large number of "nations professing the most irreconcilable religions . . . and bearing but slight resemblance in physiognomy and colour." In short, the discovery of an Indo-European base was a great boost to the advocates of the unity of mankind. By 1835, Wiseman believed, philological science, "instead of being perplexed with a multiplicity of languages," had "now reduced them to certain very large groups, each comprising a great variety of languages formerly thought to be unconnected." Indeed, the science seemed to be progressing to the point that it would diminish "still farther any apparent hostility between the number of languages and the history of the dispersion [the Tower of Babel]." The most recent findings were that the "entire Celtic family" of languages were "only a province of the Indo-European," that the Irish tongue was closely related to the Phoenician-Hebrew, and that many African words and Hebrew words had common roots.

From Thomas Young, a British Egyptologist, Wiseman borrowed a mechanism for determining the extent to which similarity of roots can indicate unity of origin. After considerable linguistic analysis, Young decided that if two languages had a single common root, little could be said about their origin. However, "if three words appear to be identical, it would then be more than ten to one that they must be derived in both cases from some parent language. . . . Six words would give more than 1700 chances to one, and eight, near 100,000." Although Wiseman found these conclusions a little "too definite and bold," he nevertheless agreed that even a small number of identical roots in two languages was a relatively sure indication that they had a common ancestor. By combining Young's probabilities with the work of Benjamin Smith Barton and German philologist Johann Vater, Wiseman became convinced that eighty-three American languages had common roots with various Asiatic, African, and European languages.[26]

In the course of his lectures Wiseman described a vast and complex hierarchy of the world's languages. Local, tribal dialects were related to each other in direct ways, and formed families of languages. These families in turn were related to one another and formed still larger groups. At the top of this pyramid was a single, primordial (but as yet undiscovered) language—the surest proof that all of mankind had proceeded from a single source.

Perhaps the most typical American response to Wiseman's book came from Moses Ashley Curtis. For once, said Curtis, orthodox Americans were not fighting a heresy from abroad. Multiple creationism was an American belief, closely tied to

American politics and racial ideas. Curtis, a Hillsboro, North Carolina, botanist and friend of Asa Gray, compared the work of a foreigner, Wiseman, with that of a thoroughbred American, Josiah Clark Nott. Curtis had to lament the fact that America was fathering and spreading heresies, rather than defending itself against foreign enemies. He saw in Wiseman the great hope of American evangelicalism. Curtis was aghast that evangelicals, in spite of their training, had not made a more aggressive use of comparative philology. Through philology, "nations which were before supposed to be severed by irreconcilable dissimilarities, have been proved to have originated in a common stock." Furthermore, "a demonstration of the common origin" of the earth's languages is "of necessity a demonstration of the unity of the human race." This kind of "collateral proof" was almost too much to hope for, and those who wished to defend orthodoxy from scientific heresy had better acquaint themselves with the new science immediately.[27]

Having determined from Wiseman that "no injury can ... accrue to Christianity from a proper study of the sciences," Curtis temporarily dropped the unity of language issue and turned to Nott's *Two Lectures,* a book that was obviously not a "proper study." Curtis found that Nott was not only an infidel, but a careless biologist as well. Nott had argued that since Negroes and Caucasians were distinct species, mulattoes were therefore hybrids or "mules," and were thus of limited fertility. Curtis demonstrated with an ample amount of evidence that mulattoes were generally just as fertile as anyone else. Curtis's arguments were challenging enough to elicit a quick reply from Nott— a reply, however, containing so much sarcasm and so little science that it reveals that Nott had been placed on the defensive.[28]

It would not be left entirely to English philologists to follow in the steps of Benjamin Smith Barton and Jefferson. At least two prominent Americans devoted parts of their lives in the 1830s and 1840s to studies of the languages of the American Indians. Neither Albert Gallatin nor Henry R. Schoolcraft was a full-time philologist. Both, however, had an extensive interest and an unusual competence in the languages of the North American Indians.

By 1836 Gallatin was an old man. Once a colorful world traveler, ambassador, and deal maker, he had retired from public life in the mid-1820s. Like his slightly older peer, Thomas Jefferson, Gallatin ended his career as an American statesman by doing the things he had always wanted to do most. He engaged in a wide variety of intellectual pursuits. His extensive correspondence with Alexander von Humboldt on various questions of anthropology led him to believe that the American Indian was the key to the unity of language question. Gallatin threw himself into the study so diligently that soon he considered publishing a dictionary of the languages of the Indians. The dictionary never materialized, but in 1836 the American Antiquarian Society helped him arrange and publish his researches as *A Synopsis of the Indian Tribes within the United States East of the Rocky Mountains.*[29]

Gallatin was no speculator. He purposely avoided the larger question of physical unity. Nevertheless, he did find an elaborate system of borrowing among the Indian languages. Gallatin's work led him to two conclusions. First, that Indian languages were "beyond a doubt" of a "common origin." Secondly, that the primordial language from which they had developed was very ancient.

Part of Gallatin's work on Indian languages was included in Henry R. Schoolcraft's *History, Condition and Prospects of the Indian Tribes of the United States.*[30] Schoolcraft did not have the time that Gallatin had for leisurely scholarship, but he probably knew more about American Indians than anyone of his day. Born in New York, he was interested at one time or another in a wide variety of technical fields, especially glass-making and geology. He ended up as an explorer, and developed such a valuable understanding of the Indians of the Northwest Territory that in 1822 he was appointed Indian Agent for the tribes of that region. By 1836 he was Michigan's Superintendent for Indian Affairs. For many years after its publication, Schoolcraft's *History, Condition and Prospects* was the best authority available on American Indians, compiled by a man who had lived among them for thirty years and had even taken an Indian wife. Schoolcraft was more speculative than Gallatin, and he suggested a mechanism for using languages to "simulate a historical chart, upon which we can trace back the tribes to the period of their original dispersion over this continent." Such a chart would show that a "single genus or family of tribes, speaking one common language," had settled the entire North Atlantic seaboard, and that only two other such families occupied the remainder of America east of the Mississippi.[31] Although Schoolcraft was not able to extend his researches far enough to find unity among these three early languages, he was convinced that future scholarship would show that a single Oriental protolanguage was the ancestor of all the native American languages.

Neither Gallatin nor Schoolcraft was particularly interested in the religious implications of their work. But both of them supplied important ammunition for later evangelicals who *did* believe that the study of Indian languages was an important support for evangelical theology. Because of the extensive and thorough work of philologists, language became evangelicalism's most effective weapon in the battle over the unity of humanity. Consequently, they, and not the polygenesists, made the most use of philological arguments. For example, Congregationalist Samuel Forry, a New York City physician, wrote his "Mosaic Account of the Unity of the Human Race, Confirmed by the Natural History of the American Aborigines" in order to show that native Americans were really Asians who had accidentally drifted across the ocean several millenia ago. He cited several examples of shipwrecked sailors who had floated aimlessly for thousands of miles before they were rescued. Having established satisfactory minimum conditions, Forry believed it was no great task to show that American Indians were really Asian. After surveying some of the physical arguments Forry turned to language. Here he found that the most striking similarity among the languages was "agglutination"—a name given by Wilhelm von Humboldt to the extensive interrelationships languages have in the structures of verb forms. Forry believed he had discovered one hundred seventy Indian words, "the roots of which appear to be the same" as roots in various other languages. Such analogy was certainly "not accidental."[32]

Forry relied heavily on Wilhelm von Humboldt's theories of the origin and development of languages. Both Wilhelm and his more famous brother Alexander had done pioneering work in comparative philology, but Wilhelm's work was the more innovative and useful. Unlike most comparative philologists of the early nineteenth century, Wilhelm was more interested in linguistic structure than he was in common root words. A thoroughgoing Romantic, Humboldt was able to find "unity" in language as easily as Cuvier and Agassiz were able to find it in fossil forms. Most Americans who read Wilhelm von Humboldt missed one important point: Humboldt's theories about the unity of language said no more about the physical unity of mankind than Agassiz's theories about the unity of the human species said about the single-creation theory. While Agassiz believed in "absolute species," Humboldt believed in "absolute language"—a language that is a "gift fallen to [men] as a result of their innate destiny." Humboldt's interest in linguistic structure derived from the fact that he looked at a particular language as itself an "organism," a complete unit incapable of being analyzed piecemeal.

Like Cuvier and Agassiz, Humboldt built his science on presuppositions that made it quite easy to separate "metaphysical" and "physical" unity. The first of these described the essential "oneness" of man, the second described his physical origin and genealogical history. For the evangelicals this kind of metaphysics was nonsense. Doctrines as "metaphysical" as Original Sin depended quite literally on the physical unity of man. When they read Wilhelm Humboldt's thesis about the unity of language, they understood only one thing: all of language must have developed from a single protolanguage; therefore, all of mankind must have a common ancestor.

Humboldt, on the contrary, found it much more difficult to justify the obvious diversity of languages than their underlying unity. Since languages are organisms and since organisms of a single species are very similar to one another, it would follow that all languages should be similar. Furthermore, Humboldt believed firmly that language is a function of man's perception of the world. Since the perceptions of all men are fundamentally similar, it would follow that languages should be similar. The organic nature of language, combined with the unity of human perception, explained language's underlying structural unity. But that was more speculation than the evangelical Americans cared for. They appropriated Humboldt's conclusions but paid little attention to the method by which he arrived at them.[33]

The science of Romantics like Humboldt was in retreat, however, as was much of the anthropology of the polygenesists. Orthodox Protestants did well in the battle over the unity of man, better than they did in any other scientific field. Eventually, scientists would universally accept as fact that all men are of one species. In a more limited way, they would come to believe even the most important thesis: that all men had originated from a single source. Ultimately, though, orthodox Protestants lost the war. The theory of evolution by natural selection would support Samuel Stanhope Smith's theory of adaptability. It would speak favorably to John Bachman and Asa Gray, and unfavorably to George Gliddon and Louis Agassiz. But Darwinian evolution so thoroughly changed the question that the evangelical victory was more awful to them than defeat would have been.

10

Coming from Nowhere

For Christians the problem of evolutionary theories has been a problem of understanding history. The entire Christian system depends on a process that has a sudden beginning, a logical development, and a definite end. The evangelical world-view insists that God and the world are absolutely different, and one of these differences is that only God is eternal, while the world is bounded by time at both ends. Every event in Christian history points either backward to the creation or forward to Christ's second coming. Christians trying to live holy lives always looked back first—to Christ, the Patriarchs, or the Apostles, as examples of Christian excellence. Then they looked forward, to the day when all time would stop. The vision of this historical process so completely dominated Christian thought that its followers have always interpreted virtually everything in terms of source, causation, process, direction, or goal. It was important to Christians that God willed the world into existence at a specific point in time, that man was created with an historical purpose, that Adam's single sinful act was the cause of all the world's misery, that the preparation of the world for Christ was a process affecting the lives of everyone, and that man was currently living in the middle of a similar current—another process with a specific goal in mind: the end of all history. Christianity's historicism is demonstrated nowhere better than in its theological debates over the Fall. It has never been enough that Christians should simply believe that man sinned and fell from God's grace. They always had to know why he fell. Did God cause man to disobey him? Did he give man free will, secretly foreknowing that eventually he would disobey? Calvinists may have gravitated toward one of these views, Arminians toward the other. But no orthodox Christian ever suggested that the Fall simply happened, that it was nothing more than an unfortunate accident.

God's historical purpose was particularly apparent in man himself. Christians believed that man was conceived by God, created in a sudden and dramatic way, and pointed in the direction his life would lead him. Man was created for a purpose. The entire human family from beginning to end was tied together in the Plan of Salvation, both the Fall and the promise. Not only was history important, man was a very important part of history.

Evolutionary theories threatened to rob man of this important position. To be sure, such theories did not always imply that man himself was the end-product of a development process. In fact, later in the nineteenth century several Protestants who reluctantly accepted evolution made man himself an exception. But few Christians in the early century bothered with such distinctions. To talk about transmutation of species was to talk about all species, including man. To accept a theory of evolution was to do more than acknowledge that many species of the original creation had long since become extinct and new ones had taken their places. To most evangelicals, the theory of evolution implied a fundamentally anti-Christian idea of man and of his purpose on earth.

At the same time, however, America's evangelicals were among the strongest spokesmen for a limited theory of development. The multiple creation theories about the origin of man on one side, and the developmental hypotheses on the other, placed orthodox Christians on a rather narrow line between two heresies. To resist suggestions that an organism could change in response to its environment rendered the present diversity of the human race inexplicable. If men could not adapt to their environment, then multiple creation was the only satisfactory means of explaining the African's blackness or the Eskimo's endomorphism. In opposition to Nott, Gliddon, and Agassiz, evangelicals like John Bachman insisted that species *could*, to a certain degree, adapt themselves to changing environments. That, however, was a risky suggestion. All that Lamarck had said was that organisms could adapt themselves to their environments, and that this capacity for adaptation was unlimited. As a result, one species changed gradually into another. Eventually the former became extinct, leaving behind only its fossil remains. The evangelical answer to Lamarck was to insist that the limits of adaptation be defined clearly: organisms could adapt, but only within a given species. The African, the Oriental, and the Caucasian were all distinctive adaptations of man to his environment, but all three were nevertheless of the same species.

The result of this limitation was that *varieties* were looked upon as artificial, as blurring gradually and insensibly from one into another, and as not particularly important except perhaps as a mechanism for determining what location a particular specimen had come from. The lines between *species*, on the other hand, were absolute and inviolable. Thus variation always approached some ill-defined limit and then stopped dead. In this way, conservative Protestant scientists tried to have things both ways— adaptation without transmutation.

Samuel Stanhope Smith had this theory of adaptation in mind in 1787 when he produced his *Essay on the Causes of the Variety of Complexion and Figure in the Human Species*. Smith believed that species were just as "absolute" as Agassiz was to believe fifty years later. He was a Scottish Realist, and species were "real" categories, just as unchangeable and permanent as the planets or the whole numbers. However, said Smith, "the Creator has adapted the pliancy of his work to meet the various situations in which he may have destined it to exist."[1] Obviously, no two individuals of the same species would live in identical situations. Since the perfect Creator makes each individual perfectly harmonious with its environment, it would follow that slight differences in environment would demand slight anatomical differences between individuals of the same species.

Later evangelicals would find that many of Smith's findings had to be updated, but in general the argument seemed good. Adaptation was a divinely directed natural process. It enabled an organism to adjust to its environment but did not permit so much adaptation that it would lose its specific identity.

Before Darwin the biggest threat to this paradigm did not come from transmutationalists but from multiple creationists. As a result evangelicals were not forced to spend a great deal of time dealing with developmental hypotheses, at least not until 1844 and the publication of Robert Chambers's *Vestiges of the Natural History of Creation.* Furthermore, if they were exposed to evolution before 1859, it was always of the directed, Lamarckian variety. Nothing as ostensibly godless as natural selection would threaten them until Darwin himself came along. For this reason, suggestions that developmental hypotheses in the earlier part of the century helped to clear the path for Darwin's theory have to be seen in perspective. The "evolution" of Erasmus Darwin, Lamarck, or later of Robert Chambers, was contained in a highly metaphysical, essentially theistic paradigm. It still held to some fundamentally Christian ideas that natural selection would reject: purpose in the universe, processes that are goal oriented, an absolute harmony of all nature, perhaps even an acknowledgment of God himself as the providential governor of the universe. Although a few people like Asa Gray claimed to see divine purpose in *On the Origin of Species,* Christians after 1859 generally faced an evolution radically different from the theories of the earlier part of the century. That is not to say, of course, that everyone recognized the difference; many evangelicals saw both evolution paradigms as atheistic heresy. However, that fact does not weaken the stated argument: to condition a Protestant to accept Lamarck was not necessarily to condition him to accept Darwin. On the contrary, his acceptance of Lamarckianism could make him all the more vehemently anti-Darwinian. In the twenty-five or so years after the publication of *On the Origin of Species,* several prominent American Protestants became believers in evolution. The majority, however, became Lamarckians.[2]

Evangelicals in the first half of the century had one thing undeniably in their favor: transmutationalists were as scorned by the scientific community as they were by the religiously orthodox. One did not have to be a conservative Protestant to believe that Lamarck or Robert Chambers were quacks. Science was not yet ready for a complete evolutionary argument, and the essays of the pre-Darwinian evolutionists were full of hypotheses, conjecture, even fantasy. As a result, the pre-Darwinian evolutionist had a hard time getting *anyone*, scientist or preacher, to take him seriously. When Carolina-born William Charles Wells stood before the Royal Society in 1813 to read a paper advocating evolution, no one in America bothered to jeer or to cheer. In fact, no one even came forth with a response.

Wells was no ordinary evolutionist. A talented physician, he was plagued all his life by his peculiar political and scientific ideas. Born to Scottish parents living in Charleston in 1757 and raised a "zealous and uncompromising Tory," Wells found his politics quite unsuitable to Revolutionary America. He moved to Edinburgh in 1775, graduated from the medical school and set up a practice. His life's work consisted of medicine together with an occasional research paper delivered before the Royal Society. Of these, only the paper delivered in 1813, an "Account of a Female of the White Race of Mankind, Part of Whose Skin Resembles that of a Negro," has much historical significance. Hannah West, the object of Wells' investigation, was born in Sussex of white parents. She herself was entirely white except for her "left shoulder, arm, and fore-arm, and hand," which were black. After a long analysis of Hannah's particular problem Wells turned to a much broader question, the cause of the African's blackness. Wells concluded that blackness made the African native more resistant to local diseases and better able to function in his environment. At the same time, he contended that the European's whiteness provided him with a similar advantage in his environment. However, Wells did not suggest that the environment or the "unconscious striving" of the organism *caused*, in any Lamarckian sense, these changes in skin color. Rather, he came up with a much more novel hypothesis. In each new generation of offspring, he suggested, there are a great many accidental varieties of one sort or another: some individuals are taller than the norm, some are shorter, some are darker or lighter. Of these "accidental varieties of man" that inhabit the black parts of Africa, "some one would be better fitted than the others to bear the diseases of the country." The result would be that "this race would consequently multiply, while the others would decrease, not only from their inability to sustain the attacks of disease, but from their incapacity of contending with their more vigorous neighbours. The colour of this vigorous race I take for granted . . . would be dark." By the same method, said Wells, the part of the human race that "proceeded to the colder regions of the earth, would in process of time become white, if they were not originally so."[3]

It was about as clear a statement of natural selection as one could find anywhere. So clear, in fact, that when Wells's essay was called to Darwin's attention, sometime between 1861 and 1866, Darwin felt obliged to mention Wells in the fourth edition of *On the Origin of Species*. Darwin recognized Wells's priority in the historical introduction, noting that Wells "distinctly recognizes the principle of natural selection, and this is the first recognition which has been indicated." However, Darwin added, Wells applied it only to human beings and only in ethnological arguments. He failed to recognize its greater implications.[4]

But Wells's hypothesis fell on deaf ears. Darwin did not even know about him until after the *Origin* had been completed. No one continued Wells's research; no one attempted to refute him; no one tried to see the theological implications of his work. In 1849, when Elisha Bartlett, a medical professor at the University of Louisville, published a biographical essay on Wells he did not even mention the "Account of a Female." Bartlett believed that Wells's most important contribution to science was his "Essay on Dew."[5]

It would be forty years before anyone else would have Wells's insights into nature's methods for choosing its survivors. But between 1813 and 1859 a few Americans made some discoveries that were difficult to explain in terms of the "absolute species" paradigm. If each species was a particular act of God's creative will, and if the lines between species were inviolable, then distinguishing varieties from species ought to be easy. In general this appeared to be true of the mammals and the higher plants. However, the distinctions between species and varieties were not as obvious among lower organisms. Of particular interest to comparative anatomists in the 1820s were the conches. Already by that time the marine shells had been divided into several genera and hundreds of species. In addition, taxonomists had identified many varieties of each species. However, as the number of catalogued conches multiplied dramatically the task of determining the lines between varieties, between species, and genera became enormously difficult. For example, should one lay in an ordered row the some forty varieties of one particular marine shell species, *Unio cornutus,* he would find that each shell compared with its nearest neighbor would "exhibit so gradual a change, as to convince the observer of their identity of species." However, if the observer should look at two shells "near the opposite extremes of arrangement . . . , they would be considered as specifically different." This problem led Philip Nicklin, a Princeton-educated Philadelphia bookseller and amateur conchologist, to suggest that the distinction between varieties, species, and genera was completely arbitrary. "The seven genera, now referred to the family of *Naiädes,*" he said concerning one particular family of shells, "are founded in artificial distinctions, and not in nature." However, Nicklin must have realized the consequences of what he was saying. He stopped at that point and did not permit himself to speculate about the nature of species. But he *did* allow the evidence to take him to one potentially unsettling conclusion about the conches: "it appears that some shells of the family of *Naiädes,* at different ages, assume different appearances in those parts which naturalists have fixed upon for the distinctive characteristics of different genera." In other words, the members of a particular genus seemed gradually to change throughout the successive generations. The seed of an extraordinary discovery was in Nicklin's hand: he had evidence that over a long period of time not merely species but entire genera change and lose their distinctive characteristics.[6]

Fourteen years later many more conches had been catalogued and the species-varieties problem was more serious than ever. The more varieties that were discovered, the more apparent it became that fixity of species was hard to see in such manifold genera. In a paper delivered in 1844 on freshwater Mollusca, Samuel Haldeman, a prominent Pennsylvania geologist, chemist, and zoologist, went much further than Nicklin. Haldeman looked at the maze of varieties and species, and the conflicting opinions about which separate types constituted distinct species, and decided that the whole concept of species needed to be reevaluated. Obviously, said Haldeman, the old idea that species includes "descent from a single pair" simply will not do, "because the first male and the first female would, by the definition, be of different species." Furthermore, the hypothesis of descent from a single pair is unverifiable. The scientist must depend on more empirical data. However, the data are difficult to read: "The proper discrimination between species and variety is one of the greatest difficulties which the naturalist has to encounter; and he who is successful in this department is entitled to a rank which comparatively few can attain." Quite clearly, said Haldeman, species are able to vary far more than Lyell or Lamarck's critics have conceded. Haldeman admitted that if one studied a few generations of a particular species, it seemed there were boundaries beyond which variation could not go. But could not "a physical agent, acting gradually for ages" eventually "carry the variation a step or two further . . . [?]" The result might be that, instead of producing four varieties, the parent generations would produce six, "the sixth being sufficiently unlike the earlier ones to induce a naturalist to consider it distinct." Haldeman continued from this point into a rather unqualified transmutationalism. That sixth variety must either survive and propagate itself, or become extinct. Often, of course, the latter happened and all that remains are a few fossils. But occasionally a new variety developed and flourished as a new type, different enough from its parents so that the naturalists would see it as a distinct species. Then, perhaps realizing that he had hypothesized too much, Haldeman qualified some of his arguments, suggesting that he intended "not to offer an opinion for or against the Lamarckian hypothesis" but was hoping only to show "the insufficiency of the standing arguments against it."[7]

Only one American of this period suggested a more general theory of evolution. French-born Kentuckian Constantine Samuel Rafinesque, having completed extensive tours of America's South and West, was quite disturbed by the great number of new species of flora constantly being discovered in previously explored regions. His four-part *New Flora and Botany of North America* attempted to bring the science up to date. Here Rafinesque described about five hundred new species of plants, trees, and shrubs that he believed had not been catalogued. In accounting for the continuing appearance of new species,

Rafinesque speculated that each was the result of "several deviations" from parent plants that became "permanently combined" into new species. "All new species are in fact such permanent deviations of growth," Rafinesque asserted. As a result of this process, the rarest species are the newest ones; they have not yet had sufficient time to establish themselves in great numbers. The more common varieties, on the other hand, are those that have been around for a long time, although Rafinesque did not suggest how long. As Rafinesque saw it, this continual process of development dictated that the botanical catalogues be continually updated.[8]

The fact that all of these men suggested a theory of evolution is important, but not as important as the fact that virtually no one responded to them. No one saw the occasional timid Lamarckian as either a scientific threat or an infidel; in fact, it appears that no one saw him at all. The reason for this was that Lamarck was not generally known in America before 1844. Lamarck, Robert Chambers, and *The Vestiges of the Natural History of Creation* all became famous together.

Part of the dramatic growth of Lamarck's infamy in America after the publication of the *Vestiges* stemmed from the fact that no one knew who its author was. Both the *Vestiges* and its sequel of 1845, the *Explanations of the Vestiges,* were published anonymously. Since reviewers did not have Robert Chambers to turn their guns on, they fired at his intellectual ancestor. But the biggest reason for the boom in antievolutionary thinking was the astonishing popularity of the *Vestiges.* Chambers brought Lamarck and the developmental hypothesis to everyone. He made it an heretical but nevertheless very popular fad. In seven months, *Vestiges* went through four editions, and by 1860 the book had sold twenty-four thousand copies, a truly incredible number for a scientific work in that period.[9] Furthermore, *Vestiges* had been written in English. Americans who could excuse Lamarck as a typical specimen of enlightened French infidelity could not dispense so easily with Chambers.

Chambers had been born in 1802 to William Chambers, a moderately wealthy manufacturer of textiles. What undoubtedly stimulated Robert's interest in the variations of species was a painful family tragedy: both he and his brother William, two years older than himself, had been born full hexadactyls, with six fingers on each hand and six toes on each foot. Both boys underwent corrective surgery. Although William made a rapid recovery Robert went through a long and tortuous convalescence, during which time he turned to the study of biology. By the time he wrote the *Vestiges*, Chambers was a successful bookseller and publisher and his personal agony was long behind him. Only the scars and his interest in biology remained.

In many ways *Vestiges of the Natural History of Creation* was an important, creative work; in many others it was a scientific fraud. Chambers was not trained as a biologist or paleontologist, and his insights were often supported by outdated and disproven evidence, many times by myths or simple tall tales.[10] What made the book so questionable from the scientific viewpoint was the vast range it tried to cover. More than a theory of evolution, the *Vestiges* claimed to be an entire cosmology. It began not with an analysis of a little aquatic slime but with a long and somewhat fanciful look at the heavens. Beginning with Laplace's nebular hypothesis, Chambers described in imaginative detail the formation of the universe and finally of the earth itself. Only after the earth had broken off from the primordial mass, cooled, and began to take its present form, did Chambers describe the process of biological development which made his book so famous.

The strength of the *Vestiges* lay in its assembly of numerous, often overlooked pieces of evidence to show that the history of the earth is also a history of biological development; its greatest weakness lay in the fact that Chambers was unable to find any natural mechanism to explain that development. He knew, along with the progressionists, that fossils became gradually more complex as one proceeds upward through the geological strata. He also knew what gave the progressionists the most difficulty: that certain forms survived the breaks in the strata, and that many extended across three or more geological layers. He knew that the earth was much older than the biblical six thousand years, and that a longer time was necessary to allow for any kind of developmental theory.[11] But although the evidence was there, he really never knew *why* it was there. He knew nothing of natural selection; he minimized the "unconscious striving" upon which Lamarck had relied. Ultimately Chambers, like Lamarck, chose a metaphysical rather than a natural explanation paradigm. The process of development, he said, all points back to a first cause—a cause that gave the universe its initial energy, which is responsible for the continual, scattered originations of life by spontaneous generation, and which controls the upward spiral of the evolutionary process.

Chambers found the proper conditions for the origin of life at the base of the ancient limestone beds where the earliest organic remains had been discovered. It took nothing more than the proper combination of warm temperature, "carbonic acid gas," and water in the atmosphere to give the earth its earliest and simplest species of plant life. Immediately these primitive organisms began developing, first into simple seaplants, then into more complex plants, simple animals, and fish. In these early stages the number of species was relatively small, but eventually offspring began to diverge and the earth became populated with a variety of forms. Then Chambers followed the increasingly complex species up through the geologic record. All parts of the earth, he said, were not in the same developmental stages at the same time. In some places dry land was being inundated. In others it was just beginning to appear. As the conditions in a certain area became ideal spontaneous generation would begin. Thus the earth is constantly going through a process of generation and development. Chambers tried to be vigorously uniformitarian. Unlike catastrophists and progressionists he believed "that the same laws and conditions of nature now apparent to us have existed throughout the whole time" of the earth's development. However, Chambers did believe that natural catastrophes had a great deal to do with the earth's formation—volcanoes and earthquakes, for example, which changed dry land into ocean, and vice-versa.

Chambers also tried to appear a convinced Christian—and not merely a Christian, but a rather superior one. He found the traditional evangelical picture of the creation to be "not in harmony" with the Mosaic record, which makes it quite clear that creation flowed "*from commands and expressions of will, not from direct acts.*"[12] Chambers saw his own supposition of a "creation by law" as giving much more justice to God than the evangelical idea of creation by fiat. On the other hand, hidden in the *Vestiges* were some simply stated, direct threats to historical Protestantism. Chambers defended spontaneous generation by arguing that life is "simply chemical."[13] He believed that living bodies are composed of little more than carbon, oxygen, hydrogen, and nitrogen; that there is no "chemical peculiarity" in the internal functioning of organisms; and that, since chemists could already manufacture urea in the laboratory, it would be only a matter of time before they would realize the "first step in organization" of the simpler organisms. In the eyes of most evangelicals this was either atheism or deism carried to its most mechanistic extreme.

Indeed, deism or whatever, it *was* a theory of the earth carried to a mechanistic extreme. Evangelicals generally recognized what Chambers did not or pretended not to: for all his generosity toward God in his system, Chambers had naturalized the development of the earth to the point that only two big issues remained. First, his principle of spontaneous generation would no longer account for the origin of life. Secondly, he had no mechanism for explaining the evolutionary process itself. Darwin, of course, would solve the latter problem; the former would never be fully explained, but its relative importance would diminish as other pieces of the biological puzzle began to fall neatly into place.

Americans, like most Britishers, were outraged by the *Vestiges*. Its handful of American supporters were scattered and contradictory; worse yet, they wrote nothing. Virtually every review published in an American journal was negative to the point of abuse.[14]

Albert Baldwin Dod, Princeton theologian and mathematics professor, found in the *Vestiges* that "the most recent discoveries are strangely blended with antiquated blunders, crude hypotheses are mingled with facts, and bold, unqualified assertions are made for which we have not one particle of evidence."[15] Dod was most fascinated by Chambers's mathematical arguments for evolution, arguments where, ironically, Chambers had come very close to developing a model for genetic mutation. As an illustration of the evolutionary process Chambers had used the famous "calculating engine" of British mathematician Charles Babbage.[16] Babbage's engine was a remarkable machine, but it had one peculiarity. When it was programmed to compute mathematical or geometric progressions it made occasional errors, apparently at random intervals. For example, when the calculating machine was programmed to compute the arithmetic progression known as "triangular numbers" ($1=1$, $1+2=3$, $1+2+3=6$, $1+2+3+4=10$, etc.), it behaved perfectly for 2,761 terms, but deviated on the 2,762nd term; it then operated perfectly for 1,430 more terms and deviated on term number 4,193. These occasional deviations, said Babbage, were "a consequence of the original adjustment" of the machine; more importantly, to a trained mathematician the deviations were really not random at all but could be "fully foreknown at the commencement" of any series.

Babbage's engine provided Chambers with the perfect analogy for the evolutionary process. The laws of creation, he suggested, have a hidden variant programmed into them, just like the variant in Babbage's machine. For long periods of time parents give birth to offspring very similar to themselves. But then suddenly and for no explainable reason the law is interrupted. Perhaps a six-toed Robert Chambers is born; perhaps a fish that breathes air from the surface. That new organism begins producing after its kind, until after a large number of generations a new deviation occurs. All that the formula needed to work itself out, explained Chambers, was time—a great amount of time. Because humans exist for only two or three of their own generations, or only a few dozen or a few hundred of the generations of small plants or insects, they are unable to observe the full impact of these programmed variations.[17]

Dod did not mind Chambers's mathematics, but he could not tolerate the analogy to nature. His mind, not much given to arguments from analogy, could find no reason why Babbage's engine could demonstrate that "at the end of some immense period a monkey may produce a man." Dod complained that Chambers was trying to make Babbage's engine do far too much. He was not looking for a simple variant, but for a planned, integrated, internally harmonious variation that would affect the entire course of nature. Dod suggested that this was roughly analogous to looking into the calculating machine and seeing "one of those plates resolving itself into types, and these types arranging themselves in the order of a page of the *Paradise Lost*, or even of the *Vestiges of Creation*."

In at least one sense, Dod was correct. Chambers had used Babbage's engine as an analogical "proof" of evolution, when at best he could use it only as a model. But in principle the Babbage analogy was clever, and Chambers did not carry it as far as Dod implied. It was precisely because the occasional variations in Babbage's series were *not* arbitrary that Chambers had used the illustration. Chambers's deism did not allow him an open-ended universe; the variations were completely predictible, built into the system from the beginning. Dod saw "blind chance" where Chambers had intended none.[18]

Another prominent Presbyterian was even harder on the *Vestiges* than Dod. Taylor Lewis, the theological reactionary whose views were generally twenty-five years behind his times, was to have his own problems with the developmental hypothesis in a few years. But he did not spare the author of *Vestiges* a single lash of his sharp tongue. Lewis could not find anything redeeming about the *Vestiges*, except that it was convincing proof of how "malignant" the "spirit of infidelity" had become. Although he spent most of his career trying to convince other evangelicals that scientific arguments have no bearing on the truths of Christianity, Lewis considered himself a rather able scientific critic. He was, however, unable to discover the scientific shortcomings of the *Vestiges*. Instead he dwelt on the author's deism and mechanism, his substitution of "law and development" for "providence and creation," and his portrayal of the world as an "immense machine." Lewis saw it as truly incredible that any monkey could produce its own kind 2,761 times when suddenly "the hidden spring is touched; the monkey loses his tail, and man comes out No. 2762." The very idea was absurd: "Is it for this that we are called upon, in the nineteenth century, to reject" the "sublime account" of the Old Testament?[19]

Francis Bowen responded to the *Vestiges* for the Unitarians. Like Lewis, Bowen was more interested in the metaphysical and religious implications of the *Vestiges* than he was in the soundness of its science. He floundered for endless paragraphs over Chambers's "striking and ingenious" metaphysical arguments and concluded that the author's intellect was "of so high an order as fairly to challenge attention and respect." He found the suggestion that "natural law" could explain every aspect of the earth's development highly seductive but ultimately preposterous. Bowen conceded the basic validity of the spontaneous generation hypothesis, but he argued that only "animalcules, or beings of very small size, and low in the scale of animated existence, can be produced . . . by the inherent qualities of matter." However, "no one will pretend, that a dog, a horse, or a man can thus be created." These higher forms needed divine guidance. To suggest "that bricks and mortar came together of their own accord" in such complex ways was to invite atheism, for "if there is no need of a bricklayer, we may discard also the brick-maker."[20]

Bowen's greatest contribution to the American understanding of the *Vestiges* was probably his identification of its author. Four years later, when Bowen reviewed Chambers's *Ancient Sea-Margins*, he compared the text of that work with the text of the *Vestiges*. Similarities in style and argument convinced Bowen that Chambers was the author of both.[21]

For all the American furor over the *Vestiges*, however, few were really able to come to terms with its scientific issues. When the *Vestiges* had been published, Asa Gray was too busy to respond. He was not at all satisfied with Bowen's "long-winded" article, nor with James D. Dana's short notice in The *American Journal of Science*. But he bit his tongue for two years, until Chambers published *Explanations: A Sequel to "Vestiges of the Natural History of Creation."*[22] Gray reviewed *Explanations* for the Unitarian *North American Review* in 1846. On the whole, it was a strange article from the man who would be America's foremost supporter of Charles Darwin only thirteen years later. Against Chambers's Lamarckianism Gray pitted old-fashioned, evangelical special-creationism. "The movements of the planets . . . show that they are under law," said Gray, superficially agreeing with Chambers; but "law" meant something different for Gray than it did for Chambers, that the planets "not only *had* a Creator, but *have* a Governor."[23] Gray objected that Chambers's evolutionary mechanism took God out of earth's history, leaving him with nothing more than its origin. Gray would actually never depart from that position; years later he would still be arguing for both design and Divine governance, insisting that those things worked themselves out in the process of natural selection.

For all of Gray's own theological problems with the *Vestiges* theory, however, his review was the most sophisticated scientific survey of Chambers's position. Gray's most serious objection to the evolutionary thesis was that, as it was stated by Chambers, it was contrary to the paleontological evidence. The *Vestiges*, strongly influenced by the Romantic biology of the early nineteenth century, made the evolutionary process from beginning to end correspond very closely with the *scala naturae* —the Great Chain of Being. In fact, the great popularity of the *Vestiges* stemmed in part from the fact that the notion of the Great Chain was deeply embedded in nineteenth-century ideas about science. Chambers merely "mobilized" what had long been a scientific and philosophical concept about the static order of nature. Chambers's evolutionary hypothesis implied that as one dug downwards through the geologic strata he would find a literal, fossilized Great Chain in exactly reversed order, indicating a process that "strictly followed the ascending steps of the natural series." But Gray found the evidence less clear. Where Chambers should have found only simple plants, there were actually higher and lower flora mixed together. In fact, the earliest evidence of plant life included fossils in the full range of orders.

In all of the *Vestiges* and the *Explanations*, Gray found "no good argument . . . against a specific creation." Throughout his essay Gray revealed the empirical, antispeculative bias that was to cause him considerable agony in the coming years. He saw the *Vestiges* as a disparagement of the "principal *working* geologists," the "ablest and soundest scientific men of our time," who do their jobs, always sticking closely to the facts. He could not tolerate the "supernumeraries" who were always waging this speculative "guerilla warfare." They, he concluded, were "unfit and disinclined for research themselves" and therefore found it "easier to *speculate* than to *examine*." Generally, said Gray, the likes of Robert Chambers were uncreative, always ready to "snatch at the results obtained by others," but because of their lack of analytic ability they "bring science itself into undeserved discredit when their unstable foundations are exposed to view."[24] Unlike Bowen, Gray minimized Chambers's creativity, noting that the nebular hypothesis came not from Chambers but from Laplace and Herschel, that transmutation itself had come from Lamarck, and that spontaneous generation was a fallacy as old as the Greek philosophers.

Gray's review of the *Explanations* did a rather good job of hiding a troubled American botanist. Like Darwin, Gray could attack and even mock Chambers's unscientific use of the data. But like Darwin, Gray knew already in the late 1840s that there was more to what Chambers said than Chambers himself realized. Gray conspicuously avoided one point that Chambers's other critics were always quick to make—that evolution was a denial of Divine planning in nature. In only a few years Gray would be sure that evolution and natural theology were not at all incompatible, that natural selection was a magnificent mechanism in which to see God's great design working itself out. That conclusion involved a great deal of evangelical back-pedalling, and Gray was the only orthodox American Protestant to make that decision before the *Origin* came to print.[25]

Most Americans, scientifically inclined or not, were outraged by the transmutation theory, more by its religious implications than by its science. At the same time, they took comfort in the fact that it could be so capably refuted—"hooted from the earth," as Lewis Warner Green told his University of Virginia audience in 1850. Every day new scientific evidence was being discovered to prove that the *Vestiges* was exactly what the critics said it was: a concoction of scientific fables, creatively assembled but ultimately indefensible and ridiculous. For Green, the real hero in combating the *Vestiges* was neither an American nor a professional scientist. Asa Gray's review may have been impressive in its erudition, but Scotsman Hugh Miller really saved the day. *The Foot-Prints of the Creator* presented catastrophic progressionism as the only alternative to the infidelity of the *Vestiges*. As far as evangelicals were concerned, Miller's was the final word. The *Vestiges*, said Green, was "shivered to atoms by a blow from the stone hammer of a Caledonian quarrier; and, for all its prodigious '*creations*,' now, no '*vestiges*' remain."[26]

A few years after the *Vestiges* controversy subsided, one of its American reviewers himself became involved in a similar debate. Taylor Lewis, opposed to Lamarckianism, opposed in fact to practically all science, attempted to solve the problems of science and the Bible by writing his own explanation of the earth's formation. Lewis insisted that the only way to look at the creation was through the Bible, because creation took place before the laws of nature were fully in effect. The study of the earth's origin was therefore a matter of biblical history and not of scientific investigation. *The Six Days of Creation* was Lewis's attempt to chart the early development of the earth using nothing but the Bible as a source. Most of Lewis's conclusions were unremarkable, typical of the findings that any evangelical interpreter of Genesis would make. One conclusion, however, was extraordinary: that the creation of plants and animals was not instantaneous but "gradual." Although Lewis would deny it, James D. Dana was sure that Lewis was advocating the developmental hypothesis.

Dana responded in four articles on "Science and the Bible" that appeared in the *Bibliotheca Sacra* during 1856 and 1857.[27] Actually, Dana's articles were not so much an attack on Lewis's transmutational theory as they were a defense of the unrestricted, objective pursuit of science. Dana believed that Lewis's exclusively scriptural analysis of the creation was blatantly antiscientific. Such research, Dana insisted, depended on *both* biblical and scientific data. In spite of that technical difference, however, the two "methods" for studying the creation yielded remarkably similar conclusions. First of all, both Lewis and Dana agreed about the natural limits of science: that it could analyze only processes, not "first causes," "origins," or "primal forces." Both writers believed that the creation took much longer than six days and that the earth was far more than six thousand years old. They even agreed largely as to the method of its creation.[28]

But they obviously disagreed on one issue. In his analysis of the work of the fifth creation day, the day that birds and fish were made, Lewis dove into some of the current issues involving species and spontaneous generation. He had great difficulty with the evangelical notion that each separate species was a distinct creation of God, "a separate spermatic word." Against this Lewis suggested something else: that "the original divine power may be supposed to have originated the new order of life in its most generic or universal germ, and all subordinate genera and species may have been developed from it." In this way, said Lewis, "species would grow out of species, as individuals out of individuals. There would be an ascent from the first rudiments of vegetable and animal life to the higher and more perfect *growths*, or *natures*."

Lewis did not really advocate the above view as the only correct interpretation of Genesis 1. He did, however, see it as a very plausible explanation, just as consistent with Scripture as the more traditional view that God had willed and created each individual species. A "development theory in the sense of species from species, as well as of individual from individual, may be as pious as any other," asserted Lewis, as long as it is regarded as "a method of God's working" and does not make the deistic mistake of acknowledging "only one divine origination." Thus Lewis's proposal was thoroughly catastrophic, involving a God who directed the evolutionary process at every point instead of merely creating the germ and leaving the laws of nature to run of their own accord. Lewis suggested a "stream of nature," which may have been in operation "for twenty-four hours, or twenty-four thousand years." At the proper time God "dropped a new power" into this stream, "varying the old flow and raising it to a higher law and a higher energy, yet still in harmony with it." This accounted for the development of all life: "a world of vegetation is the result of this chain of causation in the one period . . . , an animal creation arose in another."[29]

In spite of the fact that Lewis had soundly rejected Chambers's deistic, uniformitarian brand of evolution, Dana saw too many shades of the *Vestiges*. The most important value of the evangelical, scientific approach to earth history, snorted Dana, is that it enables Christians to see the errors of the developmental hypothesis! For all its expressed orthodoxy, Lewis's method was leading him squarely into the same dangerous heresy. Furthermore, Lewis's view of nature as "self-existent and self-propagating" but "now and then requiring a jolt from the supernatural," was entirely contrary to sound Protestantism and respectable science. It "may be an interesting myth," he suggested, but it "cannot rise to the same point of view with biblical truth or sound philosophy."[30]

Dana's own view of creation was a progressionism roughly akin to that of the Scotsman Hugh Miller. He used "Science and the Bible" to show that the geological record *and* scriptural interpretation are completely consistent with successive creations "of the tribes" occurring "at many different times" and generally "after more or less complete exterminations."[31] Using the progressionist framework, Dana followed Miller in dividing earth history into six geologic ages, beginning with the Silurian, or the "Age of Molluscs," and ending with "the Age of Man." Each of these epochs began with a special creative act and in each a new generation of organisms virtually replaced the life of the earlier age. But within an epoch there was no transmutation of species, no variation beyond the varietal.

Undoubtedly the most important thing to come out of the Dana-Lewis dialogue was not a new, American theory of evolution. No one except Dana paid much attention to Lewis's new theory. One must not look in *The Six Days of Creation* for the real significance of the controversy, but in "Science and the Bible." Here, after disposing of Taylor Lewis, Dana stated in summary form what he believed to be *the* evangelical position on biological nature. To be sure, he borrowed heavily from Hugh Miller and Arnold Guyot, but he himself was the first to put forth in simple form the creation paradigm that existed in the minds of many American Protestants.[32] Generally speaking, Dana's theory was geologically and biologically up to date. It took into account the variety and distribution of fossils. It was the result of trained biblical scholarship, the efforts of men whose special skill seemed to be to reinterpret, revise, or simply to distort the most obvious meanings of Genesis. For all its sophistication, however, the progressionism advocated by Dana and most other evangelicals in the 1850s suffered from one terrible fault: it was thoroughly catastrophist. To be antievolutionary was to be supernaturalistic in one's science. That was the handwriting that was beginning to appear on the walls of America's scientific classrooms. The antievolutionary heroes—Miller, Dana, Agassiz—were all catastrophists.

But the daily conduct of science was carrying dozens of American scientists, evangelical or not, in an irreversibly contrary direction. Silliman's cautious uniformitarianism in the 1830s and Gray's much more radical uniformitarianism as it began to develop in the early 1850s, were both sincere efforts to keep religiously orthodox scientists from talking nonsense. Catastrophism and progressionism opened the door to too many unscientific conclusions. The first reaction of many scientists, Gray included, was to close themselves off from science's deeper problems and stick closely to the business at hand. After all, there were still hundreds of flora and fauna to be discovered, described, and arranged. However, the business at hand was entirely a business of dealing with cause-effect relationships. To really avoid "hypotheses," as the Scottish Realists from an earlier generation put it, was to assume that things happened in the past just as they happen today; uniformitarianism was the ultimate in "common sense." And although many evangelicals clung tenaciously to Agassiz and other special creationists they began to realize that his was a position that violated their own long-established principles. As Agassiz and Gliddon demonstrated so clearly, even special creationism carried to its necessary conclusions generated a long list of heresies. James D. Dana was one of the few evangelicals who would, in a single lifetime, run the entire gamut from Agassiz to Darwin, going through a nervous breakdown in the process and finally concluding sometime in the 1870s that even natural selection could be consistent with the divine cosmogony.[33]

But although uniformitarianism began looking more attractive and even necessary to science, the evangelical could not accept it with some expensive trade-offs. He had already relinquished his literal Old Testament. But science wanted more than that. It demanded that "God" or "the supernatural" not be in the subject position of scientific statements. Acquiescing in this cost orthodox Protestantism dearly: if you cannot talk about God when you are talking about nature, then when *can* you talk about him?

Uniformitarianism was essential to the development of a scientific theory of evolution, but the mere acceptance of a uniformitarian model was not enough. However, evidence from a half dozen sources pointed in the same direction. When everything had been analyzed and placed into the uniformitarian framework, evolution was inescapable. The more the botanists and paleontologists learned about variation, the more they realized that it did not proceed within rigidly defined limits.[34] Although Chambers had been mistaken when he asserted that the upward progression of species in the geologic strata was in exact parallel to the Great Chain of Being, the upward progression was there nonetheless. To be sure, the evidence was not absolutely consistent. Both Hugh Miller and British geologist Adam Sedgwick had been quick to point out that many strata contained fossils in exactly the reverse of the expected order.[35]

However, as knowledge of geological inversions became more complete, it became easier for evolution's advocates to explain away the "degeneration" that Miller claimed to find.

By the mid-1850s the catastrophism of Hugh Miller, Cuvier, and Agassiz had become untenable. On the surface, catastrophism and progressionism explained the geologic record quite well: each epoch represented a new creation of species, several generations of propagation, and finally a catastrophe that obliterated all existing life forms. Progressionism suggested that God had created life on earth several times, each creation more sophisticated than the previous one. However, evolutionists had the answer to that too. Many species did not disappear at the end of an epoch. Progressionism suggested that "no fossil species, at least among the two classes of *mammalia* and *reptilia*, has any analogue among living species, or in other words, . . . every fossil species is extinct."[36] However, the geologic record revealed no such simplicity. Many species in fact extended from one epoch into the next; some transversed three or more; and a few species of *lingula* and *mollusca* had persisted from "the Silurian epoch to the present day, with so little change that competent malacologists are sometimes puzzled to distinguish the ancient from the modern species."[37] Already in 1844 Samuel Haldeman had suggested that paleontologists had been using the presuppositions of the catastrophist paradigm to distort the evidence—that they frequently catalogued virtually identical fossils as distinct species simply because they had been found in distinct strata.[38] Eventually as committed a catastrophist as Edward Hitchcock was forced to admit that at least a few ancient fossil species were still represented by living organisms.[39]

Finally were those vestigial remains that lay not buried deep in the earth, but in the bodies of living organisms. The rudimentary teeth in the jawbone of the whale, the undeveloped toes in the horse's leg, the vestiges of feet hidden beneath the skin of some snakes, the useless wings of the ostrich, and even man's own vestigial tail, all seemed to indicate that these organisms were the descendants of parents different from themselves. The progressive creationists who were confronted with Chambers's long list of rudimentary organs were hard put to find an answer. Why would God create so many organisms with these useless leftovers from nonexistent ancestors?[40]

Asa Gray's biographer has divided the respondents to *On the Origin of Species* into three groups. First were those who believed wholeheartedly that evolution and orthodoxy were incompatible, and who reveled in their discovery. The positivistic scientists of the 1860s, the Spencers and the Huxleys, saw evolution as a final step on man's road to eliminating metaphysical and theological language from his descriptions of nature. Science and religion had been in absolute conflict, and science had proved the victor.

Secondly, and at the opposite extreme, was a large group of Christians who agreed that evolution and Christianity were mutually exclusive. These, however, were stunned by the new theory. The Catholic Church, the evangelical extremists, even many of America's mainstream Protestants, gradually became convinced that Christianity could survive only by taking a firm and long-lasting stand against evolution in particular, and against all of science in general.

But there was also a third group of scholars. Asa Gray and James Dana would study evolution carefully, look at their own religious commitments, and be able to resolve the conflict. To them evolution and Christianity could be quite compatible, provided that one saw them in the proper perspective. Asa Gray devoted much of the last part of his life to proving this point. His *Darwiniana*, published in 1876, was an orthodox but evolutionary Protestant's declaration of faith. Gray found design where Princeton's Charles Hodge found only "blind chance." Gray found God's providence where Hodge found only implicit atheism. No two Americans in the nineteenth century disagreed more strongly or with more commitment.[41]

Neither of these men, however, was a Protestant extremist. Both were Presbyterian, and both of them considered themselves to be orthodox and in good standing in their churches. The Hodge-Gray debate of the 1870s was only a small part of the evidence of the substantial influence that Darwin and his theory had on American Protestantism.[42] Evolution changed the old dividing lines. Ever since the Great Awakening, American Protestants had been called "evangelical" or "liberal" on the basis of a long list of rationalistic criteria: were they trinitarian or unitarian; were they biblical literalists or moderates; did they believe in total depravity or in man's basic goodness?

But by 1860 those battles were remote in history. The Unitarian controversy was a textbook issue. Even most evangelicals were not the biblical literalists they had been in the first part of the century. Calvinism died in 1800 at Harvard; it was buried with Nathaniel Taylor at Yale; it survived only at reactionary Princeton and the small circle of colleges that Princeton provided with faculty. But only after *On the Origin of Species* were the battle lines clearly redrawn. The new questions were much more empirical, much less concerned with the niceties of American Calvinism, and much more involved with what was really on the minds of scholars: science.

Epilogue

One hundred years after John Witherspoon immigrated to America, the College of New Jersey called another Scotsman, James McCosh, to be its president. The Old School Presbyterians who actively supported the College had a strong sense of tradition. They believed, as many of the Princeton faculty were suggesting, that history was repeating itself. On 22 October 1868, five days after he had arrived in the United States, McCosh was inaugurated in front of the largest crowd that had ever assembled on the Princeton campus. The introductory address was given by Charles Hodge, Professor of Theology in the Seminary. Never before in the history of the College, proclaimed Hodge, had the trustees and the constituency been so unanimous in their support of a president. Never before were the prospects for Church unity so favorable.[1]

Hodge was exaggerating his enthusiasm somewhat. The Old School Presbyterian Church, of which he was an outspoken intellectual leader, and the New School Church based in New York were in fact on the verge of reuniting after a thirty-year split. Hodge, however, was opposed to the union. He believed that the New School had come under the influence of modern thinking: theological liberalism and theology of the feelings, extreme views of biblical criticism, and a repudiation of many of the principles of orthodox Calvinism. By 1868, however, reunion was inevitable. Charles Hodge hoped only to preserve the orthodoxy of his own Princeton, to make it a safe fortress of sound doctrine, in spite of the heresies that were beginning to extend even into his own denomination.

Hodge would have moderated his enthusiasm even more had he known that only a few days earlier the new president had decided to become a public advocate of the views of Charles Darwin. McCosh was already familiar with *On the Origin of Species* and the scientific and theological debates it had fostered. Before he was called to Princeton he had decided privately that natural selection and transmutation of species were undeniable. He had been particularly impressed with the efforts of one American Presbyterian, Asa Gray, to show that natural selection and natural theology could be perfectly compatible, if one viewed them correctly. All that remained for McCosh was to decide whether to keep his views to himself or to espouse them openly. While he was aboard the ship that carried him to America, he made up his mind. "I decided to pursue the open and honest course, as being sure that it would be the best in the end."[2]

Both Hodge and McCosh were highly esteemed surveyors of the evangelical landscape. They were, however, standing back-to-back. For Hodge, the old views were not only adequate, they were necessary for the preservation of the Christian Church. Hodge believed that the duty of theology was to do battle with the world. Theology must be defensive. It must be able to justify the rationality of its positions. To Hodge, a truly defensive theology included a heavy reliance on the "evidences" and a strong commitment to biblical literalism. That kind of theology had already served his church well for a century. The "Princeton Theology" that Hodge helped to found tried desperately to maintain that tradition.

McCosh, however, felt differently. While Hodge believed that evangelical survival depended on the maintenance of a strong orthodoxy, McCosh thought survival depended on unity. He supported Presbyterian reunion. He also believed that unity could be achieved only by compromise. McCosh was not a liberal, but he knew that no Protestant minister, no matter how powerful an orator, could hold an urban congregation together by preaching outmoded principles and dead issues. Even the Presbyterian Church, the most thoroughly Calvinistic of all New England churches, must keep up with the times. Its prosperity depended on its ability to address the problems of the 1870s, not the once great but now forgotten problems of the first and second Awakenings.

In one sense, Hodge was a better prophet than McCosh. The Presbyterian union of 1869 was the beginning of the end for orthodox Calvinism in New England. Although Hodge did not live to see it, the liberal views of the New School infiltrated the entire denomination, even Princeton Seminary itself. In the 1890s the Presbyterian Church had to endure the embarrassment of several highly-publicized heresy trials. By 1900 Presbyterian liberals obtained enough power to force a revision of the Church's long-cherished creeds. By 1929 the Church was so thoroughly dominated by evolutionary liberals and modernists that Hodge's conservative followers turned their backs on Princeton Seminary and the denomination itself.

The heroic efforts of Princeton Presbyterianism in the Gilded Age underline an important aspect of orthodoxy in the Romantic era. Scottish Realism became a dogmatic, simplistic, and impotent philosophy. "Scientific" natural theology was a self-contradiction. Perhaps it was even, as Coleridge had suggested, anti-religious. In spite of these absurdities, however, some people managed to find orthodoxy compelling. In the face of increasing hostility from science, evangelicals maintained an admirable religious integrity and stability. If, as Kierkegaard had said, religion consists of belief in the absurd, if true religious commitment requires a leap of faith, a willingness to brave contradiction and irrationality, then the orthodox Protestant of the nineteenth century was truly religious. Unlike the liberal, the evangelical realized that Christianity must maintain its uniqueness in spite of every difficulty, or else lose its identity. The evangelical still knew that "Christianity" and "Western Civilization" or "Humanism" are not synonyms. On the contrary, to be orthodox was to be deeply and sincerely committed. As his position vis-à-vis science became more and more untenable, the evangelical faced it with an increasingly eyes-closed, mind-closed confidence. He accepted what ultimately proved to be among the most indefensible of irrationalities. His was a leap of faith that Kierkegaard would have admired.

Bibliography

I. *Science, Religion, and American Periodicals, 1800–59*

Americans engaged in scholarly debates during the first half of the nineteenth century relied heavily on periodical journals. The publishing of books was a long and expensive process that many writers had to finance themselves. The community of intellectuals had grown sufficiently large that the annual meetings of the learned societies or the weekly roundtables were no longer satisfactory mechanisms for distributing information. Scholars of the period were being bombarded with ideas at an unprecedented rate. Sceptics attacked religion on a half dozen fronts, and a torrent of new scholarship and criticism was pouring in from Europe. The result of all this activity was that the period became a golden age of scholarly reviews.

Unlike the religious periodicals of the eighteenth century, the new American journals were not loaded with sermonettes or devotionals. They did not bother with church calendars, notices of important events, or lists of new ministerial candidates. They were usually not formally affiliated with any denomination. However, they were supported by the faculties of colleges and seminaries, and frequently displayed strongly sectarian sympathies.

The journals gave a reprieve to the intellectual's dying self-image: that he was a "renaissance man," a person knowledgeable in a large number of disciplines even if he was an expert in none of them. To read two or three of the better journals was to be aware of scholarly developments in every field. Only the explicitly scientific journals were too specialized for the general market.

The list below is not exhaustive. It does, however, include the most influential journals of the period and the ones that were important to this study.

The *Christian Examiner*, first published as the *Christian Disciple*, was the primary platform for Unitarian liberalism at Harvard. Its best editors during the Romantic period were Henry Ware, Jr., James Walker, Frederick Henry Hedge, and Edward Everett Hale. The scope of the *Examiner* was immensely broad, including translations of foreign articles and letters, philosophy, theology, all the sciences, exploration, politics, and the arts. The result of this breadth was that the *Christian Examiner* acquired a reputation for liberality and sophistication that really did not exist on the pages of the magazine. Its most frequent contributors were just as narrow-minded as any Presbyterian evangelical. In the wake of the Transcendentalist controversy, the *Examiner* became decidedly reactionary.

The *North American Review* had the reputation as the finest scholarly journal of its time. It generally reflected the opinion of Boston and Cambridge, representing a more conservative wing of Unitarianism and rationalistic Congregationalism than the *Christian Examiner*. Its editors included such Unitarian greats as Jared Sparks, Edward Everett, Francis Bowen, and Andrew Preston Peabody.

No individual had a stronger influence on a journal than Charles Hodge had on *The Biblical Repertory and Princeton Review*. He founded the *Review* in 1825 and edited it under various titles until 1871. Hodge tried to keep the contents of the *Review* broad, and he paid close attention to intellectual developments in Germany. However, he generally sided so completely with German evangelicals that he was unable to give Kant, Hegel, and *Naturphilosophie* fair hearings. Hodge was particularly paranoid about science. While Congregationalists like Benjamin Silliman and Edward Hitchcock were attempting to harmonize scripture with the new sciences, the *Princeton Review* rejected any such compromise as an orthodox sell-out.

The *American Quarterly Observer*, the *American Biblical Repository*, and the *Bibliotheca Sacra*, the scholarly journals produced at Andover, probably generate more surprises than the other intellectual periodicals combined. From the day Harvard's embattled conservatives formed the new seminary, Andover seemed destined to be the breeding ground of reactionary anti-intellectualism. However, its faculty did a remarkable job of holding the Unitarian controversy at arm's length while producing an impressive brigade of well-trained Bible scholars. Under competent editors such as Edward Robinson and Bela Bates Edwards, the Andover journals did very well in spite of financial difficulties. Unlike the *Princeton Review*, they contain few antiscientific reactions and few pathetic demands for worn-out positions. They represent Protestant orthodoxy at its best.

The *Literary and Theological Review* was the journal of the most conservative segment of New York Congregationalism. As a result, it drew the attention and support of many Presbyterians. Founded by Leonard Woods, Jr., as a platform for opposing the New Haven Theology, the *Literary and Theological Review* quickly became stigmatized as a one-issue journal. It survived only through the late 1830s.

The *American Review* (sometimes called the *American Whig Review*) also represented conservative Congregationalism. Although it had a wide circulation during the 1830s, younger intellectuals generally considered it to be oppressively dull. It often reviewed older books, frequently represented the views of ageing professors, and was openly hostile toward anything German. Occasionally, however, bright young scholars did publish in the *Review*, particularly if their viewpoints were strongly supportive of the intellectual status quo. Young Edward Robinson did his beginning work in the *American Review* during the late 1820s.

The *New Englander* was the journal that best represented the Standing Order of Connecticut: conservative Yale Congregationalism. Although it was never as popular nor as formidable as the Unitarian *North American Review*, the *New Englander* frequently achieved a depth and literary quality excelling that of the other journals. It reached the height of its influence during the 1850s, under able editors like Leonard Bacon, Noah Porter, and Horace Bushnell.

The *Southern Review* and the *Southern Quarterly Review* were the two major scholarly reviews of the Old South. The *Southern Review* was a short-lived (1828–32) but excellent journal devoted heavily to learning from abroad. Its contributors generally wrote competent reviews of the literature, philosophy, and science of great Europeans. The *Southern Quarterly Review* lasted much longer and had a broader circulation. It achieved the height of its prestige in the early 1850s, when it was edited by William Gilmore Simms. Both journals were more literary than scientific, but they both became deeply involved in one important scientific debate: the unity of the human race. Generally, but not always, they represented the southern position that blacks were of separate origin and inferior to whites. Unlike the northern journals, the two southern reviews were not closely representative of any particular denomination.

The *Christian Review* represented the better-educated clergy of the Baptist Church. It originated at Newton Theological Seminary, but faculty from Rochester Seminary and Brown University contributed many articles. Its scope was remarkably broad, considering the intellectual narrowness of the Baptist Church at the time. Its positions on science were generally more conciliatory than those of the Presbyterians, but not as accommodating as the Congregational and Unitarian positions.

The *Church Review* was produced by the Protestant Episcopal Church in America. It was published from 1848 under various titles and contained articles on most subjects. Its positions on science and religion were generally more conservative than those of either Unitarians or Congregationalists.

Several other journals played smaller but significant roles in the formation of this study. They include *The Panoplist*, the *General Repository and Review*, the *Christian Spectator*, the *Western Messenger*, *Brownson's Quarterly Review*, the *Dial*, the *Scriptural Interpreter*, *Putnam's Monthly Magazine*, the *Atlantic Monthly*, and others. For more information on American journals, see Frank Luther Mott, *A History of American Magazines* (Cambridge, Mass.: Harvard Univ. Press, 1957), Volumes 1 and 2.

In addition to the general intellectual and theological journals, Americans of the period produced a variety of scientific periodicals. To the credit of their editors, the scientific journals managed to keep away from the broader problems of scientific natural theology. The most important scientific journal of the period, The *American Journal of Science and Arts*, was edited by conservative Congregationalist, Benjamin Silliman. Silliman, however, did not allow his religious prejudices to interfere with the scientific discussions for which his journal provided an excellent forum.

Because they were so narrowly descriptive, the scientific journals were not as useful to this study as the general periodicals were. However, several of the better journals were important. They include The *American Journal of Science and Arts*, the *Proceedings* of the American Association for the Advancement of Science, the *Transactions* of the American Philosophical Society, the *Boston Journal of Natural History*, the *Memoirs* of the American Academy of Arts and Sciences, and the *Transactions* of the American Antiquarian Society. For more information on America's scientific journals during this period see

George H. Daniels, *American Science in the Age of Jackson* (New York: Columbia Univ. Press, 1968); and Alexandra Oleson and Sanborn C. Brown, eds., *The Pursuit of Knowledge in the Early American Republic* (Baltimore: Johns Hopkins Univ. Press, 1976).

II. *Natural Theology and the Sciences*

The close relationship between theology and science during this period led to the production of hundreds of books that can properly be called "natural theology." The following paragraphs describe only a small number of them.

Natural theology in America was modeled after the greatest of all modern natural theologies, British archdeacon William Paley's *Natural Theology,* volume 1 of *The Works of William Paley,* G. W. Meadley, ed. (Boston: J. Belcher, 1810). After Paley, Americans admired the *Bridgewater Treatises* most. Written by Englishmen and published during the middle thirties, the *Treatises* provided evangelicals with clear evidence that one could be both a careful empirical scientist and a natural theologian. The more readable American attempts to integrate science and theology include Louis Agassiz, *Essay on Classification* (London: Trübner and Co., 1857); Horace Bushnell, *Nature and the Supernatural, as Together Constituting one System of God* (New York: Scribner, 1858); Thomas Ewbank, U.S. Commissioner of Patents, *The World a Workshop* (New York: D. Appleton, 1855); Edward Hitchcock, *The Religion of Geology and its Connected Sciences* (Boston: Phillips, Sampson, and Co., 1852); and *Religious Truth Illustrated from Science* (Boston: Phillips, Sampson, and Co., 1857); Mark Hopkins, *Science and Religion* (Albany: Van Benthuysen, 1856); Taylor Lewis, *The Six Days of Creation* (Schenectady: Van Debogert, 1855); *Lectures on the Evidences of Christianity Delivered at the University of Virginia* (New York: Robert Carter, 1852); Samuel Stanhope Smith, *A Comprehensive View of the Leading and Most Important Principles of Natural and Revealed Religion* (New Brunswick: Deare and Myer, 1815); Samuel Tyler, *A Discourse on the Baconian Philosophy* (Baltimore: n.p., 1844); James Walker, *God Revealed in the Process of Creation* (Boston: Gould and Lincoln, 1856).

In addition to these was a large number of books devoted to the "evidences" of the truth of the Bible. The best of these include: Archibald Alexander, *Evidences of the Authenticity, Inspiration, and Canonical Authority of the Holy Scriptures* (Philadelphia: Presbyterian Board of Publication, 1828); Albert Barnes, *Inquiries and Sug-*

gestions in Regard to the Foundation of Faith in the Word of God (Philadelphia: Parry and McMillan, 1859); William Henry Furness, *A History of Jesus* (Boston: Crosby and Nichols, 1850); *Remarks on the Four Gospels* (Philadelphia: Carey, Lea, and Blanchard, 1836); Simon Greenleaf, *An Examination of the Testimony of the Four Evangelists, by the Rules of Evidence Administered in Courts of Justice* (Boston: Little, Brown, 1846); Andrews Norton, *The Evidences of the Genuineness of the Gospels* (Boston: American Stationers Co., 1837–44); *Internal Evidences of the Genuineness of the Gospels* (Boston: Little, Brown, 1855); Moses Stuart, *A Critical History and Defense of the Canon of the Old Testament* (Andover: Allen, Morrill, and Wardwell, 1845).

The best books dealing with the origin of the human race include: John Bachman, *The Doctrine of the Unity of the Human Race Examined on the Principles of Science* (Charleston: C. Canning, 1850); *An Examination of the Characteristics of Genera and Species as Applicable to the Doctrine of the Unity of the Human Race* (Charleston: James, Williams Gitsinger, 1855); Charles Caldwell, *Thoughts on the Original Unity of the Human Race* (New York: E. Bliss, 1830); John Campbell, *Negro-Mania, Being an Examination of the Falsely Assumed Equality of the Various Races of Men* (Philadelphia: Campbell and Power, 1851); Albert Gallatin, *A Synopsis of the Indian Tribes Within the United States East of the Rocky Mountains* (Cambridge: n.p., 1836); George Gliddon and Josiah Clark Nott, *Indigenous Races of the Earth* (Philadelphia: Lippincott, 1857); *Types of Mankind* (Philadelphia: Lippincott and Grambo, 1854); Charles Pickering, member of the United States Exploring Expedition, *The Races of Man, and their Geographical Distribution* (Philadelphia: C. Sherman, 1848); Thomas Smyth, *The Unity of the Human Races* (New York: Putnam, 1850).

Americans of the period produced a spate of books dealing with the geography of Palestine and the archeological remains in the Near East. Some of these are, Lyman Coleman, *An Historical Text-Book and Atlas of Biblical Geography* (Philadelphia: Lippincott, 1859); Asahel Davis, *Lectures on the Remarkable Discoveries Lately Made in the East, Among the Ruins: as Those of Ninevah* (Buffalo: Phinney and Co., 1852); Francis Hawks, *The Monuments of Egypt; or Egypt a Witness for the Bible* (New York, 1840); Henry L. Osborn, *Palestine Past and Present* (Philadelphia: James Challen, 1859); Stephen Olin, *Travels in Egypt, Arabia Petrea, and the Holy Land* (New York: Harper, 1843); Edward Robinson, *Biblical Researches in Palestine, Mount Sinai, and Arabia Petrea* (Boston: Crocker and Brewster, 1841); John Lloyd Stephens, *Incidents of Travel in Egypt, Arabia*

Petrea, and the Holy Land (New York: Harper, 1838); William MaClure Thomson, *The Land and the Book; or Biblical Illustrations Drawn from the Manners and Customs, the Scenes and Scenery of the Holy Land* (New York: Harper, 1859).

III. *Authorities*

A few of the secondary works important to this study deserve special mention.

Anyone interested in the early influence of Scottish Realism in America must read Douglas Sloan's *The Scottish Enlightenment and the American College Ideal* (New York: Columbia Univ. Press, 1971). Sloan's book contains as much as anyone would want to know about the influence of Common Sense Realism at Princeton. The evaluation of similar influences at Harvard has been done best by Daniel Walker Howe in *The Unitarian Conscience: Harvard Moral Philosophy, 1805–1861* (Cambridge, Mass.: Harvard Univ. Press, 1970). Howe's book is a selective study of several "moral philosophers," all of whom were strongly influenced by the Scottish Enlightenment. Both Sloan and Howe have a great deal to say about the relationship between Scottish Realism and natural theology, although neither book is particularly concerned with the sciences. For more general information on Scottish Realism and its place in American intellectual history, see Wilson Smith, *Professors and Public Ethics: Studies of Northern Moral Philosophers before the Civil War* (New York: Cornell Univ. Press, 1965); and Herbert Schneider, *A History of American Philosophy* (New York: Columbia Univ. Press, 1963).

There is no dearth of books about the Transcendentalist controversy and the debates over miracles. I have found, however, that the most exciting and useful is an anthology: Perry Miller's *The Transcendentalists: an Anthology* (Cambridge, Mass.: Harvard Univ. Press, 1950). Miller combines an excellent list of selections with superb introductions and linking paragraphs. As a result, his anthology does as good a job as any critical history of giving the reader a feeling for the important issues.

The best study of biblical scholarship in Romantic America is Jerry Wayne Brown's *The Rise of Biblical Criticism in America* (Middletown: Wesleyan Univ. Press, 1969). This useful book covers most of the men and movements but is a little light on such important issues as the influence of German scholarship on American biblical studies. For that, one would do better to consult Jürgen

Herbst, *The German Historical School in American Scholarship* (Ithaca: Cornell Univ. Press, 1965). Basic background material for biblical researches in Palestine can be found in Hermann Vollrat Hilprecht, *Explorations in Bible Lands During the Nineteenth Century* (Philadelphia: A. J. Holman, 1903). This book suffers from some of the excessive scientism that characterizes historical books of the early twentieth century, but its details are accurate and exhaustive.

The books on the science of the early nineteenth century are too numerous to count. The beginner might do well to consult such seminal books as John Theodore Merz, *A History of European Scientific Thought in the Nineteenth Century* (London: William Blackwood, 1904–12). Merz is thorough, although he might strike many readers as excessively theoretical. His work is actually more concerned with philosophies of science than with the sciences themselves. Equally important is Arthur Lovejoy's *The Great Chain of Being: A Study of the History of an Idea* (Cambridge, Mass.: Harvard Univ. Press, 1942). Lovejoy does an excellent job of following the development of this important scientific paradigm. Daniel Boorstin brings the Great Chain to America in *The Lost World of Thomas Jefferson* (New York: Henry Holt, 1948). Three important studies of the relationship between science and religious world-views in nineteenth-century Europe are Charles Coulston Gillispie, *Genesis and Geology* (Cambridge, Mass.: Harvard Univ. Press, 1951); John C. Greene, *The Death of Adam* (Ames: Iowa State Univ. Press, 1959); and Loren Eisely, *Darwin's Century* (New York: Doubleday, 1958). American science during this period is surveyed in George H. Daniels, *American Science in the Age of Jackson* (New York: Columbia Univ. Press, 1968). Daniels's book suffers from excessive reliance on the scientific journals and too little attention to European influences. Some of Daniels's later work has been discredited in a scandal over plagiarism; however, there is no reason for that unfortunate incident to detract from the value of this important book. Readers interested particularly in geology might look at George Merrill's *The First One Hundred Years of American Geology* (New Haven: Yale Univ. Press, 1924). In Merrill's book the facts are pasted rather closely together, and the reading tends to be a bit dull. In addition, the book is not very concerned with the broader issues of nineteenth-century geology. However, it contains all the names and important events. For those who would like to know more about the pre-Darwin debates over evolution in America, see John Arlo DeJong, "American Attitudes Toward Evolution Before Darwin" (Ph.D. diss., Univ. of Iowa, 1962). The debates over the unity of the human race have been covered superbly in William Stanton's *The Leopard's Spots* (Chicago: Univ.

of Chicago Press, 1960). Stanton, however, does not discuss the arguments derived from comparative philology.

Many scholarly opportunities are available in American scientific biography for the years 1800–1860. Two excellent examples of what can be done are Edward Lurie's *Louis Agassiz: A Life in Science* (Chicago: Univ. of Chicago Press, 1960); and A. Hunter Dupree, *Asa Gray* (Cambridge: Harvard Univ. Press, 1959). Both of these are clear and readable; both deal superbly with the issues.

The following works should also be of interest:

Abel, F. M. "Edward Robinson and the Identification of Biblical Sites." *Journal of Biblical Literature* 58 (1939): 365–72.

Adams, Frank Dawson. *The Development of the Geological Sciences.* Baltimore: Williams and Wilkins, 1938.

Ahlstrom, Sydney. *A Religious History of the American People.* New Haven and London: Yale Univ. Press, 1972.

Alexander, James W. *The Life of Archibald Alexander.* New York: Charles Scribner, 1854.

Alexander, Samuel Davies. *Princeton College During the Eighteenth Century.* New York: Randolph, 1872.

Alt, Albrecht. "Edward Robinson and the Historical Geography of Palestine." *Journal of Biblical Literature* 58 (1939): 373–77.

Anderson, Paul Russell, and Fisch, Max Harold, eds. *Philosophy in America: From the Puritans to James.* New York: Appleton-Century, 1939.

Bainton, Roland. *Yale and the Ministry.* New York: Harper, 1957.

Bartlett, Elisha. *A Brief Sketch of the Life, Character, and Writings of William Charles Wells.* Louisville: Prentice and Weissenger, 1849.

Bates, Ralph. *Scientific Societies in the United States.* New York: J. Wiley, 1945.

Bell, Whitfield J., Jr. *Early American Science: Needs and Opportunities for Study.* Williamsburg: Institute of Early American History and Culture, 1955.

Berry, Robert E. *Yankee Stargazer: the Life of Nathaniel Bowditch.* New York: Whittlesey House, 1941.

Blau, Joseph L. *Men and Movements in American Philosophy.* Englewood Cliffs, N.J.: Prentice-Hall, 1952.

Bowler, Peter J. "Evolutionism in the Enlightenment." *History of Science* 12 (Sept. 1974): 159–83.

Boyd, George Adams. *Elias Boudinot, Patriot and Statesman, 1740–1821.* Princeton: Princeton Univ. Press, 1952.

Bozeman, Theodore Dwight. *Protestants in an Age of Science: the Baconian Ideal and Antebellum American Religious Thought.* Chapel Hill: Univ. of North Carolina Press, 1977.

Branch, E. Douglas. *The Sentimental Years, 1836–1860.* New York: Appleton, 1934.

Brown, Roger Langham. *Willhelm von Humboldt's Conception of Linguistic Relativity.* The Hague: Mouton, 1967.

Bryson, Gladys. *Man and Society.* Princeton: Princeton Univ. Press, 1945.

Butterfield, L. H., ed. *John Witherspoon Comes to America: A Documentary History Based Largely on New Material:* Princeton: Princeton Univ. Press, 1953.

Butts, Robert E., ed. *William Whewell's Theory of Scientific Method.* Pittsburgh: Univ. of Pittsburgh Press, 1968.

Call, Richard Ellsworth. *The Life and Writings of Constantine Samuel Rafinesque.* Louisville: John Morton, 1895.

Cashdollar, Charles D. "European Positivism and the American Unitarians." *Church History* 45 (1976): 490–506.

Chadwick, John White. *Theodore Parker: Preacher and Reformer.* Boston: Houghton, Mifflin, 1900.

Charvat, William. *The Origins of American Critical Thought, 1810–1835.* Philadelphia: Univ. of Pennsylvania Press, 1936.

Cherry, Conrad. "The Structure of Organic Thinking: Horace Bushnell's Approach to Language, Nature, and Nation." *Journal of the American Academy of Religion* 40 (1972): 3–20.

Collins, Varnum. *President Witherspoon: A Biography.* Princeton: Princeton Univ. Press, 1925.

————. *Princeton.* New York: Oxford Univ. Press, 1914.

Commager, Henry Steele. *Theodore Parker.* Boston: Little, Brown, 1936.

Cooke, George W. *Unitarianism in America.* Boston: American Unitarian Assoc., 1902.

Cragg, Gerald. *Reason and Authority in the Eighteenth Century.* New York: Cambridge Univ. Press, 1964.

Cromwell, Richard S. *David Friedrich Strauss and his Place in Modern Thought.* Fair Lawn: R. E. Burdick, 1974.

Cross, Barbara. *Horace Bushnell.* Chicago: Univ. of Chicago Press, 1958.

Curti, Merle. *The Growth of American Thought.* New York: Harper and Brothers, 1943.

Davis, Merrell R. "Emerson's 'Reason' and the Scottish Philosophers." *New England Quarterly* 17 (1944): 209–28.

de Beer, Sir Gavin. *Charles Darwin: Evolution by Natural Selection.* Garden City: Doubleday, 1967.

Dillenberger, John. *Protestant Thought and Natural Science: A Historical Interpretation.* New York: Doubleday, 1960.

Dirks, John Edward. *The Critical Theology of Theodore Parker.* New York: Columbia Univ. Press, 1948.

Draper, John W. *A History of the Conflict Between Religion and Science.* New York: D. Appleton, 1875.

Ekirch, Arthur Alphonse. *The Idea of Progress in America, 1815–1860.* New York: Columbia Univ. Press, 1944.

Finnie, David H. *Pioneers East: the Early American Experience of the Middle East.* Cambridge, Mass.: Harvard Univ. Press, 1967.

Fisher, George P. *The Life of Benjamin Silliman.* New York: Charles Scribner, 1866.

Fiske, John. "Agassiz and Darwinism." *Popular Science Monthly* 3 (1873): 692–705.

Fredrickson, George M. *The Black Image in the White Mind.* New York: Harper and Row, 1971.

Frothingham, Octavius Brooks. *Transcendentalism in New England: A History.* New York, 1876.

Fulton, John F., and Thompson, Elizabeth H. *Benjamin Silliman: Pathfinder in American Science, 1779–1864.* New York: Henry Schuman, 1947.

Gabriel, Ralph Henry. *The Course of American Democratic Thought.* New York: Ronald Press, 1940.

Garfinkle, Norton. "Science and Religion in England." *Journal of the History of Ideas* 16 (1955): 376–88.

Giere, Ronald N., and Westfall, Richard S., eds. *Foundations of Scientific Method.* Bloomington: Indiana Univ. Press, 1973.

Gillispie, Charles Coulston. *The Edge of Objectivity: an Essay in the History of Scientific Ideas.* Princeton: Princeton Univ. Press, 1960.

Gilman, Daniel C. *The Life of James D. Dana.* New York: Harper, 1899.

Giltner, John H. *Moses Stuart: 1780–1852.* Ph.D. diss., Yale Univ., 1956.

Glick, Thomas F., ed. *The Comparative Reception of Darwinism.* Austin: Univ. of Texas Press, 1974.

Glover, Willis B. *Evangelical Nonconformists and Higher Criticism in the Nineteenth Century.* London: Independent Press, 1955.

Gohdes, Clarence L. F. *The Periodicals of American Transcendentalism.* Durham: Duke Univ. Press, 1931.

Gode-von Aesch, Alexander. *Natural Science in German Romanticism.* New York: AMS Press, 1966.

Grave, S. A. *The Scottish Philosophy of Common Sense.* Oxford: Oxford Univ. Press, 1960.

Greene, John C. "American Science Comes of Age, 1780–1820." *Journal of American History* 55 (1968): 22–41.

———. *The Death of Adam*. Ames: Iowa State Univ. Press, 1959.

Gundry, D. W. "The Bridgewater Treatises and their Authors." *History* 31 (1946): 140–56.

Guralnick, Stanley M. *Science and the Ante-bellum American College*. Memoirs of the American Philosophical Society, no. 109. Philadelphia: American Philosophical Society, 1975.

Hall, Courtney Robert. *A Scientist in the Early Republic: Samuel Latham Mitchill, 1764–1831*. New York: Russell and Russell, 1962.

Harris, Horton. *David Friedrich Strauss and his Theology*. Cambridge: Cambridge Univ. Press, 1973.

Harvey, Van A. "D. F. Strauss' 'Life of Jesus' Revisited." *Church History* 30 (1961): 191–211.

Hawke, David Freeman. *Paine*. New York: Harper and Row, 1974.

Hawkins, Richmond Laurin. *Auguste Comte and the United States*. Cambridge, Mass.: Harvard Univ. Press, 1936.

Himmelfarb, Gertrude. *Darwin and the Darwinian Revolution*. New York: Doubleday, 1959.

Hindle, Brook. *The Pursuit of Science in Revolutionary America, 1735–1789*. Chapel Hill: Univ. of North Carolina Press, 1956.

Hornberger, Theodore. *Scientific Thought in the American Colleges, 1636–1800*. Austin: Univ. of Texas Press, 1945.

Hudnut, William. "Samuel Stanhope Smith: Enlightened Conservative." *Journal of the History of Ideas* 17 (1956): 540–52.

Jaffe, Bernard. *Men of Science in America: the Role of Science in the Growth of our Country*. New York: Simon and Schuster, 1944.

Johnson, William Alexander. *Nature and the Supernatural in the Theology of Horace Bushnell*. Lund, Sweden: C. W. K. Gleerup, 1963.

Jones, Howard M. *America and French Culture, 1750–1848*. Chapel Hill: Univ. of North Carolina Press, 1927.

Jordan, David S., ed. *Leading American Men of Science*. New York: Holt, 1910.

Keyes, Charles. "William Maclure: Father of Modern Geology." *Pan-American Geologist* 43 (1925): 81ff.

Koch, Adrienne. *The Philosophy of Thomas Jefferson*. New York: Columbia Univ. Press, 1943.

Kuklick, Bruce. *The Rise of American Philosophy: Cambridge, Massachusetts, 1860–1930*. New Haven: Yale Univ. Press, 1977.

Loewenberg, Bert J. "The Controversy over Evolution in New England." *New England Quarterly* 8 (1935): 232–57.

———. "The Reaction of American Scientists to Darwinism." *American Historical Review* 38 (1933): 693–701.

Lovejoy, Arthur. "The Argument for Organic Evolution Before the Origin of Species." *Popular Science Monthly* 75 (1909): 499–514; 537–49.

McAllister, Ethel M. *Amos Eaton: Scientist and Educator.* Philadelphia: Univ. of Pennsylvania Press, 1946.

Maclean, John. *History of the College of New Jersey.* 2 vols. Philadelphia: J. B. Lippincott, 1877.

McCosh, James. *The Scottish Philosophy.* New York: Robert Carter, 1874.

Madden, Edward, *et al.*, eds. *Theories of Scientific Method: Renaissance Through Nineteenth Century.* Seattle: Univ. of Washington Press, 1960.

Malone, Dumas. *The Public Life of Thomas Cooper, 1783–1839.* New Haven: Yale Univ. Press, 1926.

Marcou, Jules. *Life, Letters, and Works of Louis Agassiz.* 2 vols. New York and London: Macmillan, 1895.

Marsden, George. *The Evangelical Mind and the New School Presbyterian Experience.* New Haven: Yale Univ. Press, 1970.

Martin, Edwin Thomas. *Thomas Jefferson: Scientist.* New York: Henry Schuman, 1952.

Martin, Terence. *The Instructed Vision: Scottish Common Sense Philosophy and the Origins of American Fiction.* Bloomington: Indiana Univ. Press, 1961.

Marx, Leo. *The Machine in the Garden: Technology and the Pastoral Ideal in America.* Oxford: Oxford Univ. Press, 1964.

May, Henry. *The Enlightenment in America.* Oxford: Oxford Univ. Press, 1976.

Mayr, Ernst. "Agassiz, Darwin, and Evolution." *Harvard Library Bulletin* 13 (1959): 165–94.

Mead, Sydney. *Nathaniel Taylor.* Chicago: Univ. of Chicago Press, 1942.

Meisel, Max. *A Bibliography of American Natural History; the Pioneer Century, 1769–1865.* 3 vols. Brooklyn: Premier, 1924–29; 2nd ed. New York: Hafner, 1967.

Meyer, Donald H. *The Instructed Conscience.* Philadelphia: Univ. of Pennsylvania Press, 1972.

Miller, Howard. *The Revolutionary College: American Presbyterian Higher Education, 1707–1837.* New York: New York Univ. Press, 1976.

Miller, Perry. *Jonathan Edwards.* New York: William Sloan Associates, 1949.

Millhauser, Milton. *Just Before Darwin: Robert Chambers and the Vestiges.* Middletown, Conn.: Wesleyan Press, 1959.

Mills, W. Jay, ed. *Glimpses of Colonial Society and the Life at Princeton College, 1766–1773.* Philadelphia: Lippincott, 1903.

Morais, Herbert M. *Deism in Eighteenth Century America.* New York: Columbia Univ. Press, 1934.

Morison, Samuel Eliot. *Three Centuries of Harvard, 1636–1936.* Cambridge, Mass.: Harvard Univ. Press, 1946.

Morse, Edward S. "What American Zoologists Have Done for Evolution." *Popular Science Monthly* 10 (1876): 1–16; 181–98.

Mosely, Maboth. *Irascible Genius: A Life of Charles Babbage, Inventor.* London: Hutchinson, 1964.

Olson, Richard. *Scottish Philosophy and British Physics: A Study in the Foundations of the Victorian Scientific Style.* Princeton: Princeton Univ. Press, 1975.

Peabody, Andrew P. *Harvard Reminiscences.* Boston, 1880.

Peterson, Sven R. "Benjamin Peirce: Mathematician and Philosopher." *Journal of the History of Ideas* 16 (1955): 89–112.

Pfeifer, Edward J. *The Reception of Darwinism in the United States.* Ph.D. diss., Univ. of Michigan, 1958.

Riley, Woodbridge. *American Philosophy: the Early Schools.* New York: Dodd and Mead, 1907.

———. *American Thought from Puritanism to Pragmatism.* New York: Henry Holt, 1915.

Roelker, William G. "Francis Wayland." *Proceedings* of the American Antiquarian Society 53 (1943): 27–78.

Rossiter, Margaret W. "Benjamin Silliman and the Lowell Institute: the Popularization of Science in Nineteenth-Century America." *New England Quarterly* 44 (1971): 602–26.

Russett, Cynthia Eagle. *Darwin in America: The Intellectual Response, 1865–1912.* San Francisco: W. H. Freeman, 1976.

Sandeen, Ernest R. "The Princeton Theology: One Source of Biblical Literalism in American Protestantism." *Church History* 31 (1962): 307–21.

Sanford, William. "Dana and Darwinism." *Journal of the History of Ideas* 26 (1965): 531–46.

Schneer, Cecil J., ed. *Toward a History of Geology.* Cambridge, Mass.: M.I.T. Press, 1969.

Schubert, Charles, and Levene, C. M. *O. C. Marsh: Pioneer in Paleontology.* New Haven: Yale Univ. Press, 1940.

Schweitzer, Albert. *The Quest of the Historical Jesus.* Translated by W. Montgomery. London: A. & C. Black, 1910.

Simon, W. M. *European Positivism in the Nineteenth Century.* New York: Cornell Univ. Press, 1963.

Simpson, George Gaylord. "The Beginnings of Vertebrate Paleontology in North America." *Proceedings* of the American Philosophical Society 86 (1942): 130–88.

Smallwood, William M., and Smallwood, Mabel S. C. *Natural History and the American Mind.* New York: Columbia Univ. Press, 1941.

Smith, Elwyn A. *The Presbyterian Ministry in American Culture.* Philadelphia: Westminster Press, 1962.

Sprague, William B. *Annals of the American Pulpit.* 9 vols. New York: Robert Carter, 1858.

Stanton, William. *The Great United States Exploring Expedition.* Berkeley: Univ. of California Press, 1975.

Stinespring, W. F. "The Critical Faculty of Edward Robinson." *Journal of Biblical Literature* 58 (1939): 379ff.

Struik, Dirk J. *The Origins of American Science (New England).* New York: Cameron Associates, 1957. First published as *Yankee Science in the Making.* Boston: Little, Brown, 1948.

Taylor, Alfred Edward. *David Hume and the Miraculous.* Cambridge, Eng.: Cambridge Univ. Press, 1927.

Thwing, Charles F. "Professor Francis Bowen." *Harvard Register* 3 (1881): 249–53.

Todd, Charles L., and Robert Sonkin. *Alexander Bryan Johnson: Philosophical Banker.* Syracuse: Syracuse Univ. Press, 1977.

Todd, Edgeley W. "Philosophical Ideas at Harvard, 1817–1837." *New England Quarterly* 16 (1943): 63–90.

Trinterud, Leonard J. *The Forming of an American Tradition: A Reexamination of Colonial Presbyterianism.* Philadelphia: Westminster Press, 1949.

Tyler, Moses Coit. *Three Men of Letters.* New York: Putnam, 1895.

Walters, Raymond, Jr. *Albert Gallatin.* New York: Macmillan, 1957.

Ward, Charles Henshaw. *Charles Darwin: the Man and his Warfare.* Indianapolis: Bobbs-Merrill, 1927.

Welch, Claude. *Protestant Thought in the Nineteenth Century.* New Haven: Yale Univ. Press, 1972.

Wells, Ronald Vale. *Three Christian Transcendentalists.* New York: Columbia Univ. Press, 1943.

Wertenbaker, Thomas Jefferson. *Princeton, 1746–1896.* Princeton: Princeton Univ. Press, 1946.

West, Robert Frederick. *Alexander Campbell and Natural Religion.* New Haven: Yale Univ. Press, 1948.

Westfall, Richard S. *Science and Religion in Seventeenth-century England.* New Haven: Yale Univ. Press, 1958.

White, Edward A. *Science and Religion in American Thought: the Impact of Naturalism.* Stanford: Stanford Univ. Press, 1952.

White, Andrew D. *A History of the Warfare of Science with Theology in Christendom.* New York: Appleton, 1896.

Wilbur, Earl Morse. *A History of Unitarianism.* 2 vols. Cambridge, Mass.: Harvard Univ. Press, 1952.

Williams, Daniel Day. *The Andover Liberals: A Study in American Theology.* New York: Octagon, 1970.

Wilson, John Albert. *Signs and Wonders Upon Pharaoh: A History of American Egyptology.* Chicago: Univ. of Chicago Press, 1964.

Woods, David Walker. *John Witherspoon.* New York: Revell, 1906.

Wortham, John David. *The Genesis of British Egyptology, 1549–1906.* Norman: Univ. of Oklahoma Press, 1971.

Wright, Benjamin Fletcher, Jr. *American Interpretations of Natural Law.* Cambridge, Mass.: Harvard Univ. Press, 1931.

Wright, Conrad. *The Beginnings of Unitarianism in America.* Boston: Starr King Press, 1955.

———. "The Religion of Geology." *New England Quarterly,* 14 (1941): 335–58.

Youmans, W. J. *Pioneers of Science in America.* New York: Appleton, 1896.

Notes

Chapter 1

1. Varnum Collins, *President Witherspoon: A Biography* (Princeton: Princeton Univ. Press, 1925), p. 76.

2. Ibid., p. 77.

3. Thomas Reid, *Essays on the Intellectual Powers of Man*, reprinted from the 1785 edition in Sir William Hamilton, ed., *The Philosophical Works of Thomas Reid* (Edinburgh: James Thin, 1895), 1: 293.

4. Thomas Reid, *An Inquiry into the Human Mind, on the Principles of Common Sense*, printed from the first edition of 1764, in Sir William Hamilton, ed., *The Philosophical Works of Thomas Reid*, 1: 209.

5. Reid, *Essays on the Intellectual Powers*, p. 328.

6. See Douglas Sloan, *The Scottish Enlightenment and the American College Ideal* (New York: Columbia Univ. Press, 1971), p. 115. Also, Henry May, *The Enlightenment in America* (Oxford: Oxford Univ. Press, 1976), pp. 62ff; and Howard Miller, *The Revolutionary*

College: American Presbyterian Higher Education, 1707–1837 (New York: New York Univ. Press, 1976), pp. 164–67 and *passim*; and Donald H. Meyer, *The Instructed Conscience* (Philadelphia: Univ. of Pennsylvania Press, 1972).

7. Herbert W. Schneider, *A History of American Philosophy* (New York: Columbia Univ. Press, 1963), pp. 193ff.

8. Reid, *Inquiry into the Human Mind*, p. 97.

9. The biographical information concerning Smith comes from William B. Sprague, *Annals of the American Pulpit* (New York: Robert Carter, 1858), 3:335ff. See also, Howard Miller, *The Revolutionary College, passim.*

10. Sloan, *Scottish Enlightenment*, pp. 146ff. Sloan's discussion of Samuel Stanhope Smith presents a more complete picture of the status of science at Princeton during Smith's administration.

11. For a detailed analysis of Kames's position, see Winthrop Jordan, "Introduction," Samuel Stanhope Smith, *An Essay on the Causes of the Variety of Complexion and Figure in the Human Species* (Cambridge, Mass.: Harvard Univ. Press, 1965), pp. xx, ff.

12. Henry Home, Lord Kames, *Sketches of the History of Man* (Edinburgh: W. Creech, 1774).

13. Smith, *An Essay on the Causes*, p. 188.

14. Jordan, "Introduction," p. xix.

15. Elwyn A. Smith, *The Presbyterian Ministry in American Culture* (Philadelphia: Westminster Press, 1962), p. 113.

16. Ibid., p. 114.

17. Ibid., p. 132.

18. See Sloan, *Scottish Enlightenment*, p. 182.

19. James W. Alexander, *The Life of Archibald Alexander* (New York: C. Scribner, 1854), pp. 314–15. See also, Henry May, *The Enlightenment in America*, pp. 347ff.

20. Samuel Stanhope Smith, *A Comprehensive View of the Leading and Most Important Principles of Natural and Revealed Religion* (New Brunswick: Deare and Myer, 1815), p. 68.

Chapter 2

1. For a full-length study of the influence of Scottish Realism at Harvard during this time see Daniel Walker Howe, *The Unitarian Conscience: Harvard Moral Philosophy, 1805–1861* (Cambridge, Mass.: Harvard Univ. Press, 1970). See also, Bruce Kuklick, *The Rise of American Philosophy: Cambridge, Massachusetts, 1860–1930* (New Haven: Yale Univ. Press, 1977), chapters 1 and 2. The influ-

ence of Scottish Realism on British thought, especially on the exact sciences, is described in Richard Olson, *Scottish Philosophy and British Physics: A Study in the Foundations of the Victorian Scientific Style* (Princeton: Princeton Univ. Press, 1975).

2. For the development of the Unitarian Controversy in America, see Conrad Wright, *The Beginnings of Unitarianism in America* (Boston: Star King Press, 1955); and Earl Morse Wilbur, *A History of Unitarianism* (Cambridge, Mass.: Harvard University Press, 1952), volume 2.

3. Sydney Mead, *Nathaniel Taylor* (Chicago: Univ. of Chicago Press, 1942).

4. Ethan Allen, *Reason the Only Oracle of Man* (Bennington, Vt.: Haswell and Russell, 1784), p. 51.

5. David Freeman Hawke, *Paine* (New York: Harper and Row, 1974), p. 7.

6. Thomas Paine, *The Age of Reason* (Parts I and II, Paris, 1784–1785; Part III, London: D. I. Eaton, 1811); the quotation is from a modern American edition: (New York: Bobbs-Merrill, 1948), p. 15. See also, Henry May, *The Enlightenment in America*, pp. 116–32.

7. Elias Boudinot, *The Age of Revelation; or, the Age of Reason Shown to be an Age of Infidelity* (Philadelphia, 1801), p. xx. Evangelicals were fond of writing full-length attacks on Paine. For another, see Uzal Ogden, *Antidote to Deism: the Deist Unmasked*, n.p., 1795. See also, Henry May, *The Enlightenment in America*, pp. 252–77.

8. See Gerald Cragg, *Reason and Authority in the Eighteenth Century* (Cambridge, Eng.: Cambridge Univ. Press, 1964).

9. Edward Everett, "Character of Lord Bacon," *North American Review* 16 (1823): 300.

10. Albert Barnes, "The Works of Lord Bacon," *Quarterly Christian Spectator* 4 (1832): 539.

11. George H. Daniels, *American Science in the Age of Jackson* (New York: Columbia Univ. Press, 1968), p. 65. Daniels's book, particularly chapters 3 and 4, is an extensive analysis of Baconian science in America. See also, Theodore Dwight Bozeman, *Potestants in an Age of Science: the Baconian Ideal and Antebellum American Religious Thought* (Chapel Hill: Univ. of North Carolina Press, 1977).

12. John Brazer, "A Review of the Argument in Support of Natural Religion," *Christian Examiner* 19 (1835): 140.

13. Ibid., p. 145.

14. Samuel Tyler, "Influence of the Baconian Philosophy," *Biblical Repertory and Princeton Review* 15 (1843): 493, 505. See also, Richard Olson, *Scottish Philosophy and British Physics*.

15. A longer analysis of the *Bridgewater Treatises* can be found in Charles Coulston Gillispie, *Genesis and Geology* (New York: Harper, 1951), pp. 209ff.; and D. W. Gundry, "The Bridgewater Treatises and their Authors," *History* 31 (1946): 140–56.

16. William Whewell, *Astronomy and General Physics Considered with Reference to Natural Theology.* The quotation comes from the American edition: (Philadelphia: Carey, Lea and Blanchard, 1833), p. 14.

17. Thomas Chalmers, *On the Power, Wisdom, and Goodness of God as Manifested in the Adaptation of External Nature to the Moral and Intellectual Constitution of Man* (London: W. Pickering, 1833), 1: 5.

18. Mark Hopkins, "Argument from Nature, for the Divine Existence," *American Quarterly Observer* 1 (1833): 321. See Donald H. Meyer, *The Instructed Conscience*, pp. 16–17 and *passim.*

19. Warren Burton, "Divine Agency in the Material Universe," *Christian Examiner* 18 (1835): 315. Burton is probably not very representative of orthodox, analytic Unitarianism. He became quite enamored of Transcendentalism and eventually with Swedenborg. From 1841 to 1844 he was associated with Brook Farm.

20. Samuel Gilman, "Brown's Philosophy of Mind," *North American Review* 19 (1824): 9.

21. Anon., "Brown's Philosophy," *American Quarterly Review* 4 (1828): 4.

22. Leonard Woods, Jr., "Christianity and Philosophy," *Literary and Theological Review* 1 (1834): 674.

23. Ibid., p. 681.

24. Johnson's contributions to the banking industry in the state of New York are recounted in M. M. Baggs, *The Pioneers of Utica* (Utica: n.p., 1877); and Charles L. Todd and Robert Sankin, *Alexander Bryan Johnson: Philosophical Banker* (Syracuse: Syracuse Univ. Press, 1977). Johnson's most lasting contribution in economic theory was *An Inquiry into the Nature of Value and of Capital*, reprint ed., Joseph Dorfman, ed. (New York: Augustus M. Kelley, 1968).

25. Johnson's works on language are: *The Philosophy of Human Knowledge, or a Treatise on Language* (New York: G. and C. Carvill, 1828); *A Treatise on Language: or the Relation which Words Bear to Things* (New York: Harper, 1836); *The Meaning of Words: Analyzed into Words and Unverbal Things, and Unverbal Things Classified into Intellections, Sensations, and Emotions* (New York: D. Appleton, 1854); *The Physiology of the Senses: or How and What we See, Hear, Taste, Feel and Smell* (New York and Cincinnati: Derby and Jackson, 1856).

26. Johnson, *A Treatise on Language*, pp. 57–73.

27. See Daniels, *American Science*, p. 69. Daniels suggests that this list would be the typical nineteenth-century American moral philosopher's idea of a "philosophical hall of fame."

28. Samuel Tyler, "The Baconian Philosophy," *Biblical Repertory and Princeton Review* 12 (1840): 358.

29. Ibid., p. 362.

30. Tyler, "Psychology," *Biblical Repertory and Princeton Review* 12 (1840): 258.

31. Quoted in Ibid., p. 238.

32. Johnson, *Treatise on Language*, p. 140.

33. Clement Long, "Mental Philosophy," *American Quarterly Observer* 1 (1833): 112. Abercrombie was a prominent Edinburgh physician and scientist.

34. Jonathan Edwards, "The Great Christian Doctrine of Original Sin Defended," in *The Works of President Edwards* (New York: Leavitt and Allen, 1856), 2: 488–90.

35. For more on Edwards's response to Newtonian and Lockean philosophy, see Perry Miller, *Jonathan Edwards* (New York: W. Sloane, 1949). Miller argues that Edwards's modifications of rationalistic Puritan Calvinism were not a return to sixteenth-century Calvinism at all, but a new, "modernized" Calvinism built on essentially empirical principles. See also "Jonathan Edwards as a Thinker," in Clarence H. Faust and Thomas H. Johnson, eds., *Jonathan Edwards* (New York: Hill and Wang, 1962), especially pp. xxxii and following.

36. Warren Burton, "Divine Agency in the Material Universe," *Christian Examiner* 18 (1835): 315–21.

37. Tyler, "On Philosophical Induction," *American Journal of Science* 55 (1848): 319–22.

38. Andrews Norton, "A Discourse on the Latest Form of Infidelity," delivered at the Cambridge Divinity School, 19 July 1839 (Cambridge, Mass.: J. Owen, 1839); quoted by Andrew P. Peabody, in "Mr. Norton's Discourse," *Christian Examiner* 27 (1839): 233. Peabody was pastor of the South Parish Unitarian Church, Portsmouth, New Hampshire. In 1860 he became professor of Christian Morals at Harvard.

39. Peabody, "Mr. Norton's Discourse," p. 233.

Chapter 3

1. Francis Bowen, *Lowell Lectures on the Application of Metaphysical and Ethical Science to the Evidences of Religion*, delivered at

the Lowell Institute, Boston, 1848–49 (Boston: Little, Brown, 1849), p. 6. See Donald H. Meyer, *The Instructed Conscience*, pp. 17–20, and *passim*. Bowen's influence on American philosophy, especially at Harvard, is discussed in Bruce Kuklick, *The Rise of American Philosophy*, pp. 28–45.

2. Immanuel Kant, *Critick of Pure Reason*, 2nd ed., trans. by F. Haywood (London: W. Pickering, 1848).

3. Bowen, *Lowell Lectures*, p. 89.

4. Joseph Haven, Jr., "Natural Theology," *Bibliotheca Sacra* 6 (1849): 52. In 1850 Haven would become professor of mental and moral philosophy at Amherst College.

5. Archibald Alexander, *Evidences of the Authenticity, Inspiration, and Canonical Authority of the Holy Scriptures* (Philadelphia: Presbyterian Board of Publication, 1826); Mark Hopkins, *Lectures on the Evidences of Christianity Before the Lowell Institute, 1844* (Boston: T. R. Marvin, 1861).

6. James Richards, *Lectures on Mental Philosophy and Theology* (New York: Dodd, 1846).

7. Edward Hitchcock, *Religious Lectures on Peculiar Phenomena in the Four Seasons* (Amherst: J., S. and C. Adams, 1850), p. 34.

8. Hitchcock, *Religious Lectures*, "Introduction," pp. v–vi.

9. Hitchcock, *Religious Truth Illustrated from Science* (Boston: Phillips, Sampson, 1857), pp. 35–36.

10. See Leonard Woods, Jr., *Works* (Boston: John P. Jewett, 1851), lecture VII, p. 78.

11. For example, Thomas Reid himself, who had argued that "no reasoning . . . which is built on analogy, can be regarded as conclusive." See Woods, *Works*, lecture VII, p. 78.

12. *Lectures on the Evidences of Christianity Delivered at the University of Virginia, During the Session of 1850–1851* (New York: Robert Carter, 1852).

13. For example, see George Ide Chace, "On the Natural Proofs of the Immortality of the Soul," *Bibliotheca Sacra* 6 (1849): 48ff. Chace was professor of chemistry, geology, and physiology at Brown.

14. Joseph Haven, Jr., "Natural Theology," *Bibliotheca Sacra* 6 (1849): 645.

15. James Walker, *God Revealed in the Process of Creation* (Boston: Gould and Lincoln, 1856). In 1853 Walker had become the president of Harvard.

16. Edward Hitchcock, *The Religion of Geology and its Connected Sciences* (Boston: Phillips, Sampson, and Co., 1852), p. 3.

17. For example, William Buckland suggested "millions and millions of years" in *Geology and Mineralogy Considered with Reference*

to Natural Theology (London, 1836), 1: 21–22. Lyell refused to speculate, but the uniformitarian process he conceived required at least several million years. See Francis Haber, *The Age of the World* (Baltimore: Johns Hopkins Press, 1959), particularly chapter 4, "The Biblical Age of the Earth Surrendered," pp. 187ff. During the 1840s, Louis Agassiz lectured that the age of the earth "is as if one were gently to rub a silk handkerchief across Plymouth Rock once a year until it were reduced to a pebble." See Ralph Henry Gabriel, *The Course of American Democratic Thought* (New York: Ronald Press, 1956), pp. 170–71.

18. For more on Bushnell's rearing and education, see Barbara Cross, *Horace Bushnell* (Chicago: Univ. of Chicago Press, 1958); Nathaniel Taylor's elaborate modifications of New England Calvinism are discussed in Sydney Mead, *Nathaniel Taylor* (Chicago: Univ. of Chicago Press, 1942).

19. Evangelicals who understood the implications of Kant's and Coleridge's strictures on metaphysics were, quite obviously, disturbed. See: anon., "Science and Religion," *The Church Review and Ecclesiastical Register* 5 (1852–53): 329–48; or anon., "The Essence and End of Infidelity," *Christian Review* 20 (1855): 548–68.

20. Quoted in Claude Welch, *Protestant Thought in the Nineteenth Century* (New Haven: Yale Univ. Press, 1972), p. 115. Welch discusses Coleridge throughout chapter 5.

21. Samuel Taylor Coleridge, *Aids to Reflection*, ed., James Marsh, 2nd ed. (Burlington: Chauncey Goodrich, 1840), p. 187.

22. Perry Miller, *The Transcendentalists: An Anthology* (Cambridge, Mass.: Harvard Univ. Press, 1950), p. 34. Marsh was professor of philosophy and president of the University of Vermont.

23. See James Marsh's "Preliminary Essay" in his edition of the *Aids to Reflection*. The quotation is from pp. 25–26.

24. Essays on Coleridge that appeared in the *Christian Examiner* during the 1830s include: "Coleridge's Literary Character," *Christian Examiner* 14 (1833): 108ff; and the Rev. Leonard Withington, "The Present State of Metaphysics," *Christian Examiner* 6 (third series, 1834): 609ff.

25. Noah Porter, Jr., "Coleridge and his American Disciples," *Bibliotheca Sacra and Theological Review* 9 (1847): 117–71.

26. Cross, *Horace Bushnell*, p. 112.

27. Horace Bushnell, *God in Christ* (Hartford: Brown and Parsons, 1849).

28. See chapter 6 of this book for more on the mathematical evidences of design.

29. Bushnell, *God in Christ*, pp. 21–22.

30. Ibid., pp. 38–43.

31. Cross, *Horace Bushnell*, p. 99.

32. *God in Christ*, pp. 48–49.

33. Ibid., p. 57.

34. See Cross, *Horace Bushnell*, p. 111.

35. Edwards Amasa Park, "The Theology of the Intellect and that of the Feelings," *Bibliotheca Sacra* 7 (1850): 533–69.

36. Quoted in William Alexander Johnson, *Nature and the Supernatural in the Theology of Horace Bushnell* (Lund, Sweden: C. W. K. Gleerup, 1963), p. 227.

Chapter 4

1. Radical deists, such as Thomas Paine, thought that the Bible was little more than a collection of myths and superstitions. However, more moderate deists like Jefferson believed that the ethical parts of the Bible ought to be preserved as a normative Christian document. Jefferson himself cut out and assembled the teachings of Christ, together with other ethical passages as he saw fit, into the "Jefferson Bible." For his own description of this see his letter to John Adams, Monticello, 13 October 1813.

2. Bacon's entire statement is illuminating: "Sacred Theology (which in our idiom we call Divinity), is grounded only upon the word and oracle of God, and not upon the light of nature; for it is written, 'Coeli enarrant gloriam Dei;' but it is not written, 'Coeli enarrant voluntatem Dei' "; from *The Advancement of Learning*, in *The Works of Francis Bacon* (Philadelphia: M. Murphy, 1889), 1: 239.

3. Thomas Paine, *The Age of Reason* (New York: Liberal Arts Press, 1948), p. 3.

4. Samuel Tyler, "Connection Between Philosophy and Revelation," *The Biblical Repertory and Princeton Review* 17 (1845): 386.

5. For example, Archibald Alexander's *Evidences of the Authenticity, Inspiration, and Canonical Authority of the Holy Scriptures* (Philadelphia: Presbyterian Board of Publication, 1826).

6. Andrews Norton, *The Evidences of the Genuineness of the Gospels*, 3 vols. (Boston and Cambridge, Mass.: J. B. Russell, 1837–44).

7. Norton, *Internal Evidences of the Genuineness of the Gospels* (Boston: Little, Brown, 1855).

8. Unitarians believed that textual criticism supported their own positions on one issue in particular: the doctrine of the trinity. George R. Noyes's review of J. Scott Porter's *Principles of Textual Criticism*

with their Application to the Old and New Testaments (Christian Examiner 48 [1850]) made a great deal of the fact that "Higher Criticism" had discovered that the Bible verse most explicitly in support of the trinitarian position, 1 John 5:7 ("There are three that bear witness of me in heaven, the Father, the Son, and the Holy Ghost: and these three are one." KJV), was spurious—probably added by an early medieval trinitarian during the debates over the divinity of Christ.

9. Bela Bates Edwards, "Remarks on Certain Erroneous Methods and Principles in Biblical Criticism," *Bibliotheca Sacra* 6 (1849): 185ff.

10. Benjamin B. Smith, "Theology a Strictly Inductive Science," *Literary and Theological Review* 2 (1835): 93–94.

11. Leonard Woods, Jr., *Letters to Unitarians* (Andover, 1822), pp. 18–21. Jürgen Herbst says that Woods "contended that theology differed from physics only in that in addition to the facts of observation and experience it knew the facts of revelation." *The German Historical School in American Scholarship* (Ithaca: Cornell Univ. Press, 1965), p. 83.

12. Samuel Tyler, "Connection Between Philosophy and Revelation." See also Benjamin Morgan Palmer, *Baconianism and the Bible* (Columbia, S. C.: n.p., 1852).

13. For example, Taylor Lewis and Eleazor Lord argued that studies of the creation must be exclusively biblical, not scientific. One cannot attempt to verify the Bible with science, or vice-versa. See chapter 7 of this study.

14. Tyler, "Connection," p. 405.

15. See Moses Stuart, "Are the Same Principles of Interpretation to be Applied to Scripture as to Other Books?" *American Biblical Repository* 2 (1832): 124–37.

16. See Jerry Wayne Brown, *The Rise of Biblical Criticism in America* (Middletown, Conn.: Wesleyan Univ. Press, 1969). particularly chapter three on Moses Stuart and Andover, pp. 45ff.

17. Stuart, "Are the Same Principles," pp. 125–29. Twenty years later Stuart's successor, Calvin E. Stowe, supported his teacher's position. See "The Right Interpretation of the Sacred Scriptures," *Bibliotheca Sacra* 10 (1853): 36–37.

18. Quoted from Stuart's manuscript lectures on "Hermeneutics," series VI. The lectures are included in the Stuart Papers, Andover-Newton Theological Seminary. A microfilm copy is in the Yale Divinity School library. See Brown, *Rise of Biblical Criticism*, p. 45.

19. Edward Hitchcock, "The Connection Between Geology and the Mosaic History of the Creation," *American Biblical Repository* 6 (1835): 294.

20. Moses Stuart, "Critical Examination of Genesis one with Reference to Geology," *American Biblical Repository* 7 (1836): 49.

21. Edward Hitchcock, "Remarks on Professor Stuart's Examination of Genesis one in Reference to Geology," *American Biblical Repository* 7 (1836): 452–53.

22. K, "Remarks on Professor Stuart's Examination of Genesis one," *American Journal of Science* 30 (1836): 114.

23. See Moses Stuart, *A Critical History and Defense of the Canon of the Old Testament* (Andover: Allen, Morrill, and Wardwell, 1845).

24. For more on Noyes, see Brown, *Rise of American Biblical Criticism*, chapter 7.

25. Buckminster is discussed rather thoroughly in Brown, *Rise of American Biblical Criticism*, chapter 1.

26. Andrews Norton, "Defense of Liberal Christianity," *General Repository and Review* 1 (1812): 2.

27. See Norton's manuscript *Lectures*, no. 10. The papers are in the Harvard University archives; a microfilm copy is in the library at Union Theological Seminary. See also, Brown, *Rise of American Biblical Criticism*, pp. 75ff.

28. Norton, *Evidences of the Genuineness of the Gospels* and *Internal Evidences of the Genuineness of the Gospels, supra.*

29. Norton, *Evidences*, 1: clix–clxi.

30. See, for example, an article by "A. L." entitled "Norton on the Genuineness of the Gospels," *Christian Examiner* 22 (1837): 206ff.

31. Moses Stuart, "The Evidences of the Genuineness of the Gospels," *American Biblical Repository* 11 (1838): 265.

32. Stuart, "Evidences," pp. 340–42.

33. One good discussion of Strauss appears in Albert Schweitzer's classic *The Quest of the Historical Jesus* (New York: Macmillan, 1948), pp. 68–120; see also, Van A. Harvey, "D. F. Strauss' Life of Jesus Revisited," *Church History* 30 (1961): 191ff; and Horton Harris, *David Friedrich Strauss and his Theology* (Cambridge, Eng.: Cambridge University Press, 1973).

34. See Schweitzer, *Quest*, p. 32.

35. The one American who came closest to sharing Paulus's view that Christ's miracles could be given rational explanations was William Henry Furness, whose *Remarks on the Four Gospels* was published in Philadelphia in 1836. Furness's position is ambiguous, but he appears to say that he believes in miracles but fails to see their apologetic value. He tried to solve the scientific and historical problems of miracles by suggesting that they came about by natural causes unknown to man. He modified and restated his position in 1850, when

he published *A History of Jesus* (Boston: Crosby and Nichols, 1850). This work offered the same sorts of explanations that Paulus gave in his *Life of Jesus*, with the added suggestion that Jesus hallucinated the temptation in the wilderness and the transfiguration. Such a pathological explanation of Christ's motives was a little more than most Unitarians could handle. A. P. Peabody thought it speculative, neglectful of the testimony of the four evangelists, and fatal to the inspired Word, for "Without miracle there is no revelation." (A. P. Peabody, "Furness' History of Jesus," *North American Review* 71 [1850]: 464ff).

36. For more on Strauss's mythological historiography see Richard S. Cromwell, *David Friedrich Strauss and his Place in Modern Thought* (Fair Lawn, N.J.: R. E. Burdick, 1974); see also, Van A. Harvey, "D. F. Strauss' Life of Jesus Revisited"; and Horton Harris, *David Friedrich Strauss and his Theology*.

37. Charles Hodge, "Strauss' Life of Jesus," *Biblical Repertory and Princeton Review* 9 (1837): 198.

38. H. B. Hackett, "Critique on Strauss' Life of Jesus," *Bibliotheca Sacra* 2 (1844): 48ff. Although he was educated a Congregationalist, Hackett converted to the Baptist Church. He taught at Brown, then went to Newton Seminary in 1839. He ended his career at the Baptist's Rochester Theological Seminary. Jerry Wayne Brown (*Rise of Biblical Criticism in America*) apparently overlooked this important article when he said that the *Bibliotheca Sacra* contains "scarcely any notice" of Strauss' work (*Rise of Biblical Criticism*, p. 148). Nevertheless, the point that evangelicals did not respond very heavily to Strauss ought to be well taken.

39. Another important American article on Strauss was G. R. Noyes's, "Causes of the Decline of Interest in Critical Theology," *Christian Examiner* 43 (1847): 325–40. Noyes criticized his colleagues for their failure to keep up with German scholarship. Implicit in Noyes's essay is the recognition that biblical criticism was badly in need of a refutation of Strauss. Both German and American "refutations" thus far had been unsatisfactory. Noyes appealed to Americans for a concentration of effort in right-minded criticism that would put biblical science back on the right track.

40. George E. Ellis, "The Mythical Theory Applied to the Life of Jesus," *Christian Examiner* 41 (1846): 343–44. A similar position was taken by Unitarian Stephen Bullfinch in "Strauss' Life of Jesus:—the Mythic Theory," *Christian Examiner* 39 (1845): 164.

41. Simon Greenleaf, *An Examination of the Testimony of the Four Evangelists, by the Rules of Evidence Administered in Courts of Justice* (Boston: Little, Brown, 1846), p. 22. Greenleaf was highly re-

garded as a scholar of the law of evidence. His *Treatise on the Law of Evidence* (Boston: Little, Brown, 1842–53) was widely used by lawyers and judges well into the twentieth century.

42. Of course Strauss made a great deal of the hypothesis that the synoptic Gospels were *not* independent at all but were "editions" of a single source document, probably most similar to Mark. Strauss believed that the Gospel of John was of even more questionable origin.

43. Francis Bowen, "The Truth of Christianity," *North American Review* 63 (1846): 382.

44. Theodore Parker, "Strauss' Life of Jesus," *Christian Examiner* 28 (1840): 273ff.

45. Parker, "The Transient and Permanent in Christianity," *Works*, Centenary Edition (Boston: American Unitarian Association, 1908), 4: 11.

46. Parker, *A Discourse on Matters Pertaining to Religion* (Boston: Little, Brown, 1842). Parker came to similar conclusions regarding the Old Testament in what he considered to be his greatest contribution to biblical scholarship: his translation and expansion of Willhelm Martin De Wette's *A Critical and Historical Introduction to the Canonical Scriptures of the Old Testament*, 2nd ed. (Boston: Little, Brown, 1850). With this work Parker felt that he had "accomplished something for the students and friends of science" (1: iii). Here he came to some additional heterodox conclusions; for example, that the books of Samuel contain "numerous inconsistencies . . ., which can be explained only on the supposition that the author drew from various sources, whose testimony was imperfect, and often conflicting." (1: 222).

47. See Brown, *Rise of Biblical Criticism*, pp. 161–62.

48. A. P. Peabody, "Mr. Parker's Discourse," *Christian Examiner* 31 (1841): 98ff.

49. "Mr. Parker's Discourse," *Christian Review* 7 (1842): 163–65. The Baptist reviewer blamed the infidelity of Parker on "Infant baptism, the Half-way covenant, union of church and state, and too little regard to piety, formerly, as a qualification in candidates for the ministry."

50. J. H. Morrison, "Parker's Discourse," *Christian Examiner* 32 (1842): 337ff. The author is identified as "J. M. Merrick" in Poole's *Guide to Early American Periodicals*; but probably correctly as John Hopkins Morrison in John White Chadwick, *Theodore Parker: Preacher and Reformer* (Boston: Houghton, Mifflin, 1900). Morrison was the editor of the *Monthly Religious Magazine*.

51. Noah Porter, "Theodore Parker," *New Englander* 2 (1844):

371–72. Porter was pastor of the second Congregational Church, Springfield, Mass. In the seventies he would become one of Yale's more prominent and conservative presidents.

52. Parker, "Thoughts on Theology," *The Dial* 2 (1842): 497–98. The article is a review of Tübingen professor J. A. Dorner's *Historical Development of the Doctrine of the Person of Christ* (Stutgart, 1839). For more on Parker and Comte, see Charles D. Cashdollar, "European Positivism and the American Unitarians," *Church History* 45 (1976): 490–506.

Chapter 5

1. That is, except for the Unitarians themselves, who supported miracles and scriptural infallibility, but denied the divinity of Christ on purely exegetical grounds.

2. Roland Bainton, *Yale and the Ministry* (New York: Harper, 1957), p. 107.

3. For a good survey of the relationship between European catastrophist geologists and interpretations of Genesis, see Charles Coulston Gillispie, *Genesis and Geology*, pp. 98–120.

4. Ethan Allen, *Reason the Only Oracle of Man* (Bennington, Vt: Haswell and Russell, 1784), p. 235.

5. David Hume, *An Inquiry Concerning Human Understanding* (LaSalle: Open Court Publishing Company, 1966). The Inquiry was originally published in 1777. Alfred Edward Taylor has made a detailed analysis of Hume's argument against miracles in *David Hume and the Miraculous* (Cambridge, Eng.: Cambridge Univ. Press, 1927).

6. Samuel Stanhope Smith, *A Comprehensive View of the Leading and Most Important Principles of Natural and Revealed Religion* (New Brunswick: Deare and Myer, 1815), pp. 79–85. Actually, the tale of the Dutch navigator came from John Locke, *An Essay Concerning Human Understanding* (1690), Book IV, chapter 15.

7. Timothy Dwight, *Theology; Explained and Defended in a Series of Sermons* (Middletown, Conn: Clark and Lyman, 1919), 2: 459.

8. Dwight had a pitiable lack of originality and an infamous ability to borrow cleverly from other people's material. Moses Coit Tyler attacked this vice in his *Three Men of Letters* (New York: Putnam, 1895), p. 116.

9. George Campbell, *A Dissertation on Miracles: Containing an Examination of the Principles Advanced by David Hume, Esq: in an Essay on Miracles* (Edinburgh: A. Kincaid and J. Bell, 1762), p. 41.

10. Charles Pettit M'Ilvaine, *The Evidences of Christianity in their External or Historical Division: Exhibited in a Course of Lectures* (New York: American Tract Society, 1832).

11. More refutations of Hume's position: Alexander Campbell, *Popular Lectures and Addresses* (Philadelphia: James Challen and Son, 1863); Mark Hopkins, *Lectures on the Evidences of Christianity Delivered Before the Lowell Institute, 1844* (Boston: T. R. Marvin, 1861); James McCosh, *The Supernatural in Relation to the Natural* (New York: Robert Carter, 1862). McCosh's response to Hume's argument was perhaps the most straightforward of all: "In a court of law, the testimony of a thousand witnesses, that they did not see a particular individual commit a murder, cannot set aside the testimony of two credible witnesses, that they saw the deed done." (p. 127).

12. Orville Dewey, "Discourse on Miracles," *Christian Examiner* 21 (1836): 102–7.

13. George Ripley, "Martineau's Rationale of Religious Inquiry," *Christian Examiner* 21 (1836): 248–49. The article was ostensibly a review of James Martineau's *Rationale of Religious Inquiry* (London: Whittaker, 1836).

14. *Boston Daily Advertiser*, 5 November 1836 (vol. 42, no. 13933). Perry Miller sees this as one of the nation's first important controversies over "academic freedom." See *The Transcendentalists: an Anthology* (Cambridge, Mass.: Harvard Univ. Press, 1950), pp. 160ff.

15. *Boston Daily Advertiser*, 9 November 1836 (vol. 42, no. 13936).

16. William Henry Furness, *Remarks on the Four Gospels* (Philadelphia: Carey, Lea, and Blanchard, 1836), pp. 177ff.

17. Samuel Osgood, "A Word on Miracles," *Western Messenger* 1 (1836): 777.

18. William G. Elliot, "On Miracles, etc," *Western Messenger* 2 (1837): 312–18.

19. Martin Luther Hurlbut, "Theory of Miracles," *Christian examiner* 23 (1837): 110.

20. Francis Bowen, "Locke and the Transcendentalists," *Christian Examiner* 23 (1837): 170–94.

21. See George Ripley, *The Latest Form of Infidelity Examined* (Boston: Munroe, 1839).

22. See Charles Coulston Gillispie, *Genesis and Geology*, pp. 51–52; 56ff; chapters 2 and 3, *passim*.

23. A Hunter Dupree, *Asa Gray* (New York: Atheneum, 1968), p. 153.

24. Gillispie, *Genesis and Geology*, p. 103. Buckland's *Vindiciae Geologicae* was published at Oxford in 1820.

25. I can find no basis for George H. Daniels's belief that "Edward Hitchcock, in one of his periods at least, came as close as any eminent American to the extreme uniformitarian position of Lyell." (*American Science in the Age of Jackson*, p. 194). That was certainly not Hitchcock's position in the mid-1850s, his most productive years, when he wrote that "in the natural history of our globe, we meet with phenomena explicable only by miraculous intervention." ("Special Divine Interpositions in Nature," *Bibliotheca Sacra* 11 [1854]: 787).

26. "Geology," *American Quarterly Review* 6 (1829): 103–4.

27. Gillispie, *Genesis and Geology*, p. 121.

Chapter 6

1. Francis Wayland, "A Discourse on the Philosophy of Analogy," in Joseph Blau, ed., *American Philosophic Addresses, 1700–1900* (New York: Columbia Univ. Press 1946), pp. 348ff.

2. Francis Wayland, *The Elements of Moral Science* (Boston: Gould, Kendall, and Lincoln, 1835).

3. Wayland, "Discourse," p. 356. Not all of the orthodox were as optimistic about the philosophy of analogy as Francis Wayland. Harvard logician Levi Hedge cautioned the readers of his *Elements of Logic* against excessive analogy, for "the evidence employed in [it] is wholly *indirect* and collateral;—the coexistence of two qualities in one subject affording no direct [evidence] of their coexistence in any other." Hedge concluded that "analogy is an unsafe ground of reasoning; and its conclusions should seldom be received, without some degree of distrust. When things resemble each other in several circumstances, we are apt to suppose the similitude more extensive than it really is." Hedge believed that analogy's only proper use was "to defend and illustrate truths already admitted on other evidence." (*Elements of Logick; or a Summary of the General Principles and Different Modes of Reasoning* [Boston: Hilliard, Gray, Little, and Wilkins, 1829], pp. 84ff).

4. See chapter 3 of this study.

5. George H. Daniels documents this preoccupation in *American Science in the Age of Jackson*, chapter 5.

6. Nathaniel Bowditch, *The American Practical Navigator* (Washington: U.S. Government Printing Office, 1802).

7. See Laplace's *Celestial Mechanics*, Nathaniel Bowditch, ed., (New York: Chelsea Publishing Company, 1829, 1832, 1834, 1839). For more on Bowditch, see Robert E. Berry, *Yankee Stargazer: the Life of Nathaniel Bowditch* (New York: Whittlesey House, 1941).

8. Benjamin Peirce, "Bowditch's Translation of the Mécanique Céleste," *North American Review* 48 (1839): 144–45.

9. Peirce, "Bowditch's Translation," 171–72.

10. *Proceedings*, American Association for the Advancement of Science 2 (1849): 446–47.

11. Ibid., pp. 438–44.

12. Thomas Hill, "The Scientific Meeting at Cambridge," *Christian Examiner* 47 (1849): 331.

13. Joseph Tracy, "On the Idea of an Infinite Series, as Applicable to Natural Theology," *Bibliotheca Sacra* 7 (1850): 617–21.

14. Mary Somerville, *On the Connexion of the Physical Sciences* (London: John Murray, 1824); "On the Connexion of the Physical Sciences," *American Quarterly Review* 16 (1834): 429.

15. Thaddeus William Harris, "Man and Nature," *Christian Examiner* 53 (1852): 116–18. Harris, another follower of Agassiz, was Asa Gray's chief competitor for the Fisher Professorship of Natural History in 1842. See Dupree, *Asa Gray*.

16. A more complete discussion of German *Naturphilosophie* is contained in Frederick Copleston, S. J., *A History of Philosophy* (New York: Doubleday, 1965), 7: part one.

17. George Daniels discusses the ideas of such empiricists, among them Samuel Tyler. Characteristically, they identified science with taxonomy. *American Science in the Age of Jackson*, pp. 65ff.

18. As T. W. Harris said, "Every child should be early taught the utmost precision of observation." It is the "visible facts" of nature which direct men to (quoting Agassiz) "the immaterial principle with which each is endowed, and which determines the constancy of species from generation to generation." ("Man and Nature," p. 125).

19. Georges Cuvier, *The Animal Kingdom* (1st American ed. (New York: Carvill, 1831).

20. Louis Agassiz, "Contemplations of God in the Kosmos," *Christian Examiner* 50 (1851): 3.

21. Ibid., p. 10.

22. See Lorenz Oken, *Lehrbuch der Naturphilosophie* (Jena: F. Frommann, 1809–11). Oken did have at least one follower in the United States. See anon., "Physical Science, in its Relation to Natural and Revealed Religion," *The Southern Quarterly Review* 19 (1851): 449.

23. Louis Agassiz, *Contributions to the Natural History of the*

United States (London: Trubner and Co., 1857–62). Part one contains the *Essay on Classification*. See also, Agassiz and Augustus A. Gould, *Principles of Zoology* (Boston: Gould, Kendall, and Lincoln, 1848). Here Agassiz argues many of the same positions.

24. Agassiz, *Essay*, pp. 4–11.

25. Ibid., pp. 187ff.

26. James Dwight Dana, "Agassiz's Contributions to the Natural History of the United States," *American Journal of Science* 75 (1858): 341.

27. This was quite relevant to the one point where Agassiz and Dana still had significant differences—the unity of origin of the human race.

28. James Dwight Dana, "Thoughts on Species," in *Bibliotheca Sacra* 14 (1857): 854ff, and in *American Journal of Science* 24 (1857): 305ff. Quotes are from the *American Journal of Science*, pp. 307–9.

29. Dana, "Thoughts on Species," pp. 308–9. This piece of reasoning made Asa Gray sceptical. He suggested to Dana that his entire argument might be based on an equivocation of the word *species*. "In reasoning from *inorganic species* to organic species," he wrote Dana, "and in making it tell *where* you want it, and *for what* you want it to tell, you must be sure that you are using the word *species* in the same sense in the two. . . . That is what I am not yet convinced of." Gray to Dana, 7 November 1857.

30. John Harris, *The Pre-Adamite Earth* (Boston: Gould and Lincoln, 1859), p. 62.

31. Dana, "Thoughts on Species," pp. 312–16.

32. See, for example, Oliver Wendell Holmes, Sr., "Agassiz's Natural History," *Atlantic Monthly* 1 (1857–1858): 320–33. Writing for the nonscientific public, Holmes praised Agassiz for tracking "the warm foot-prints of Divinity throughout all the vestiges of creation." (p. 323). See also, Ian F. A. Bell, "Divine Patterns: Louis Agassiz and American Men of Letters. Some Preliminary Explorations," *Journal of American Studies* 10 (1976): 349–81.

33. Miller (1802–56), trained as a mason, had no formal education as a geologist. He turned to writing about geology and natural theology in response to Robert Chambers' *Vestiges of the Natural History of Creation*. See Hugh Miller, *The Foot-Prints of the Creator; Or, the Asterolepis of Stromness* (Boston: Gould, Kendall, and Lincoln, 1850); and *The Testimony of the Rocks; or Geology in its Bearings on the Two Theologies, Natural and Revealed* (Boston: Gould and Lincoln, 1857).

34. See William Sanford, "Dana and Darwinism," *Journal of the History of Ideas* 26 (1965): 531–46.

Chapter 7

1. Samuel Miller, *A Brief Retrospect of the Eighteenth Century* (New York: T. and J. Swords, 1803), 1: 12.

2. Ibid., 1: 186–89.

3. The "watershed" hypothesis comes from Gillispie, *Genesis and Geology*, pp. 41ff.

4. Miller rejected as anti-Christian even thoroughly Wernerian ideas, because they "rejected the Mosaic account of the deluge" and "have been compelled to seek for other means of immerging the present continents in the ocean." (*Brief Retrospect*, 1: 187). For a more general discussion of the *Brief Retrospect*, see Henry May, *The Enlightenment in America*, pp. 337ff. An excellent, illustrated account of theories of the earth during the eighteenth century can be found in John C. Greene, *The Death of Adam* (Ames: Iowa State Univ. Press, 1959), pp. 17–76.

5. However, the Neptunists who had the Genesis account strongly in mind apparently did not include Werner himself, who was a deist. Werner, in fact, called his own work "geognosy" in order to distinguish it from the excessively speculative "geology" of his contemporaries. His disciples, notably Richard Kirwan (*Geological Essays* [London: D. Bremner, 1799]) and Robert Jameson (*System of Mineralogy* [Edinburgh: n.p., 1808]) were most instrumental in weaving Genesis and geology together. This led to a misunderstanding of Werner's own position, which was exacerbated by the fact that Lyell misrepresented Werner's work as excessively theological (*Principles of Geology* [London: J. Murray, 1830–33], 1: 69). See Leroy E. Page, "Diluvialism and Its Critics in Great Britain in the Early Nineteenth Century," *Toward a History of Geology*, Cecil J. Schneer, ed. (Cambridge, Mass.: M.I.T. Press, 1969).

6. For a more detailed analysis of Werner's position, see Gillispie, *Genesis and Geology*, chapter 2, *passim*.

7. One scholar makes a great deal of MaClure's budding uniformitarianism. Charles Keyes, "William MaClure: Father of Modern Geology," *Pan-American Geologist* 43 (1925): 81ff.

8. MaClure attempted to justify his extensive changes of Werner's classification system in a letter to Silliman, 22 August 1818, reprinted in The *American Journal of Science* 1 (1818): 209.

9. See William MaClure, *Observations on the Geology of the United States of America* (Philadelphia: Abraham Small, 1817).

10. James Hutton, *Theory of the Earth* (Edinburgh, 1795), 1: 200.

11. See Gillispie, *Genesis and Geology*, p. 48ff; and John C. Greene, *The Death of Adam*, pp. 76–85.

12. John Playfair, *Illustrations of the Huttonian Theory of the Earth*, 1802.

13. See Ethel M. McAllister, *Amos Eaton: Scientist and Educator* (Philadelphia: Univ. of Pennsylvania Press, 1946).

14. Eaton's *Conjectures* was appended to his *Index to the Geology of the Northern States*, (Leicester, Mass.: H. Brown, 1818). See also, George Merrill, *The First One Hundred Years of American Geology* (New Haven: Yale Univ. Press, 1924), pp. 59ff.

15. Benjamin Silliman, "Notice of Eaton's Index to the Geology of the Northern States," *American Journal of Science* 1 (1818): 69–70.

16. Robert Bakewell, *An Introduction to Geology; Comprising the Elements of the Science in its Present State*, with notes by Benjamin Silliman, 1st American ed., from the 3rd British ed. (New Haven: H. Howe, 1829), p. 46. See Stanley M. Guralnick, *Science and the Ante-bellum American College*, *Memoirs* of the American Philosophical Society, no. 109 (Philadelphia: American Philosophical Society, 1975). One earlier American text, Bowdoin geologist Parker Cleaveland's *Elementary Treatise on Mineralogy and Geology* (Boston: Cummings and Hilliard, 1816), had received wide use through the early 1820s. By the time of Silliman's edition of Bakewell, however, it was considered badly outdated. See Guralnick, *Science and the Ante-bellum American College*, pp. 180–81.

17. Bakewell, *An Introduction to Geology*, pp. 135–38.

18. Some of the less secular texts included William Buckland, *Reliquiae Diluvianae*, 2nd ed. (London: J. Murray, 1824); Richard Kirwan, *Elements of Mineralogy* (London: n.p., 1784); Robert Jameson, *System of Mineralogy*, including an *Elements of Geognosy* (Edinburgh: n.p., 1804–8).

19. Silliman did not alter Bakewell's text; he simply appended his own conclusions.

20. Silliman, "Outline," pp. 3–4.

21. Even Silliman conceded that some rocks appear to be igneous, and not aqueous, in origin, "Outline," p. 54.

22. Silliman, "Outline," p. 50.

23. For an extensive exposition of the long-day theory, see Hugh Miller, *The Testimony of the Rocks*, pp. 197ff. Miller created a detailed correspondence between geologic epochs and individual creation days. He believed that the first creation day corresponded to the Azoic, that the second was the Silurian, the third was the Car-

boniferous, the fourth combined the Permian and Triassic, and the fifth included the Oolitic and Cretaceous periods.

24. Even Werner defined the diluvial in terms of floods *in general.*

25. Silliman, "Outline," pp. 69–74. The evidence from Humboldt to which Silliman referred came from The *American Journal of Science* 2 (1820): 3.

26. The second American edition of Bakewell's *Geology* was based on the fourth London edition. It was published in New Haven by H. Howe in 1833. Lyell's name appears several times in Bakewell's text.

27. Silliman, "Consistency of Geology," in Robert Bakewell, *An Introduction to Geology* (New Haven, 1833), p. 458.

28. According to George H. Daniels, Silliman's work of this period, together with his publication of the *American Journal of Science*, may well have made him "the greatest single influence in the development of an American scientific community" (*American Science in the Age of Jackson*, p. 18). By the early 1840s, Silliman's professional influence was beginning to decline, but he remained immensely popular with laymen. See Margaret W. Rossiter, "Benjamin Silliman and the Lowell Institute: the Popularization of Science in Nineteenth-Century America," *New England Quarterly* 44 (1971): 602–26.

29. At least one southern author other than Cooper found Silliman's work "at least twenty years behind the knowledge of the day." While not a deist, and himself a firm believer that Genesis and geology could be harmonized, this reviewer was outraged by the lengths to which Silliman was willing to carry this effort. ("Geology," *Southern Review* 6 [1830]: 285).

30. Thomas Cooper, *The Connection Between Geology and the Pentateuch: in a Letter to Professor Silliman* (Columbia, S.C.: n.p., 1836), preface. For more on Cooper, see Dumas Malone, *The Public Life of Thomas Cooper, 1783–1839* (New Haven: Yale Univ. Press, 1926).

31. Cooper, *Connection*, p. 1.

32. Ibid., pp. 55–60.

33. Another response to Silliman's Bakewell was much more positive about Silliman's work and about the harmonization effort in general. "Geology," *American Quarterly Review* 6 (1829): 73ff; and 7 (1830): 361ff.

34. Edward Hitchcock, "The Connection Between Geology and Natural Religion," *The Biblical Repository* 6 (1836): 114–15.

35. The Jameson edition was published in Edinburgh: William

Blackwood, 1813; the Mitchill edition was published in New York: Kirk and Mercein, 1818. See also, Georges Cuvier, *A Discourse on the Revolutions of the Surface of the Globe, and the Changes thereby Produced in the Animal Kingdom* (London: Whittaker, Treacher, and Arnot, 1829).

36. Although James Hutton's position is frequently identified as the basis of the extreme uniformitarianism of Lyell, many geologists— notably Cuvier—found the necessity for catastrophist theory in Hutton's work. In explaining how strata containing marine fossils could be found in elevated dry land, Neptunists and Vulcanists developed opposing theories. Werner believed that the seas were formerly at a higher level than they are now; as they evaporated, they receded from some of the land they once covered. Hutton, on the other hand, suggested that the land had been raised up by internal pressure, and had thus been transformed from ocean floor to dry land. This Huttonian belief, says Leonard G. Wilson, made it "almost necessary" that geologists "accept the occurrence of catastrophes during geological history, for they found the strata not only elevated to form hills and mountains but also in inclined, even vertical positions, and frequently bent and distorted in an extravagant way." For Conybeare and Phillips (*Outlines of the Geology of England and Wales* [London: n.p., 1822]), "The acceptance of the occurrence of violent convulsions during the past history of the earth appears . . . to have been a consequence of the acceptance of the Huttonian theory of the earth." Thus, when Lyell began his study of geology in 1816 under Buckland, he learned theories that in general were "both Huttonian and catastrophic." For more on this, see Leonard G. Wilson, "The Intellectual Background to Charles Lyell's "Principles of Geology, 1830–1833," in Cecil J. Schneer, ed., *Toward A History of Geology* (Cambridge, Mass.: M.I.T. Press, 1969), pp. 426ff.

37. I have used Samuel L. Mitchill's edition of Cuvier's *Theory: Essay on the Theory of the Earth; to which are added Observations on the Geology of North America, by S. L. Mitchill* (New York: Kirk and Mercein, 1818), p. 166.

38. However, Cuvier did mention the Pentateuch in his work. He believed that it was legitimately written by Moses and that its account of the Deluge was the best of all flood epics. *Theory*, pp. 146ff.

39. Others who used Cuvier to the same end include: Thomas Chalmers, "Remarks on Cuvier's Theory of the Earth," *Miscellanies* (New York: Robert Carter, 1848); William Buckland, *Vindiciae Geologicae* (Oxford: Oxford Univ. Press, 1820).

40. Edward Hitchcock, "On the Connection Between Geology and Natural Religion," *American Biblical Repository* 5 (1835): 113–37; 439–51. The quotation is from p. 117.

41. Edward Hitchcock, "The Connection Between Geology and the Mosaic History of the Creation," *American Biblical Repository* 6 (1835): 275–315.

42. The two-creation theory was not without its own problems; such as, what accounts for the fact that sun, moon, and stars were not created until the fourth day of the second creation? Hitchcock disregarded that objection.

43. Hitchcock, "Connection," 327.

44. Moses Stuart, "Critical Examination of Some Passages in Genesis I, with Reference to Geology . . .," *American Biblical Repository* 7 (1836): 46ff. Hitchcock answered Stuart's criticisms in "Remarks on Professor Stuart's Examination of Genesis One with Reference to Geology," *American Biblical Repository* 7 (1836): 448ff.

45. Buckland's book was published in Philadelphia in 1837. See anon., "Buckland's Geology," *Christian Review* 2 (1837): 552ff. Another critic who was favorable to the two-creation view was the reviewer of the third American edition of Bakewell's *Geology*, in the *New York Review* 5 (1839): 457ff.

46. John Pye Smith's book was published in New York in 1840. See Matthew Boyd Hope, "The Relation between Scripture and Geology," *The Biblical Repertory and Princeton Review* 13 (1841): 385. In 1846 Hope would become professor of rhetoric at Princeton; in 1854 he would additionally acquire the chair of political economy.

47. Edward Hitchcock, *Elementary Geology* (Amherst: J. S. and C. Adams, 1840).

48. Rufus P. Stebbins, "Scripture and Geology," *Christian Examiner* 29 (1841): 353.

49. Edward Hitchcock, *The Religion of Geology* (Boston: Phillips, Sampson, 1851), pp. 62–63.

50. Rufus P. Stebbins, "The Religion of Geology," *Christian Examiner* 53 (1852): 56.

51. Edward Hitchcock, "The Historical and Geological Deluges Compared," *American Biblical Repository* 9 (1837): 92–93.

52. Edward Hitchcock, "The Historical and Geological Deluges Compared," *American Biblical Repository* 10 (1837): 335–36.

53. Ibid., 336 and 353.

54. Edward Hitchcock, "The Historical and Geological Deluges Compared," *American Biblical Repository* 11 (1838): 2–5. The illustrations from Buckland were contained in his *Reliquiae Diluvianae*,

2nd ed. (London: J. Murray, 1824) and also his *Bridgewater Treatise, Geology and Mineralogy Considered with Reference to Natural Theology* (London: W. Pickering, 1836; Philadelphia: Carey, Lea, and Blanchard, 1837).

55. Edward Hitchcock, "The Historical and Geological Deluges Compared," *American Biblical Repository* 11 (1838): 2–27. However, by 1851, when *The Religion of Geology* was published, Hitchcock was considerably less sure about the cause of the deluge; he refused to suggest one (p. 142).

56. A few English writers had done the same thing. See, for example, William Cockburn, *The Bible Defended Against the British Association* (London: n.p., 1839).

57. Eleazor Lord, *The Epoch of Creation, the Scripture Doctrine Contrasted with the Geological Theory* (New York: Scribner, 1851), p. x.

58. Ibid., p. 35.

59. Anon., "Lord's Epoch of Creation," *New Englander* 9 (1851): 510.

60. Taylor Lewis, *The Six Days of Creation; or, the Scriptural Cosmology, with the Ancient Idea of Time-Worlds, in Distinction from Worlds of Space* (Schenectady: Van Debogert, 1855), p. 1. Lewis was thoroughly committed to the view that science and theology have nothing to say to each other. As a result, he abhorred the "scientific" natural theology of the 1840s and 1850s. He wrote, for example, that the *Bridgewater Treatises* "have made more infidels than they have ever cured." Lewis, "Vestiges of Creation," *American Whig Review* 1 (1845): 537. Another writer who shared Lewis's views about the exclusivity of science and religion was William T. Hamilton, pastor of the Government Street Church in Mobile, Alabama, and author of *The Friend of Moses* (New York: Dodd, 1852). Hamilton based his whole defense of Genesis on the Huttonian argument that "geology treats of the changes effected on the earth's surface, *since its creation*. About the *origin* of the earth, it teaches, and it can teach, literally nothing."

61. Lewis, *Six Days*, pp. 2–4.

62. Ibid., p. 393.

63. See Conrad Wright, "The Religion of Geology," *New England Quarterly* 14 (1941): 354.

64. For a longer analysis of the Dana-Lewis controversy, see Morgan B. Sherwood, "Genesis, Evolution, and Geology in America Before Darwin: the Dana-Lewis Controversy, 1856–57," *Toward a History of Geology*, Cecil J. Schneer, ed. (Cambridge, Mass.: M. I. T.

Press, 1969). Dana's response to Lewis is contained in four articles entitled "Science and the Bible," two of which appear in *Bibliotheca Sacra* 13 (1856); and two in *Bibliotheca Sacra,* 14 (1857).

65. Thomas A. Davies, *Cosmogony, or the Mysteries of Creation* (New York: Rudd and Carleton, 1857), pp. 34–36.

66. Stebbins, "The Religion of Geology," *Christian Examiner* 53 (1852): 58.

67. Edward Hitchcock, *Report on the Geology, Mineralogy, Botany, and Zoology of Massachusetts* (Amherst: J. S. and C. Adams, 1832); for more on the state geological surveys, see George Perkins Merrill, *The First one Hundred Years of American Geology* (New Haven: Yale Univ. Press, 1924).

Chapter 8

1. Edward Gibbon, *The History of the Decline and Fall of the Roman Empire* (New York: Harper, n.d.), 1: 245.

2. Constantin Francois Volney, *Travels in Egypt and Syria* (London: n.p., 1786). Volney is more famous as the author of *Ruins: or a Survey of the Revolution of Empires* (London: n.p., 1791). That book, which was translated into English by Thomas Jefferson and Joel Barlow (Richmond: James Lyon, 1799), rejected all supernaturalism in religion.

3. For example, Yale chemist and physicist Denison Olmsted wrote an essay on the "Meteorology of Palestine" (*New Englander* [1859]: 450ff) in order to substantiate the Bible's claim that Palestine has violent extremes of weather, thus causing abundant harvests followed by absolute famines.

4. The development of the "Deutero-Isaiah" theory goes back to Johann Gottfried Eichhorn's *Einleitung in Das Alte Testament* (Leipzig: n.p., 1780–83), 3: 76.

5. Chateaubriand's book was published in Paris in 1811; Lamartine's was published in Paris in 1835.

6. See Gotthilf Neinreich von Schubert, *Reise in Das Morgenland in den Jahren 1836 und 1837* (Erlangen: n.p., 1838–39); and Johannes Ludwig Burckhardt, *Travels in Syria and the Holy Land* (London: J. Murray, 1822). Some examples of British travels in Palestine before Robinson are: Charles Leonard Irby and James Mangles, *Travels Through Nubia, Palestine, and Syria in 1817 and 1818* (London: T. White, 1823); and Claudius James Rich, *Memoir on the Ruins of Babylon* (London: n.p., 1815). For more on the state of the science in the first quarter of the century, see H. V. Hilprecht, *Explorations in*

Bible Lands During the Nineteenth Century (Philadelphia: A. J. Holman, 1903).

7. Henry A. S. Dearborn, *A Memoir on the Commerce and Navigation of the Black Sea, and the Trade and Maritime Geography of Turkey and Egypt* (Boston: Wells and Lilly, 1819). A more complete description of Dearborn's work, together with descriptions of some other books, can be found in David H. Finnie, *Pioneers East: the Early American Experience in the Middle East* (Cambridge, Mass.: Harvard Univ. Press, 1967).

8. Finnie, *Pioneers East*, p. 14.

9. Nathaniel Parker Willis, *Pencillings by the Way* (Philadelphia: Carey, Lea, and Blanchard, 1836).

10. [John Lloyd Stephens], *Incidents of Travel in Egypt, Arabia Petrea, and the Holy Land* (New York: Harper, 1837). Stephens's *Incidents* has been republished with an introduction by Victor Wolfgang von Hagen (Norman: Univ. of Oklahoma Press, 1970).

11. E. W. Hengstenberg, *Egypt and the Books of Moses*, R. D. C. Robbins, trans. (Andover and New York: Carter, 1850). It was reviewed in America by Robert Davidson, pastor of the First Presbyterian Church, New Brunswick, New Jersey. See "Egypt and Ninevah," *Biblical Repertory and Princeton Review* 22 (1850): 260ff. William Osburn, *Ancient Egypt, Her Testimony to the Truth of the Holy Bible* (London, n.p., 1846). Francis L. Hawks, *The Monuments of Egypt; or, Egypt a Witness for the Bible* (London: n.p., 1850). William Maclure Thomson, *The Land and the Book; or Biblical Illustrations Drawn from the Manners and Customs, the Scenes and Scenery of the Holy Land* (New York: Harper, 1859). Other important American books include: James Ewing Cooley, *The American in Egypt* (New York: Appleton, 1842); John P. Durbin, *Observations in the East, Chiefly in Egypt, Palestine, Syria, and Asia-Minor* (New York: Harper, 1845); William Francis Lynch, *Narrative of the United States Expedition to the River Jordan and the Dead Sea* (Philadelphia: Lea and Blanchard, 1849); Stephen Olin, *Travels in Egypt, Arabia Petraea and the Holy Land* (New York: Harper, 1843).

12. Edward Robinson, "On the Exodus of the Israelites out of Egypt," *American Biblical Repository* 2 (1832): 743. Robinson reaffirmed his conclusions in his *Biblical Researches*.

13. Robinson, "On the Exodus," p. 755.

14. Edward Robinson, "The Land of Goshen, and the Exodus of the Israelites," *American Biblical Repository* 15 (1840): 306ff.

15. Edward Robinson, "The Destruction of Sodom and Gomorrah," *American Biblical Repository* 15 (1840): 24–33.

16. Charles A. Lee, "On the Geology of Palestine, and the De-

struction of Sodom and Gomorrah," *American Biblical Repository* 16 (1840): 324–52.

17. Published in Boston by Crocker and Brewster.

18. For example, Robinson had a measurable influence on the Swiss archeologist Titus Tobler, author of *The Topography of Jerusalem and its Environs* (Berlin: n.p., 1853). See H. V. Hilprecht, *Explorations in Bible Lands During the Nineteenth Century* (Philadelphia: A. J. Holman and Co., 1903).

19. Stephens, *Incidents of Travel*, 2: 137. For more information on the early lack of critical method, see F. M. Abel, "Edward Robinson and the Identification of Biblical Sites," *Journal of Biblical Literature* 58 (1939): 365ff.

20. Stephens, *Incidents of Travel*, 2: 163.

21. Albrecht Alt, "Edward Robinson and the Historical Geography of Palestine," *Journal of Biblical Literature* 58 (1939): 374ff.

22. Robinson, *Biblical Researches*, 2: 64–80. F. M. Abel, "Edward Robinson and the Identification of Biblical Sites," also mentions several sites that Robinson correctly identified for the first time. See also W. F. Stinespring, "The Critical Faculty of Edward Robinson," *Journal of Biblical Literature* 58 (1939): 379ff. Stinespring attempted to answer the allegations of Frederick Jones Bliss, an archeologist who delivered the 1903 Ely Lectures at Union Theological Seminary. Bliss had suggested that Robinson rejected so many traditional locations because of his excessive anti-Catholicism. Stinespring could find no such bias; he affirmed that in most cases Robinson, and not the Old Church tradition, was correct. See F. J. Bliss, *The Development of Palestine Exploration* (New York: Scribner's, 1907).

23. Robinson, *Biblical Researches*, 2: 328; and 1: 415ff. W. F. Lynch, leader of the United States Expedition to the River Jordan and the Dead Sea, 1847, was as determined as Robinson to take a critical view of the geography of Palestine, but even he was convinced that the Church of the Holy Sepulchre was on the correct spot. Lynch's argument made some sense: since there were Christians in Jerusalem continuously since New Testament times, is it likely that they would have forgotten or changed the location of Christ's interment, any more than that the Jews would "forget the site of the temple?" Lynch thereupon attacked the "presumptuous cavillers" who doubted everything the Holy Land guides told them. "For their peace of mind here, I hope that they may never know how much they have injured a cause, of which some of them are the professed champions." There is no explicit reference to Robinson's *Researches*, but Robinson's work is obviously what Lynch had in mind. See W. F. Lynch, *Narra-*

tive of the United States Expedition to the River Jordan and the Dead Sea (Philadelphia: Lea and Blanchard, 1849).

24. See F. M. Abel, "Edward Robinson and the Identification of Biblical Sites." David Finnie, *Pioneer's East*, generally takes a contrary position. His book praises the less critical travelers, such as William Maclure Thomson, and attacks Robinson for being too pedantic and technical. Finnie evidently had no access to the several articles devoted to Robinson that appear in the *Journal of Biblical Literature* 58 (1939).

25. G. E. Ellis, "Robinson's Biblical Researches in Palestine and Mount Sinai," *Christian Examiner* 31 (1842): 222ff.

26. Charles Hall, "Review of Robinson's Biblical Researches," *American Biblical Repository* 18 (1841): 427ff.

27. Joseph Addison Alexander, "Robinson's Biblical Researches," *Biblical Repertory and Princeton Review* 13 (1841): 583ff.

28. William Maclure Thomson, *The Land and the Book*, p. 674.

29. Austen Henry Layard, *Ninevah and its Remains* (London: J. Murray, 1849); *Discoveries Among the Ruins of Ninevah and Babylon* (New York: Harper, 1853), reviewed by Bela Bates Edwards, "Ruins of Ancient Ninevah," *American Biblical Repository* 9 (1837): 139ff. An excellent biography of Layard is Gordan Waterfield's *Layard of Ninevah* (New York: Praeger, 1968).

30. See Leonard Woolsey Bacon, "Layard's Discoveries," *New Englander* 11 (1853): 462.

31. Thomas Laurie, "Testimony of Assyrian Inscriptions to the Truth of the Scriptures," *Bibliotheca Sacra* 14 (1857): 147ff. For more on the American response to Layard, see Phillip Andrew Kildah, "British and American Reaction to Layard's Discoveries in Assyria, 1845–1860, (Ph.D. diss., University of Minnesota, 1959). The most important American responses included clergyman Daniel P. Kidder's *Ninevah and the River Tigris* (New York: Lane and Scott, 1851); and Asahel Davis, *Lectures on the Remarkable Discoveries Lately Made in the East, Among the Ruins; as Those of Ninevah* (Buffalo: Phinney and Company, 1852).

32. Robinson, "Egyptian Hieroglyphics," *American Quarterly Review* 1 (1827): 438ff.

33. As evangelicals already knew in the thirties, ancient Egyptians believed that history repeated itself in cycles of 36,525 years. The historian Menetho, it was suspected, had "created" much of the earlier history (the antediluvian part) in order to fill out the cycle. By supposing this, Robinson and later Alonzo Chapin were able to bring the Egyptian chronology into relatively close harmony

with the biblical chronology. See Chapin, "Connection Between Egyptian and Jewish History," *Quarterly Christian Spectator* 8 (third series, 1836): 340.

34. Robinson, "Egyptian Chronology," *American Quarterly Review* 1 (1827): 520.

35. Robinson, "Egyptian History," *American Quarterly Review* 4 (1828): 34.

36. Ibid., p. 38.

37. Robinson, "Egyptian Chronology," p. 531.

38. Modern historians generally place the Hyksos in the fifteenth and sixteenth Dynasties. They apparently came from Assyria and spoke Chaldee, the language of Abraham.

39. Generally, Chapin's "Connection between Egyptian and Jewish History" is a very confused account (*Quarterly Christian Spectator* 8 [1836]: 337ff). See also his more detailed "Comparison of the Biblical and Egyptian Chronologies," *Quarterly Christian Spectator* 9 (1837): 193ff.

40. George Gliddon, *Ancient Egypt* (New York: J. Winchester, 1843).

41. Anon., "Egyptian Antiquities," *Church Review* 3 (1850), 14.

42. Josiah Clark Nott, *Two Lectures on the Connection between the Biblical and Physical History of Man* (New York: Bartlett and Welford, 1849).

43. Karl Richard Lepsius, *Chronologie der Aegypter* (Berlin: Nicolaische Buchhandlung, 1849).

44. Nott, *Two Lectures*, pp. 78–80.

45. Nott, "Ancient and Scripture Chronology," *Southern Quarterly Review* 18 (1850): 388.

46. "Parson-skinning" was the term Nott applied to his attacks on Clergymen. See William Stanton, *The Leopard's Spots* (Chicago: Univ. of Chicago Press, 1960), pp. 137ff. Howe's suggestion came in a review of Nott's work that appeared in the *Southern Presbyterian Review* 3 (1850).

47. Moses Ashley Curtis accused Nott of "setting up" his opponents in this way: "Why does he never mention," said Curtis, that "the Septuagint chronology is as authoritative as Ussher's . . .? Why does he assume the year 2348 (B.C.) as "our date" of the Deluge, as if we were necessarily committed to it, and thus leave the unlearned to infer that Menes, whose era he puts at 2750 (B.C.) must have reigned in Egypt 400 years before the Deluge, when by the Septuagint chronology, his time would be 500 years *after* the Deluge?" in "Unity of the Races," *Southern Quarterly Review* 7 (1849): 396.

48. Nott, "Ancient and Scripture Chronology," pp. 422–23.

Chapter 9

1. Romans 5:12.

2. Henry Bronson, "Review of Thoughts on the Original Unity of the Human Race," *Quarterly Christian Spectator* 3 (1831): 57.

3. Matthew Boyd Hope, "On the Unity of the Human Race," *Biblical Repertory and Princeton Review* 22 (1850): 316. Hope was reviewing John Bachman's *The Doctrine of the Unity of the Human Race, Examined on the Principles of Science* (Charleston: C. Canning, 1850).

4. Samuel Stanhope Smith, *An Essay on the Causes of the Variety of Complexion and Figure in the Human Species* (New Brunswick, 1810).

5. Samuel George Morton, *Crania Americana; or, a Comparative View of the Skulls of the Various Aboriginal Nations of North and South America, to Which is Prefixed an Essay on the Varieties of the Human Species* (Philadelphia: J. Dobson, 1839), p. 3. Actually, *Crania Americana* was so ambiguous on the unity question that the reviewers could find nothing unorthodox. The reviewer for The *American Journal of Science* even believed that "the unity of the human species is assumed by Dr. Morton." "Morton's Crania Americana," *American Journal of Science* 38 (1840): 344.

6. Morton, *Crania Americana*, p. 260.

7. M. B. Hope, "On the Unity of the Human Race, "*Biblical Repertory and Princeton Review* 22 (1850): 315–18. Another supporter of the exclusively biblical approach was Thomas A. Davies. See his *Cosmogony, or the Mysteries of Creation* (New York: Rudd and Carleton, 1857), p. 35.

8. Generally, there were two methods for defining "species" in the first half of the nineteenth century. One relied heavily on the "common stock" or common ancestry concept—the idea that all the members of a species had descended from the same parent stock. To be sure, anatomists in practice identified species on the basis of physical characteristics, but they used these only as a mechanism for demonstrating that two organisms were "really" of the same stock. The other, "ideal" notion of species was that a species represents a single creative act or expression of God's mind. According to Agassiz, God "conceived" the idea of a certain organism and then created it, perhaps in only one place, but perhaps in a number of places and even at different times. Therefore this initial creation was not limited to a single pair but to a number of individuals sufficient to cover the entire range of distribution of that particular species. In this case again, Agassiz in practice identified species by looking at anatomical

differences and similarities, but only to "discover" whether or not two organisms were of the same species. Both groups, therefore, used taxonomy as a mechanism for *identifying* species they believed existed absolutely in nature, not as a mechanism for *defining* them. Evangelical John Bachman came as close as anyone to a truly empirical definition of species, but even he could not divest himself completely of the "common stock" idea: "Species we define as applying to those individuals resembling each other in definition and general structure. In wild animals, as a general rule, they must approach the same size; but both in wild and domesticated animals they must have the same duration of life, the same period of utero-gestation, the same average number of progeny, the same habits and instincts, in a word, they belong to one stock that produce fertile offspring by association." *Unity of the Human Race Examined*, p. 19.

9. Alonzo Bowen Chapin, "Chronology and its Adjuncts," *Church Review* 6 (1853): 384.

10. Genesis 9:25.

11. Anon. "Canaan Identified with the Ethiopian," *Southern Quarterly Review* 2 (1842): 328. For a similar view, see Samuel Davies Baldwin, *Dominion, or the Unity and Eternity of the Human Race* (Nashville: E. Stevenson, 1857).

12. For more on Bachman, see Stanton, *The Leopard's Spots*, pp. 123–26.

13. See Thomas Smyth, *The Unity of the Human Races Proved to be the Doctrine of Scripture, Reason, and Science: with a Review of the Present Position and Theory of Professor Agassiz* (New York: Putnam, 1850). Quotations in this chapter are taken from the edition included in Smith's *Works*, vol. 8 (Columbia: Bryan, 1910). Smyth claimed that his own attacks on Nott ante-dated Bachman's arguments, even though Smyth's book was published later. Smyth defended his claim by citing earlier sources of his work. See his preface, pp. 31–32. For more on Agassiz's distinction between "type" and "origin" questions, see Agassiz, "The Diversity of Origin of the Human Races," *Christian Examiner* 49 (1850): 110.

14. Smyth, *Works*, 8: 80.

15. See Ibid., 8: 17.

16. McCosh to Smyth, n.d.; reprinted in Ibid., 8: 14.

17. *Virginia Lectures on the Evidences of Christianity* (New York: Carter, 1853), pp. 419, 431.

18. Thomas Jefferson, *Notes on the State of Virginia*, in *The Writings of Thomas Jefferson* (Washington, D.C.: Taylor and Maury, 1854), 8: 345ff.

19. Benjamin Smith Barton, "Hints on the Etymology of Certain

English Words," *Transactions*, American Philosophical Society, vol. 6 (21 October 1803), pp. 151ff.

20. Louis Agassiz, "The Diversity of Origin of the Human Races," *Christian Examiner* 49 (1850): 140.

21. George Gliddon and Josiah Clark Nott, eds., *Types of Mankind* (Philadelphia: Lippincott and Grambo, 1854); and *Indigenous Races of the Earth* (Philadelphia: Lippincott, 1857).

22. Maury, "On the Distribution and Classification of Tongues," *Indigenous Races of the Earth*, pp. 25–86.

23. James Cowles Prichard, *Researches into the Physical History of Mankind* (London: n.p., 1813). The second edition was expanded into two volumes (London: John and Arthur Arch, 1826).

24. Julius Klaproth, *Asia Polyglotta* (Paris: n.p., 1823). Klaproth, a close friend of Wilhelm von Humboldt, was at this time a professor of Oriental languages at the University of Berlin.

25. See Prichard, *Researches* (1826), 2: 606–11. For more on Prichard, see John C. Greene, *The Death of Adam*, pp. 238–44.

26. Nicholas Cardinal Wiseman, *Twelve Lectures* (London: n.p., 1835), pp. 7–62. Wiseman borrowed some of this material from Alexander von Humboldt, *Vues de Cordillères* (Paris: F. Schoeel, 1818).

27. Moses Ashley Curtis, "Unity of the Races," *Southern Quarterly Review* 7 (1845): 372–448.

28. [Josiah C. Nott], "Dr. Nott's Reply to 'C,' " *Southern Quarterly Review* 8 (1845): 148–90.

29. Albert Gallatin, *A Synopsis of the Indian Tribes Within the United States East of the Rocky Mountains* (Cambridge, Mass.: n.p., 1836). See also, Samuel Latham Mitchill, "The Original Inhabitants of America Shown to be the Same Family and Lineage with those of Asia," *Archaelogia Americana: Transactions and Collections of the American Antiquarian Society* 1 (1820); and James Haines M'Culloh, *Researches on America* (Baltimore: Coale and Maxwell, 1816); and *Researches, Philosophical and Antiquarian, Concerning the Aboriginal History of America* (Baltimore: F. Lucas, 1829). M'Culloh was one of the first Americans to suggest that the Indians were actually displaced Asians.

30. Henry R. Schoolcraft, *History, Condition and Prospects of the Indian Tribes of the United States (or Ethnological Researches Respecting the Red Men of America)* (published by authority of Congress, 1854).

31. This information comes from the revised, one-volume edition of the *History, Condition and Prospects* (Philadelphia: Lippincott, 1857).

32. Samuel Forry, "Mosaic Account of the Unity of the Human Race, Confirmed by the Natural History of the American Aborigines," *American Biblical Repository* 22 (1843): 77.

33. For Humboldt's theory of language, see: Wilhelm von Humboldt, *Linguistic Variability and Intellectual Development,* trans. by George C. Buck and F. A. Raven (Miami: University of Miami Press, 1971). See also, Roger Langham Brown, *Willhelm von Humboldt's Conception of Linguistic Relativity* (The Hague: Mouton, 1967).

Chapter 10

1. Samuel Stanhope Smith, *Essay on the Causes of the Variety of Complexion and Figure in the Human Species* (New Brunswick: J. Simpson, 1810), p. 54.

2. For example, James McCosh, president of Princeton; and Augustus Hopkins Strong, president of Rochester Theological Seminary.

3. William Charles Wells, "Account of a Female of the White Race of Mankind, Part of Whose Skin Resembles that of a Negro," *Two Essays* (London: n.p., 1818), especially pages 430–36. For more on Wells, see Edward S. Morse, "What American Zoologists Have Done for Evolution," *The Popular Science Monthly* 10 (1876): 4; John C. Green, *The Death of Adam*, pp. 244–47.

4. See Loren Eisely, *Darwin's Century* (New York: Doubleday, 1958), pp. 119–25.

5. Elisha Bartlett, *A Brief Sketch of the Life, Character, and Writings of William Charles Wells* (Louisville: Prentice and Weissinger, 1849).

6. Philip Nicklin, "Conchological Observations on Lamarck's Family of Naiädes," *Transactions,* American Philosophical Society 3 (1830), pp. 396–98.

7. Samuel Haldeman, "Enumeration of Recent Fresh-water Mollusca," *Boston Journal of Natural History* 4 (1844): 474–79.

8. C. S. Rafinesque, *New Flora and Botany of North America* (Philadelphia: n.p., 1836–38); see also, J. Stanley Grimes, *Phreno-Geology: the Progressive Creation of Man Indicated by Natural History* (Boston: J. Munroe, 1851).

9. See Eisely, *Darwin's Century*, p. 133.

10. See Gillispie, *Genesis and Geology*, p. 155. Chambers drew support from outdated experiments with galvanism and Cooke's refuted experiments with spontaneous generation.

11. For more of Chambers's arguments, see Eisely, *Darwin's Cenutry,* pp. 135ff.

12. Robert Chambers, *Vestiges of the Natural History of Creation* (London: J. Churchill, 1844), p. 155. Quotations come from the 1949 edition, published in New York by Humanities Press; introduction by Gavin de Beer.

13. Chambers, *Vestiges,* p. 170.

14. In addition to the reviews discussed, see also anon., "Vestiges of Creation and its Reviewers," *New Englander* 4 (1846): 113ff.

15. A. B. Dod, "Vestiges of Creation," *Princeton Review* 17 (1845): 515.

16. See Maboth Moseley, *Irascible Genius: A Life of Charles Babbage, Inventor* (London: Hutchinson, 1964).

17. Chambers, *Vestiges,* pp. 209–11.

18. Dod, "Vestiges of Creation," p. 524.

19. Taylor Lewis, "Vestiges of Creation," *The American Review* (later, *The American Whig Review*) 1 (1845): 538.

20. Francis Bowen, "A Theory of Creation," *North American Review* 60 (1845): 439.

21. Francis Bowen, "Recent Theories in Geology," *North American Review* 69 (1849): 256.

22. Robert Chambers, *Explanations: A Sequel to the "Vestiges of the Natural History of Creation"* (London: J. Churchill, 1845).

23. Asa Gray, "Explanations of the Vestiges," *North American Review* 62 (1846): 470.

24. Ibid., p. 478.

25. See Asa Gray, "Darwin on the Origin of Species," *Atlantic Monthly* 6 (1860): 109–16; 229–39.

26. See Lewis Warner Green, *Virginia Lectures on the Evidences of Christianity* (New York: Carter, 1853), p. 472. Hugh Miller's response to Chambers is contained mainly in chapter 7 of *The Foot-Prints of the Creator* (Boston: Gould and Lincoln, 1856). Chambers, however, is discussed *passim.*

27. See James D. Dana, "Science and the Bible," *Bibliotheca Sacra* 13 (1856); and 14 (1857).

28. Morgan B. Sherwood has made a lengthy analysis of the controversy in "Genesis, Evolution, and Geology in America before Darwin: the Dana-Lewis Controversy, 1856–1857," in *Toward a History of Geology,* Cecil J. Schneer, ed. (Cambridge, Mass.: M.I.T. Press, 1969), pp. 305ff.

29. Lewis, *The Six Days of Creation* (Schenectady: G. Y. Van Debogert, 1855), pp. 214–16.

30. James D. Dana, "Science and the Bible," *Bibliotheca Sacra* 13 (1856): 103.

31. Ibid., p. 119.

32. See Arnold Guyot, *The Earth and Man: Lectures on Comparative Physical Geography, in its Relation to the History of Mankind,* trans. by C. C. Felton (Boston: Gould, Kendall, Lincoln, 1849). Guyot, a Neuchâtel born friend of Agassiz, came to America in 1848. This book is his collected Lowell Lectures. In 1855 he became geographer at Princeton.

33. See William Sanford, "Dana and Darwinism," *Journal of the History of Ideas* 26 (1965): 531–46.

34. See Arthur Lovejoy, "The Argument for Organic Evolution Before the Origin of Species," *Popular Science Monthly* 75 (1909): 499–514; 537–49.

35. Ibid., 539; Hugh Miller, *Foot-Prints of the Creator,* pp. 227–28.

36. From Marie Jean Flourens, one of Cuvier's students, professor of comparative anatomy at the French Museum, and general secretary of the French Academy of Sciences. He is quoted in Lovejoy, "Argument," p. 543.

37. Quoted from Huxley's "Address to the Geological Society," 1862, in Lovejoy, "Argument," p. 543.

38. Haldeman, Enumeration of Recent Fresh-water Mollusca," pp. 481.

39. Edward Hitchcock, *The Religion of Geology and its Connected Sciences* (Boston: Phillips, Sampson, and Co., 1852), p. 55.

40. Chambers, *Vestiges,* pp. 193–95.

41. See Charles Hodge, *What is Darwinism?* (New York: Scribner and Armstrong, 1874).

42. See Dupree, *Asa Gray,* p. 360.

Epilogue

1. See William Milligan Sloane, *The Life of James McCosh* (New York: Scribner's, 1896), p. 187.

2. Quoted in Mark DeWolfe Howe, *Classic Shades* (Boston: Little, Brown, and Company, 1928), p. 145; see also Sloane, *The Life of James McCosh,* p. 234.

Index